Democracy for Busy People

Democracy for Busy People

KEVIN J. ELLIOTT

THE UNIVERSITY OF CHICAGO PRESS   CHICAGO AND LONDON

The University of Chicago Press, Chicago 60637
The University of Chicago Press, Ltd., London
© 2023 by The University of Chicago
All rights reserved. No part of this book may be used or reproduced in any manner
whatsoever without written permission, except in the case of brief quotations in critical
articles and reviews. For more information, contact the University of Chicago Press,
1427 E. 60th St., Chicago, IL 60637.
Published 2023
Printed in the United States of America

32 31 30 29 28 27 26 25 24 23   1 2 3 4 5

ISBN-13: 978-0-226-82630-1 (cloth)
ISBN-13: 978-0-226-82632-5 (paper)
ISBN-13: 978-0-226-82631-8 (e-book)
DOI: https://doi.org/10.7208/chicago/9780226826318.001.0001

Library of Congress Cataloging-in-Publication Data

Names: Elliott, Kevin J., author.
Title: Democracy for busy people / Kevin J. Elliott.
Description: Chicago : The University of Chicago Press, 2023. | Includes bibliographical
    references and index.
Identifiers: LCCN 2022040913 | ISBN 9780226826301 (cloth) | ISBN 9780226826325 (paperback) |
    ISBN 9780226826318 (ebook)
Subjects: LCSH: Political participation—Social aspects—United States. | Americans—
    Political activity—Social aspects. | Time management—Political aspects—United States. |
    Elections—Social aspects—United States. | Democracy—United States. | Equality.
Classification: LCC JK1764 .E455 2023 | DDC 323/.0420973—dc23/eng/20220923
LC record available at https://lccn.loc.gov/2022040913

♾ This paper meets the requirements of ANSI/NISO Z39.48-1992 (Permanence of Paper).

FOR MY MOTHER

Contents

CHAPTER ONE

The Demands of Democratic Citizenship

The Difficulty of Participation

Democracy is a fragile thing. The millenarian optimism about democracy that followed the collapse of communism has long since faded into dread of an unknown future. The future is dimmed in large part due to the recession of democracy in many parts of the world during the first decades of the twenty-first century. Yet the latest tide of democratic deconsolidation has mostly not occurred through the familiar high dramas of military coups or revolutionary overthrows of democratic regimes. Instead, it has taken the form of elected governments rewriting the often invisible, technical rules of the political game to keep themselves in power (Levitsky and Ziblatt 2018).

This has been the pattern in the United States. Since 2010, numerous states have enacted policies burdening the exercise of the franchise (Herd and Moynihan 2018, 43–70). The first wave of these policies introduced burdensome identification requirements for voting, as well as the elimination of polling places and the restriction of early voting (Lockhart 2019). The latest round has specifically targeted measures instituted to make voting easier, such as mail or no-excuse absentee voting. Both Iowa and Georgia substantially reduced the amount of time voters and election authorities have to apply for, send out, and return mail-in ballots, making it more likely for citizens to miss these voting deadlines (Fowler 2021; Brennan Center for Justice 2021). Many of these changes were designed to create new hoops for citizens to jump through to vote. For instance, in Florida, a 2021 law shortened the period during which voters can automatically receive absentee ballots by mail and requiring them to reregister as absentee every election (Mazzei and Corasaniti 2021). Registration itself has also been made more difficult in states like Florida and Georgia, where citizens now must supply identification information that not everyone has—such as a driver's license number—either to be added to the voter roll or to request an absentee ballot. States have also taken steps likely to lead to faulty purges of the voter rolls, at best forcing voters to reregister, and at worst disenfranchising those who are errantly purged and unable to register again in time for the election. Most notable about these vote suppression efforts taken as a whole is that they do not operate by outright banning citizens from voting. Instead, they work by making it harder and more complicated to vote.

At the same time that American states are burdening the franchise, democratic innovations that involve difficult and time-consuming forms of participation have exploded in interest among scholars, civil society organizations, and—increasingly—even some governments. There seem to be more and more amazing examples every year of ordinary citizens in randomly selected deliberative forums being tasked with difficult and high-stakes challenges, such as writing new constitutions (as in Iceland), reforming electoral systems (as in Canada and the Netherlands), considering measures for addressing major public policy challenges like climate change (as in France), revising constitutional provisions governing major issues like marriage equality and abortion (as in Ireland), and reviewing ballot initiatives to inform voters (as in Oregon) (Warren and Pearse 2008; Fournier, Van der Kolk, et al. 2011; Farrell and Suiter 2019; Landemore 2020; Gastil and Knobloch 2020). Yet these innovative reforms often ask their citizen participants for substantial amounts of free time and significant travel far from home, demanding much more time and effort than the conventional institutions of electoral democracy. Other proposals for reform, such as randomly selected issue-specific legislatures (Guerrero 2014) or liquid democracy, where citizens delegate their votes to issue-specific experts (Blum and Zuber 2016), also raise the burden on ordinary citizens by multiplying the issues and centers of power citizens need to pay attention to. Like efforts to suppress the vote, these reforms end up drastically raising the cost and complexity of being a good democratic citizen.

There is obviously no comparison to be made in terms of intention here between the advocates of vote suppression schemes and those of democratic innovations. The legislators behind contemporary vote suppression efforts seem to have thoroughly instrumentalized democracy, seeing its value solely in terms of partisan advantage and so as disposable. The reformers who are thinking about, studying, and doing the hard work of enacting democratic innovations, on the other hand, are firmly committed to furthering the core democratic ideals of equality and collective self-rule for all, even when democracy produces results they may personally dislike. Yet there is a vitally important way in which these policies are of a piece. Though we cannot compare them on the basis of their designers' intentions, there is nonetheless something comparable in their *consequences*. Both these species of reform have the effect of making it harder for people to participate in democratic processes, especially those who are busy.

Compared to the demands of deliberative institutions that ask for a substantial amount of citizens' time, even waiting hours to vote is easier. Compared to needing to designate a proxy for every imaginable political issue, as in liquid democracy, conventional voting for candidates and parties is incomparably simpler. Indeed, survey evidence suggests that citizens are significantly less supportive of democratic innovations that involve more than a single meeting (Christensen 2020). These citizens seem to sense what preoccupies me: that many of these democratic innovations, if generalized, would effectively make it harder for many, if not most, people to actually participate in politics.

This brings me to the central concern of this book: when we make it hard or confusing to participate, we *reduce democratic inclusion*. Increasing the difficulty of participation means not only adding practical or administrative burdens to it but also increasing the demandingness of participation itself. When people have to devote substantial amounts of time and effort to take part, they are less likely to do so, leading to their absence from politics and the creation of a less inclusive body of active citizens. This is not an original observation (Chambers 2009), but it seems too often to be overlooked and undervalued amid the enthusiasm for the latest promising innovation cooked up by democratic theorists or activists. I confess to regularly experiencing this enthusiasm myself. Yet even in the grip of such enthusiasm, I often find myself thinking about my mother.

Unequal Busyness and Democratic Equality

For most of her life, my mother was not a good democratic citizen. She voted maybe once a decade and knew next to nothing about the issues, parties, candidates, or wider political context. This ignorance wasn't due to any infirmity or lack of ability. In the ordinary run of life, my mother is punctilious and thoughtful. But as a single working mother without a college degree, she was *busy*. Not busy the way a high-powered lawyer or other successful professional is. She was not plowed under with work imposed by a demanding work ethic and culture. She was busy in more mundane ways — if she didn't pick up the child, shop for groceries, cook the meal, do the dishes, pay the bills, clean the house, tend the child, track the household budget, etc. — it simply wouldn't get done. And after doing all of this every day, day after day, without break or assistance, she also had to find time to rest and recuperate her energies to prevent depression and burnout, at which she was only ever partly successful. She was busy the way millions of people around the world are: swamped by meeting the everyday demands of life while maintaining a modicum of sanity.

It is extremely unlikely that my mother at that time would have opted to participate in a democratic innovation like a deliberative forum even if she had been invited. Nor would she have bothered to parcel out her vote, issue by issue, to trusted surrogates. There was little time in her busy life for anything of as uncertain value as politics. Reasons against participation could be found in every household task that had to be completed during the all-too-short evenings and weekends she would have been asked to sacrifice.

When we make participation more difficult, in whatever way we do so, we lock busy people out of democracy. Demanding forms of participation, and participatory institutions that require them, create subtle yet effective patterns of exclusion. This is a problem for many well-understood reasons. For example, inclusion aids the quality of democratic decision-making by introducing greater diversity of ideas and information into the process (Page 2007; Landemore 2013). It is also essential that people be present in politics or else their voices and interests stand a sickening chance of being overlooked and ignored (Phillips 1998). I say much more about the importance of inclusion as a bedrock democratic value in chapter 4. For now, I simply contend that it does not matter *how* citizens are excluded from taking an active part in politics — whether through nefarious efforts to undermine democracy or well-meaning ones to improve it. When the democratic arena is emptied of citizens, for whatever reason, democracy is diminished.

My concern throughout this book is with busy people like my mother was when I was a child. Busy people for me are not the jet-setters with

clogged calendars full of high-stakes meetings. They are the people wag-
ing a constant battle against burnout, bills, and the neglect of their loved
ones. Busyness in this sense overlaps with poverty and many other forms
of disadvantage, such as those attached to race and gender. This is because
these other categories of disadvantage often materialize in terms of ex-
tra burdens of time and necessary work—they take the form of "unequal
busyness," in other words. When a woman faces mounting sexist disre-
spect at work and must take the time to process it, or a woman of lower
socioeconomic status and also of color is expected to take care of her own
children as well as those of a rich family that employs her, or a disabled
person must meticulously choreograph a seemingly simple trip to the gro-
cery store, or a Black American must process yet another police shooting
that reminds them of their subordinate status under America's political
and criminal punishment institutions, their time is burdened and they are
made busy by it. This is what I mean when I say that busyness overlaps
with other categories of disadvantage; busyness is often the *currency* of
disadvantage. It gets heaped upon some groups, while others are spared.
Addressing busyness and its implications for democratic empowerment,
then, can help to address many categories of social disempowerment and
disadvantage.

Yet busyness is not identical with these other forms of disadvantage
either. Each of them involves unique challenges requiring specific rem-
edies, and it is not my intention to claim busyness addresses them in their
entirety. Racial and sex-based oppression, and disadvantages due to disability and prejudice, would likely leave substantial remainders even after busyness is comprehensively addressed. Nonetheless, progress against
the inequality occasioned by busyness is also progress against many other
forms of injustice and inequality.

Busy people are, for me, then, the people who are relatively disadvantaged in a given time and place in terms of the time and attention they
devote to politics. They have many things they care about and must devote
themselves to in life, and those things occupy enough of their time, energy,
and attention to often leave politics a minor concern indeed. The factors
leading to this disadvantage will often track other markers of social disadvantage, such as race, sex, socioeconomic status, immigration status, and
disability, as I just discussed, but my focus is on busyness as a common
currency of disadvantage, if an imperfect one.

The problem of busyness as I mean it is easily misunderstood and requires clarification. To some, the busyness of democratic citizens like my

mother seems like a problem of material scarcity to be solved mainly by economic redistribution and the provision of public services, like child or elder care. But this does not resolve the problem. Although unequal busyness as I mean it overlaps with traditional forms of disadvantage like poverty, it is in fact a more general problem that would obtain even in a universally developed world that had an ideal distribution of wealth and a perfect social welfare state. Even in a world of fully automated luxury communism (Bastani 2019), in other words, some people will always have children, aged parents, or disabled loved ones—and want to care for them themselves. Some will always choose to take on service roles in their clubs and churches, become coaches for Little League teams, or pursue enthralling artistic or do-it-yourself projects, while others do not.

Even if we could conquer material scarcity and make sure all shared in that prosperity fairly, people's time and attention is and always will be finite, and they will choose to use it differently. People will always make choices, forge dependencies, or be imposed upon by circumstances that differentially burden the two resources absolutely essential for democratic citizenship: *time* and *attention*. This persistent unequal busyness means that citizens will always devote unequal time and attention to politics. A world of abundance cannot alleviate this unequal busyness because it involves scarcity in resources that cannot be manufactured and because it is a product of people's choices and the widely varying circumstances of individual human lives. People thus make different choices and face different circumstances that shape their lives and yet are not fundamentally changeable by policy or institutions, and these choices and circumstances determine how much time, attention, and energy they end up devoting to democratic citizenship.

Yet these choices and circumstances do *not* affect their entitlement to democratic equality. Regardless of how busy they are, everyone remains entitled to have their views and interests considered in collective decision procedures equally alongside everyone else's. When some people are attentive to politics and others are not, however, the inevitable result is political inequality, since those with the time and inclination will take advantage of participatory opportunities—including those created by democratic innovations—and so become disproportionately empowered compared to those busy with other things. This would perhaps not be concerning if this busyness were distributed equally among all of society's members. Yet we know that countless forms of social power operate to specially burden racial and ethnic minorities, women, poor people, migrants, and disabled people, among others, occupying more of their time and attention with the basics of navigating the world. Misfortune too generates lasting unequal burdens since some have the support to weather or recover from it quickly, while others must stagger on bearing physical, mental, and financial debilities.

Democratic reformers and theorists have sought to address these kinds of deep inequalities with radically new democratic institutions that aim to empower ordinary citizens at the expense of professional politicians and bureaucrats. Yet new and demanding opportunities to participate in democratic processes often come to be dominated by those with the greatest relevant advantages, including education, income, and status—as well as time and attention. Instead of empowering the disadvantaged, they put more tools for maintaining power in the hands of the already advantaged members of society. This is due to what I call the "paradox of empowerment." The way the paradox works is that participation is costly, and so those who can most afford to pay those costs are the most likely to participate. This means that, other things equal, we would expect new institutions of democratic participation to be dominated by those with the most relevant advantages, paradoxically empowering those who are already powerful and advantaged in society and intensifying the marginalization of those who are busy and disadvantaged. As I explain in detail in chapter 3, the paradox of empowerment is not a mere theoretical possibility. We observe it operating in a variety of settings, from developing countries, to public schools, to the segregated US South, to democratically innovative citizen assemblies. In all these cases, supposedly democratic empowerment served to reinforce the power of more advantaged groups, promoting democratic inequality.

The point of highlighting unequal busyness is not to imply that people are naturally anti-political, and just want to be left alone to ignore politics. This view would imply that mobilization efforts aimed at recruiting politically passive citizens into politics are not worthwhile. When others have attended to the paradox of empowerment, they have often indeed made the mistake of assuming that passivity is fixed because people are "just like that," and so incapable of more demanding modes of citizenship (Cain 2015). I emphatically reject the naturalization of political apathy this assumption implies and argue instead that mobilization efforts are democratically essential, and I explore some promising approaches in the second part of the book. Instead of naturalizing apathy and fixing it as something that simply must be accommodated, I offer a principled argument for why individuals are *entitled* to undemanding modes of democratic citizenship as a matter of justice, rather than as a concession to a supposedly incorrigible reality of political apathy. In other words, I explain why it would be *good* to limit democracy's demands, not just why it must be done out of concession to an unchangeable reality.

The point of emphasizing busyness is that people are not *entirely* political—that no matter how expansively we define politics and the political, there is something that is *not* politics—and that devoting one's time and attention to these nonpolitical areas of social life will seem immensely worthwhile for many. At whatever level of systematic effort to recruit citizens into active citizenship one cares to theorize, there will be differential uptake and response to it. Some will respond and enthusiastically take up politics as a topic worth their time and attention; others will respond tepidly, persuaded to engage but not enthused with the democratic spirit. Still others will respond not at all, continuing to see politics as a burden generally not worth their time, at least when compared to their other endeavors. The result will be predictable participatory inequality between these groups, though, as I will suggest, the relative sizes of these groups will vary as a function of mobilization efforts and institutions.

This brings us to the core problem of this book: people are unequally busy, and this generates democratic inequality since busier citizens are effectively excluded from participation. The disempowerment of the busy is, in turn, exacerbated when participation is made onerous and demanding, as it is in many of the democratic innovations most celebrated today. I argue that if we recognize inclusion's proper importance to democracy, we must seek out a different direction of democratic reform, one that prioritizes mobilizing institutions that reach citizens where they are and that make participation as simple and easy as possible. I emphasize one particular way to make participation simple and easy that has been almost entirely neglected in political science and democratic theory: making participation cognitively tractable for busy citizens. This means simplifying participation and the choices faced by citizens, as well as elements of the political system itself.

Democratic institutions can be designed in ways that expect more or less from citizens in terms of effort and participation. Power can then be concentrated in institutions that are easy to engage with, or in less accessible ones. So, for example, if a democracy concentrates power in in-person assemblies that meet in the evening, when young children need to be fed and put to bed, that will affect who can attend and thus who is empowered. If a democracy concentrates power in electoral institutions that make voting easy, it shapes who is empowered differently. The design of democracy's participatory institutions thus determines who is empowered. I will be arguing throughout this book that democratic equality and inclusion require that democracies be designed to empower busy people, even if that means abandoning or diluting some of the more complex and participatory designs favored by reformers today.

If citizens vary in their busyness, how much of a participatory burden can they be expected to bear for democracy? Just how much democratic citizenship can we expect of them? It turns out that when we think of the predicament facing democracy in terms of unequal busyness, we generate a need for a new model of democratic citizenship that can accommodate the varying levels of interest and attention that citizens bring to it. Thinking of citizenship in terms of a highly demanding ideal, for instance, flattens the diversity we encounter in the world and does so in a way certain to generate democratic inequality. So, what kind of ideal would be appropriate for a world of unequally busy citizens? Is there a minimum of what can be expected of them? Is there a maximum? The first part of the book considers these questions.

The model of citizenship that emerges from this discussion is focused on citizens being attentive to politics and prepared to participate in it. This model, called "stand-by citizenship," unlocks a new agenda for institutional reform, one focused on making participation not just technically accessible for busy people, but practically and cognitively tractable for them as well by scaffolding the individual's participation with intermediary bodies like political parties. Exploring this reform agenda constitutes the second half of the book and emphasizes revitalizing the highly accessible and cognitively tractable institutions of electoral democracy, rather than pursuing sortition or deliberative reforms, as is more common in much recent democratic theory and in many reform efforts.

Is Inequality from Unequal Busyness a Problem?

The central problem of this book is that citizens are unequally busy and that this creates democratic inequality. Yet some might doubt that this kind of inequality is actually problematic. Is this, one might ask, a *type* of political inequality that should concern us in the same way disenfranchisement or an unregulated campaign finance system does? Or is the inequality

here somehow legitimate—as many believe the inequality between representatives and their constituents is due to electoral accountability? In this
section, I consider a potentially powerful reason to dismiss the inequality
generated by unequal busyness based on emphasizing the value of the
opportunity to participate rather than participation per se. I find this argument insufficient and conclude that this kind of inequality should concern
us deeply in the design of democratic institutions.

One of the most straightforward arguments for dismissing inequality
resulting from differing levels of busyness is that, insofar as it is a product
of informed choices made in a context where there is a real opportunity
for all to participate, such inequality is simply not a problem. Rather, it
is a product of people using their political freedom as they see fit, and if
the consequences include widespread political inequality, then so be it.
Such inequality might simply have to be accepted, even if it generates
serious complications for the ideal of democratic equality. Note that this
argument relies upon two key assumptions: (1) equal opportunity to participate and (2) that citizens make an informed choice not to participate.

In a counterfactual democracy that systematically eradicated *every*
conceivable barrier to participation, including by guaranteeing sufficient
resource endowments to all, *and* had a perfect system of civic education,
this argument might make some sense. In most imaginable realities, however, it will first run into countless informal barriers to participation that
render it specious (Parvin 2018). The list of such barriers hardly needs
elaboration. Lynn Sanders (1997) details the ways that supposedly inclusive deliberation can effectively exclude many people, such as those less
skilled at presenting their thoughts in the form of rational, reasonable
arguments and those without the material preconditions required to participate in deliberation. Iris Marion Young (2000, 53) too details subtle
yet powerful ways that seemingly open institutions can yet incorporate
exclusionary pressures, such as by utilizing terms of discourse not shared
by all, discounting testimony and other forms of political communication
favored by marginalized groups, and dismissing the participation of some
as out of order. Miranda Fricker (2007) develops similar insights into a
full-fledged theory of "epistemic injustice," analyzing the underappreciated ways that some speakers are denied a fair hearing. This is to say
nothing of the less subtle institutional barriers to participation that have
recently spread across the United States that I discussed above, such as
the closing of polling places, elimination of early voting days, and the imposition of onerous voter identification and registration requirements, all

of which can help invisibly generate apparent political silence. On top of and in addition to these other phenomena lies that of unequal busyness. Many have conflicting demands on their time and attention and do not or cannot prioritize politics even when it touches their lives closely. Clearly, wanting to be heard is often not enough to actually be heard in the democratic process.

It seems to me that informal barriers to participation are sufficiently persistent, numerous, and protean as to, at best, render untenable any line of argument that relies upon equality of opportunity to dismiss inequalities in participation and power. At worst, this line of argument amounts to little more than ideological cover for silencing inconvenient voices. This forecloses legitimizing the democratic inequality that results from unequal busyness on the basis of equal opportunity to participate. Yet this is not the only problem with that argument. It is also far from clear that citizens who do not participate do so out of informed choice.

I think again here of my mother. People are often not aware of having made decisions that never come to their attention. This was my mother's situation with regard to politics, and it remains the situation of millions of other democratic citizens. They are not politically passive, apathetic, ignorant, or disinterested because they made a conscious decision to ignore politics. They are passive, apathetic, etc. because politics never became something that they even thought about. Like most social behaviors, being interested in politics is something we learn in families and at school (Prior 2018). But of course, the bare existence of people like my mother, who had never thought seriously about politics, proves that not everyone learns about it from these core sources of early socialization. Becoming an active citizen—or not—is thus subject to what Peter Bachrach and Morton Baratz (1962) famously term "nondecision-making." Nondecision-making occurs when certain issues are kept off the agenda, such that decisions are effectively "made" without the decision-makers even being aware that other alternatives exist. This is the situation that citizens who have not been socialized into politics by their families or educational milieus often find themselves in with respect to politics. These citizens ignore politics not because they've made a conscious decision to do so, but rather because they were not properly informed that *not* ignoring it—that giving it their attention—was a real option for them. They were not informed that they even faced a choice, in other words. And even if they were aware of it, they did not—and indeed, could not—have known *enough* about what the choice meant for it to have been sufficiently informed.

It is important not to misunderstand my purpose in pointing out that people don't always choose to ignore politics and avoid participation. I am *not* saying that those who ignore politics necessarily make a mistake, or act inauthentically due to false consciousness, or the like. Nor is my point that being properly informed would transform them all into energized model citizens. Though I do argue against political apathy as it is often understood in chapter 2, one of my aims is to secure institutional conditions in which citizens can responsibly determine their own level of political engagement as a *real* choice. The problem thus isn't that some citizens are nonpolitical; it is, rather, that some citizens are *unthinkingly* nonpolitical. What we want are institutions that can ensure that every citizen is given a real and enduring invitation into political engagement, and an invitation that remains standing should someone not be ready to engage at a given time. We should create a supportive institutional environment, in other words, that regularly reaches out to every citizen so that busy people like my mother have multiple real opportunities to enter (or reenter) the political arena.

We thus cannot take political silence or absence as an exercise of freedom that must simply be accepted. Truly equal opportunities to participate will likely never be forthcoming and, in the absence of systematic recruitment and mobilization institutions, there will always be citizens whose nonparticipation is a function of ignorance, inertia, and unchosen habit, not of informed choice. There are too many invisible ways that not participating in democratic processes can be involuntary and self-sustaining for an argument based on opportunity or choice to go through.

Moreover, even if we posit *perfect* equality of opportunity and perfect information about politics, there is still reason to reject the compatibility with democracy of an unequal division of political influence resulting from unequal busyness. Consider a situation in which a polity had perfectly open democratic institutions, no informal barriers to participation whatsoever, and a universally informed citizenry, yet wherein only 10 percent of eligible citizens bestirred themselves to take even the least part in public affairs. In that situation, only that activist elite would have *any* say at all over collective decisions; they would effectively be ruling over the other 90 percent. Should we consider such an "aristocracy of activists" a legitimate democracy? It seems to me that we must say no. There has to be a point at which the formal trappings of democracy, such as procedural guarantees and sufficient resource endowments, on their own fail to qualify a regime as democratic. A case like this, where political apathy is nearly universal and therefore all influence is in the hands of a few, makes for a clear example. If this is right, one cannot dismiss busyness-induced democratic inequality even in a counterfactual world where true equality of opportunity has been achieved.

One of the issues this book explores is whether being more dedicated to politics entitles one to greater political power, as in the aristocracy-of-activists example I just mentioned. Intuitions about this question vary widely, but it is not a question that I have ever seen explicitly addressed before. Some seem to assume that having the will or desire to influence politics unproblematically entitles one to greater say compared to those who lack such a will or desire. Yet the latter group still has interests that could be advanced or sacrificed politically; they have views that could be represented or ignored. They could be exploited or protected from exploitation by political means. Even when one seems, through their conduct, to say they have no interest in politics, politics (as it is often said) nonetheless takes an interest in them. If democratic equality means anything, it seems to stand for the idea that everyone's interests and views are deserving of equal consideration; this is what justifies universal suffrage and political equality more generally, since it is thought equal power will secure equal consideration. But if we allow one's intrinsic dedication to politics to govern the amount of political influence one has, we endanger this equality. It is a core assumption of this book that there is a real problem here for those who view equality as the core value of democracy.[1] And it is my position that we must not allow habitual patterns of political motivation to erode democratic equality.

There are a host of reasons for the democratic inadmissibility of apathy that I detail in chapter 2. For now, suffice it say that a regime in which vast numbers of citizens are apathetic while others are disproportionately empowered would struggle to qualify as a democracy, or at least to remain one. The openness of democratic processes and varying willingness to participate is thus not a reason to dismiss the democratic inequality generated by unequal busyness.

Institutions, Information, and Empirical Evidence

Perhaps the most important part of my mother's story, and one that most influences this book, is how her unawareness of politics changed. Because

---

1. Adequately adjusted, the same can be said if we endorse the view that collective self-government is the core democratic value, because unequal busyness results in some of society governing the rest rather than everyone doing so together.

she is not still a bad democratic citizen—she now takes a regular interest in politics and has at times been highly involved politically. Yet this
change did not occur until she reached middle age. The particulars of her
emergence from political unawareness were idiosyncratic, following from
the major political events of the early 2000s, specifically 9/11 and the Iraq
War, and from conversations about these and other events with me after
I entered college and began to understand more about the world. Over
the following years, she would deepen her awareness of, and engagement
with, US politics on her own, trying out different modes of citizenship,
such as by joining and becoming involved with the local branch of a political party and volunteering for state and national campaigns. Today, she
keeps close tabs on political developments in her state and in national
politics and remains periodically active in politics.

My mother's transformation illustrates that political apathy and ignorance are not fixed or immutable. It is no one's destiny to view politics
as something that doesn't concern them. Like any social phenomena, it
has an etiology, an environment, and equilibria. It may even have a life
cycle; born in the darkness of ignorance, nourished by cynical slogans and
uncivic habits and habitats, weakened by the undeniable connectedness
of our fates, and finally expiring in the searing dawn of an unjust war or
disastrous financial crisis. Apathy thus can be destabilized and replaced,
and an attentive citizen born.

I am interested in the conditions that encourage the accidents of fate
helping to birth attentive citizens—a sort of pro-natalism for stand-by citizenship. But rather than focusing on the formal education system or political culture, I propose to focus on political institutions. Institutions shape
the quotidian environment that people like my mother occupy, and they
can either fill that environment with political actors and messages that try
to reach citizens like her, or fail to do so. I ask, then: What institutional
conditions generate the most conducive circumstances to encourage citizens like my mother *was* to become citizens like my mother *is*? How can
we chart a course from apathy to attention using institutions? Moreover,
how can we do so while making sure to leave no one behind?

Although this book does not reach strong conclusions about the merits of actively participating in democratic processes as I suggested in the
last section, it does reach such conclusions about being *attentive* to those
processes and *prepared* to engage them should the need arise. This sort of
orientation is captured in the idea of stand-by citizenship elaborated in
chapter 4. The second part of this book is primarily concerned with ques-

tions of institutional design focused on how to build a democracy that empowers busy citizens, like my mother was, including especially how to cultivate stand-by citizenship. This content makes the book an exercise in what Jeremy Waldron (2016, 8) has called "political political theory," meaning in particular that it is concerned with the normative choices we must make about our institutions and their processes. I contend that the ability to cultivate stand-by citizenship and empower busy people in other ways is perhaps the most important task in the design of democracy's participatory institutions.

A key part of this institutional approach involves combining empirical evidence about the functioning of democratic institutions with normative and theoretical analysis. Particularly in part II, I draw extensively from empirical studies of institutions, as well as from history. In this, I largely depart from many approaches in political theory, such as those that rely on abstract principles and thought experiments or that mine classic texts for fresh insights. As valuable and insightful as these other approaches often are, there is also value in seeing what an alternative approach that makes greater use of the insights of the other subfields of political science can teach us.

My use of empirical evidence is, however, often critical, informed by the limitations of some research methods and the ways that choices in inquiry design can determine or efface certain possibilities or interpretations. Among the growing group of political theorists who engage with empirical evidence, this approach is seldom taken. Often lacking the methodological training to identify better or worse sorts of evidence and research designs, theorists and philosophers sometimes erroneously take empirical findings at face value. My own approach differs from this one because I do not always accept empirical evidence at face value, but rather interrogate it where methodological concerns are relevant or interpret it in ways the original authors may not.

Yet in doing so, I am intensely aware of the dangers of motivated reasoning and confirmation bias. Motivated reasoning operates in part through the selective application of scrutiny to evidence that disconfirms one's existing beliefs, or that is inconvenient to a point one is making. Confirmation bias operates partly by pushing some questions out of the scope of what is investigated. When one uses empirical evidence critically, as I do, these pathologies are a very real risk, since I might unfairly scrutinize evidence running contrary to my argument or fail to question evidence that supports it. I have sought throughout this book to use empirical evidence responsibly and critically. Yet I remain aware of the limits of my ability to detect missteps in this regard. I therefore trust that the reader will judge whether I have succeeded in avoiding these dangers.

One of the unique emphases of my institutional approach is the way that institutions can help address the problem of political information. I mentioned above how my mother knew little about politics, as a result of not being interested in it. Because of this unfamiliarity with politics, some political philosophers today would say that she had something of an obligation to refrain from engaging in politics (Brennan 2011). Lacking information about the issues and candidates, as well as social scientific knowledge about how the world works, she could not responsibly use her vote, these critics would say.

Yet institutions decisively shape the information environment of politics, making what is going on clearer or more opaque to citizens. Citizens are not isolated atoms, floating alone through space and forced to shift for themselves in the task of becoming informed. Rather, they are embedded in a more or less rich ecosystem of institutions that can, in certain situations, operate to enrich the information environment and directly help citizens learn what they need to know to make political decisions. It is thus wrong to look only at the qualities and characteristics of individuals, such as the number of political trivia questions they can answer, when considering the problem of political information.

Institutional context also shapes what sorts of decisions ordinary citizens are called on to make—for example, do they mostly elect party-affiliated representatives or vote directly on policy? This further affects the kind and amount of information they might need (Lupia 2006). I focus on the ways that elections and especially parties shape the epistemic climate of democracy. I contend that, in the right institutional environment, citizens being critically attentive to politics is sufficient for them to make defensible political decisions. This focus on institutional environment also reveals a key disadvantage of "government by mini-public," or proposals to replace electoral-representative institutions with randomly selected deliberative assemblies (Landemore 2020). Such arrangements would eviscerate this environment, leaving citizens with the impermissibly demanding task of following every detail of politics themselves.

This book does not present a complete blueprint for a democracy for busy people. Instead, it focuses first on general questions that must be answered about such a democracy, and then offers a sketch of the institutions most useful for it. The general questions considered in the first part include: How far must democracy be prepared to accommodate the busyness of citizens? Why should democracy accommodate busyness in the first place? Shouldn't it just follow the requirements of democracy or justice by some plausible account? Does a democracy for busy people have any particular value at its heart? Answering these questions sets the parameters of a democracy for busy people and generates organizational principles for its institutions. These principles then form the basis of the second part of the book, which considers the promise of certain broad categories of democratic institutional forms for a democracy for busy people, with emphasis on elections, mandatory voting, annual elections, political parties, and deliberative mini-publics.

Democratic Citizenship as an Office

Throughout this book, I am concerned with democratic citizenship in a distinctive sense as an *office*—an institutional position associated with formal and informal powers, burdens, demands, and expectations. My account focuses on the demands and expectations associated with the role of citizen. This section explains this approach as a theoretical framework that integrates individual citizens, democratic theory, and democratic institutions, supplying a conceptual tool for addressing the ethics of democratic citizenship and institutional design.

Approaching citizenship as an office differs from the common way of thinking about it as a *status*. As a status, citizenship is about membership and standing, entailing rights of protection against certain kinds of treatment and guarantees of certain entitlements. As an office, however, citizenship is a formal part of a wider landscape constituted by institutions and practices in which citizens play some functional role. I want to focus on how the way we lay out that landscape determines the shape of the citizen's role and the expectations associated with it.

This account of citizenship begins with its requirements or demands. So, what are the demands of citizenship? They are not, first of all, conduct required for basic social order, such as law-abidingness. Nor are they the extraordinary demands made, for instance, in time of war like conscription since there is nothing distinctively democratic about these. Nor is the focus on the unique and more demanding tasks associated with specialized roles like representative, journalist, activist, or bureaucrat (Sabl 2002). The concern is, rather, the acts needed of ordinary citizens to support a specifically democratic politics.

The most common source of these demands is an institutional arrangement that includes formal and informal ways to authoritatively incorporate input from ordinary citizens in making collective decisions. Stripped to essentials, this is what democracy is. These ways might include institutions like elections, deliberative mini-publics, participatory budgeting, town meetings or other plenary assemblies as well as informal or quasi-institutionalized practices like protesting, joining a political association or civil society group, or even revolutionary activity. A democracy is constituted by a particular arrangement of these institutions and practices. This means a democracy could be more representative, by relying more exclusively on elections and parties, or more participatory, by deploying institutions and practices that disintermediate decision-making.

These different arrangements thereby serve to *encode expectations* for ordinary citizens because collective decision-making (in a genuine democracy) will crucially depend at some stage upon citizens *actually* making use of at least some institutional opportunities for participation. Consider, for instance, elections. If no one turned out to vote, elections would fail to elect representatives and (representative) democracy would be functionally crippled. A democracy incorporating elections, then, encodes the expectation that citizens will vote and, indeed, could not subsist without such participation.

In any given democratic arrangement, some institutions and practices are more central or important than others. This reveals that particular democratic arrangements or theories configure the office of democratic citizenship in one way or another—arrangements that make deliberative institutions more central configure the office in deliberative ways, for example. This means that the office of democratic citizen and the duties and expectations associated with it are *relative* to the specific practices and institutional arrangements that characterize a polity's particular democracy.

The other main source of the demands of citizenship is democratic theory. Democratic theories give rise to demands in both direct and indirect ways. Indirectly, they do so by recommending particular arrangements of institutions and practices that encode expectations and configure citizenship in particular ways, as above. Directly, democratic theories expect or demand conduct from ordinary citizens to secure the value of democracy or for democracy to fulfill the principles that justify it; that is, the *worth* or *legitimacy* of democracy is often at stake in citizens discharging these duties, adding an ethical dimension to them.

The reason for this is that democracies rely on their citizens in ways other regimes do not since they involve ordinary citizens in making au-

thoritative decisions and because the values or principles justifying democracy are usually linked to this involvement. The point here is that if, to
use the election example again, no one turned out to vote, representative
democracy would be crippled not just functionally but also *normatively*
since there would be scant legitimacy in elections with zero turnout. These
expectations are thus central to the normative core of most if not all democratic theories, revealing that fulfilling the ethical demands of citizenship
encoded in a democracy's practices and institutions is *necessary* for democracy to realize its worth, or be justified.

In sum, democratic citizenship can be configured in different ways
according to different institutional and theoretical backdrops. This suggests a distinctive approach to conceptualizing democratic citizenship as
an office, an institutional position associated with formal and informal
powers, burdens, and expectations. I have referred to the latter of these—
expectations—as "demands" in this section and will do so throughout the
argument to come. The idea that citizenship is associated with demands on
our time and resources and that these demands can be modulated through
institutional design is a core assumption of this book.

This approach provides a theoretical framework that has been missing
from the literature on the ethics of democratic citizenship. It borrows from
the notions of role morality used in professional ethics—and pioneered
by Andrew Sabl in the political sphere—and extends them to the role of
democratic citizen. Though scholars like Lisa Herzog and Bernardo Zacka
have used a similar approach in studying more technical and specialized
roles in bureaucratic organizations, I expand its use to that of citizens in
the more diffuse organizational setting of mass democracy (Herzog 2018;
Zacka 2017). Pathbreaking work in the ethics of democratic citizenship by
scholars like Eric Beerbohm (2012) and Jason Brennan (2011) have provided few general-purpose theoretical tools for thinking about the role of
citizens and how their role relates to the wider democratic institutional
and theoretical context. Thinking of citizenship as an office uniquely
synthesizes individual-level obligations and society- or system-wide institutions and norms. This synthetic approach also aims to contribute to
meso-level theorizing about social organizations that refuses to reduce individuals to functionalist cogs, but rather maintains their ethical character
(Herzog 2018). The framework also improves on the moralist philosophical approach taken by many theorists, who go about democratic ethics
with abstract arguments for particular rights or obligations in isolation
from the wider institutional context in which the individual is enmeshed.
This moralist approach comes with the disadvantage of generating many

seeming dilemmas and false problems caused by using a myopic frame of reference where a more expansive and integrative approach can populate myriad ways to address tensions, as I show throughout this book.

Outline of the Argument

The argument of the book is structured in two parts. Chapters 2–4, comprising part I, "How Much Democratic Citizenship," explore general questions defining the parameters of democracy for busy people. This inquiry takes place largely in terms of the ethics of democratic citizenship, using the framework of citizenship as an office. The argument considers whether citizenship has a minimum or a maximum and advances a standard that can reasonably be expected of all, regardless of their busyness.

Chapter 2, "Democracy's Floor: The Case against Apathy," explores whether there is any minimum threshold to democratic citizenship by considering whether political apathy can be justified in a democracy. I consider prominent arguments celebrating apathy in different ways from more than a century of democratic theory, including arguments from Bernard Berelson, Robert Dahl, and Jason Brennan. I argue that there are more and stronger arguments against apathy than in its favor, and that some arguments defending apathy are actually compatible with a situation where no citizen is entirely a stranger to politics. I lay out four arguments against apathy: (1) one based on the existence of injustice that we could help remedy; (2) one based on equality; (3) one based on harm to others; and (4) one based on how apathy undermines political stability. These arguments draw from the work of scholars like Beerbohm, Tommie Shelby, Hannah Arendt, and Sheri Berman, among others.

In these arguments, I highlight neglected ways that mechanisms of collective action interact with apathy, such as how apathy differentially pervades social networks, mobilizing some and demobilizing others politically. The chapter concludes by outlining an ethics of political apathy and identifies five conditions anyone who wanted to be politically apathetic would have to meet. I conclude that there are two defensible forms of apathy: one that meets the five conditions but that is likely to be extremely rare and another, based on the work of Jeffrey Green, that is temporary and intended to restore one's participatory spirit. In both cases, citizens must at least occasionally pay attention to politics, ruling out the most thoroughgoing forms of apathy as incompatible with democracy.

Whereas chapter 2 considers how low the minimum of democratic citizenship could be, chapter 3, "When Does Democracy Ask Too Much? Realism and the Paradox of Empowerment," considers the maximum that democracy can expect from its citizens in terms of participation and political engagement. Realist critics since Walter Lippmann and Joseph Schumpeter have worried that democracy, as conceived in political theory, expects too much from its citizens. They claim that the mismatch between democratic ideals and empirical reality necessitates revising down the demands of democratic theory. Yet this line of argument is vulnerable to the objection that citizens' capacities can always be improved by education or institutional reform, and so that projects that limit democratic aspirations are unduly concessive and conservative. I circumvent this powerful objection by offering a *principled* argument—rather than one based on probabilistic inferences from empirical research—for why the demands of democracy might be too heavy for ordinary citizens. Drawing on Julie Rose's work on the entitlement to free time, I argue that democracy asks too much of citizens when it infringes on their moral right to control their time, and that limiting democracy's demands can, paradoxically, empower busy and marginalized citizens who otherwise struggle to participate when participation is costly or demanding. This latter part of the argument relies upon the paradox of empowerment, a documented phenomenon whereby new opportunities to participate in collective governance become dominated by the most privileged members of a social group. The paradox illustrates that limiting democracy's demands on citizens is often emancipatory, and—counterintuitively to many democratic theorists—empowering, particularly for busy and disadvantaged citizens. The argument concludes that it is imperative to seek institutional arrangements that can empower citizens while simultaneously economizing on their participation.

The previous two chapters make a case for, on the one hand, a level of citizenship that excludes apathy and, on the other, the importance of limiting democracy's demands of ordinary citizens. Chapter 4, "The Citizen Minimum: Inclusion and Stand-By Citizenship," makes a case for how to go about promoting democratic equality in line with these requirements. It begins by arguing that inclusion, as part of a wider ideal of democratic equality, should be put first in the design of democratic institutions, against theorists like Iris Marion Young who want to subsume equality and inclusion. I am concerned with inclusion in the sense of what it means to be a democratic citizen. This is an important dimension of inclusion that has been overlooked in recent debates that have been preoccupied with global democracy and migration, in which the main question is *who* ought to be included as citizens and by what principle. I emphasize cases of "informal inclusion" whereby groups make themselves politically consequential even when they are not formally enfranchised, such as women in late nineteenth and early twentieth century reform movements. Such cases suggest that individuals are politically included when they pay attention to politics, and I develop an account of the minimum of democratic citizenship starting from this insight called stand-by citizenship. This account critically engages with Green's notion of political spectatorship by emphasizing citizens' surveillance of politics yet also, and contrary to Green, requiring that citizens remain prepared to participate should the need arise.

Stand-by citizenship is the culmination of part I because it economizes on the time and efforts of citizens, in line with chapter 3's conclusions, and yet does not collapse into apathy, as chapter 2 requires. Stand-by citizenship comprises the least demanding form of citizenship compatible with democracy and so defines a minimum that is to be expected of all citizens, regardless of their busyness or other obligations, and one that is also maximally inclusive due to its minimal demands. I defend stand-by citizenship from allegations that it is too minimal to be an attractive model of democratic citizenship and conclude by suggesting three ways to measure it. This concludes part I of the book.

Part II, "Democratic Institutions for Busy People," is composed of the last three chapters and explores the institutions likely to be most useful in a democracy for busy people. The discussion of part I identified four principles that can help guide the arrangement of democracy's participatory institutions, and these are gathered in a brief introductory section of chapter 5. The rest of the chapter, entitled "How to Democratize Elections: Annual Elections and Mandatory Voting," focuses on elections and on ways that they can be democratized to improve the uptake of popular views and promote stand-by citizenship among all citizens. I first enumerate the core advantages of elections from the perspective of a democracy for busy people. These advantages include that elections generate a huge coordinated social event able to draw the attention of virtually every citizen to politics for a time and also that they are based on the single most egalitarian form of participation, as voting is cheap, easy, and accessible.

I then explore in detail three categories of electoral institutions that can help elections to be simultaneously more responsive to ordinary citizens and also to reach every citizen and nudge them toward stand-by citizenship. The first category encompasses election administration and some features of constitutional design, such as the complexity of chains of responsibility. The second electoral institution is mandatory voting. I offer a novel argument for mandatory voting as a tutelary institution aimed at reaching every citizen to thereby nudge them toward paying politics periodic attention. Next, drawing on work from Elizabeth Cohen on the political value of time, as well as from the historical experience of the Revolutionary-era American states, I argue that manipulating the length of elected officials' term in office, as by making elections annual, can shorten the leash of accountability between constituents and representatives, in ways that transform the relationship and make it more democratic.

Chapter 6, "Engines of Inclusion: Political Parties in Competition," argues that political parties are another major piece of a democracy for busy people and may be the most powerful of all due to the way they mobilize citizens and cognitively scaffold citizens' engagement with politics. Although elections make it easy for citizens to participate, they ultimately still rely upon citizens to come to them. Parties, on the other hand, can reach citizens where they are and mobilize them, at least when they are forced to compete with each other. This chapter contributes to a growing literature in political theory on parties by exploring the ways that parties make politics tractable and understandable to ordinary citizens, facilitating stand-by citizenship and inclusion. Although theorists like Nancy Rosenblum, Lea Ypi, and Jonathan White emphasize the power of parties to mobilize voters, I suggest that much of this mobilizing power comes not from get-out-the-vote efforts but rather through promoting politics' cognitive tractability and accessibility. Yet parties do not make politics tractable for voters automatically. Contrary to the previous celebrations of parties in political theory, I emphasize that their salubrious effects on democracy are conditional on *competition*. Drawing from the history of urban political machines of the United States in the nineteenth and twentieth centuries, I show that parties mobilize voters, but only when they are forced to compete with each other. Indeed, competitive pressure renders parties capable of remarkable feats aimed at mobilizing new and potential voters. Ensuring that parties cannot take electoral wins or voters for granted by forcing them to compete is essential to preventing them from degenerating into corrupt political cartels only interested in protecting core supporters and from succumbing to spirals of polarization. I thus argue for multipartyism as a key tool for ensuring robust competition against the argument of Frances Rosenbluth and Ian Shapiro who regard two-party systems as superior.

Many democratic theorists today favor reforms based on deliberation and sortition, and this raises the question of what role they could play in a democracy for busy people. Chapter 7, "Putting Deliberation and Sortition in their Place," uses empirical evidence, including an original analysis of data from Canada, to argue that they are unlikely to play a central role in any democracy that puts inclusion first because they cannot be the mass-scale aids to the cultivation of stand-by citizenship that democracy needs and because they threaten the institutional scaffolding and mobilization resources that make politics accessible to busy people. Although I show that there is substantial evidence that mini-publics can cultivate stand-by citizenship among those who participate in them, there is little or no evidence that they do so for nonparticipants. Spreading their influence would therefore require the multiplication of deliberative institutions, which creates a dilemma.

One horn of the dilemma is that, if multiplied deliberative institutions are made authoritative, they may displace electoral institutions, as Hélène Landemore and Alexander Guerrero have advocated, with the result of shredding the ecosystem of information-generating and engagement-stimulating institutions, like parties, that make politics an everyday part of citizens' lives. This would have, I argue, a massive demobilizing effect on the public. The other horn of the dilemma is that, if multiplied deliberative bodies are left advisory, they will either be captured by the already politically engaged, or the quality of their deliberation may be degraded. In either case, they will fail to reach the citizens most in need of a nudge toward stand-by citizenship. Drawing from the work of John Gastil, I argue that deliberation and sortition are likely to find their most plausible place as supplemental helpmates to electoral democracy, such as through improving the quality of the check on elected legislatures provided by direct democracy. This constitutes a valuable service to any democracy, including one for busy people, but surely falls short of reinventing it. Deliberation and sortition thus find their place in a distinctly secondary role to electoral democracy, I conclude, at least in a democracy that puts inclusion first.

PART I

How Much Democratic Citizenship?

CHAPTER TWO

Democracy's Floor

The Case against Apathy

Is democracy better off if some people stay out of politics? Can democracy benefit from the apathy of some of its citizens? Political scientists and theorists have long thought so. In the middle of the twentieth century, Bernard Berelson and his Columbia school colleagues argued that apathy among some citizens powers a potent mechanism of democratic stability. More recently, Jason Brennan has argued the quality of democratic decision-making is harmed by inclusion, since inclusive decision-making counts the input of citizens who are poorly informed and badly motivated, as out of destructive partisanship. Democracy is better off without them, Brennan says.

In this chapter, I argue that these long-standing views of apathy are confused at best, and wrong—dangerously so—at worst. Apathy is neither good for democracy, nor do democratic citizens have a right to be politically apathetic. *Something* is required from all of us as democratic citizens. Though I make some comments as to what this level of engagement entails, I leave its full elucidation to chapter 4.

So, why should individuals living in democratic societies pay any attention to politics in the first place? It is, after all, a core feature of liberal democratic practice today that the decision whether to participate is left entirely up to the individual. Indeed, objections to the most common form of compulsory political participation—mandatory voting—is often framed in terms of violating a right to withhold one's input from electoral contests (Lever 2010). This suggests that there is a widespread implicit belief that it is up to the individual whether to pay politics any attention at all. This, in turn, seems to suggest that political apathy, understood as giving politics no thought or concern, is a legitimate form of democratic citizenship. Implicit in existing liberal democratic practice, therefore, is something like a "right to apathy," whereby individuals could opt to disengage from or ignore their democracy's politics and play no part whatsoever in it, not even that of passive observer.[1] At least one philosopher has recently argued that citizens ought to "ignore politics," effectively defending a right to apathy (Freiman 2021).

It is important to be clear about what is meant by "apathy" here. To be apathetic in my sense is to be utterly inattentive to politics; it is to refrain from giving politics any space in one's mind or awareness. It means not just refraining from political participation, but also refraining from the activities of someone in the habit of political engagement such as "regularly reading opinion pieces, watching news and debates, studying social science and political philosophy, taking steps to reduce one's partisan bias, attending rallies, discussing and linking to political articles on Facebook" (Freiman 2021, 135). Just as most of us are unaware of developments in, say, the world of competitive quilting, politically apathetic people are simply unaware of, and uninterested in, what is happening in politics.

What apathy does *not* include by this account, therefore, is a conscious or reflective rejection of participating in politics, a rejection that might or might not be paired with paying (even disgusted) attention to politics. Such cynical political orientations are often classified as a species of apathy. But this is not correct, as many individuals in this position care very much about political developments, but, for whatever reason, find no avenue of political participation worthwhile. Thus, apathy is not the same as passivity, since passivity encompasses a wider group and includes those who are not apathetic in my sense. Choosing to observe politics but not participate does *not* make one apathetic. Only being unmindful of politics does. And lest we think that there are no apathetic citizens in this sense, between 1948 and 2008, on average 13 percent of Americans, or about one in eight, reported the lowest possible level of interest in public affairs (American National Election Studies 2021).[2] Apathy in the sense I am concerned with is thus a small but hardly trivial phenomenon.

1. I take for granted that there is sufficient scope in modern societies to enable citizens to avoid politics in daily life. This of course involves making assumptions about what counts as politics, assumptions which might be controversial. At present, all that matters is that politics is not coincident with the entire social realm.

2. After 2008, a different question was used by the American National Election Studies (ANES) to measure political interest. On average, 6–7 percent fell into the lowest category

One underappreciated argument for a right to apathy is that it is key to pursuing one's own idea of the good life. Our lives have what I have called elsewhere a moral economy (Elliott 2018b). This economy comprises how we divide our time, energy, and resources between different projects in different spheres of our lives. Do we devote ourselves to religious fellowship? To a career? To family? These choices structure our lives and determine whether one's life is well spent. A life's moral economy therefore constitutes a cornerstone of one's conception of the good life.

The idea that a life has a moral economy suggests a justification for the standard liberal belief that choices about structuring one's life should be left to the individual. The reason we think such decisions are important is in some sense because we think individuals ought to have control over their life's moral economy, an idea we often articulate in terms of autonomy.[3] No one else is as well situated to ensure that one's moral economy is structured to best promote one's own idea of happiness.

It is clear, then, why a duty to pay attention to politics might be problematic. It interferes with the individual's control over their own moral economy by laying claim to a portion of it in the name of democracy. How could this interference be justified, then, if at all? I argue that no citizen has a right to be politically apathetic in the sense of paying politics no attention whatsoever. Apathy undermines democratic equality, imposes harms on other citizens, and is unfair to those who need the individual's help to combat social and political injustice. It may even undermine the stability of democratic regimes.

This chapter focuses on contrasting views regarding the value of apathy for democracy starting in the middle of the twentieth century. This is because, although the topic is an important one in democratic theory, there has never to my knowledge been a systematic analysis of the major arguments for and against political apathy as such. This may have something to do with a widespread belief among democratic theorists and

---

of political interest using this new measure. However, another item querying "interest in the election" found a similarly sized group of totally uninterested citizens to the older interest question: 13 percent or more. There is reason to worry that none of these questions constitute very good measures of interest in politics (Shani 2012). They nonetheless provide a *very* rough sense of the scale of political apathy.

3. The language of moral economy highlights the utilitarian (or eudaimonic) approach to justifying the right of individuals to noninterference, as opposed to an autonomy-based approach. I do not believe the difference in these approaches affects the argument.

reformers that apathy is simply unjustifiable, and so not worth discussing seriously. Yet when politics becomes polarized and toxic, and so repellent to many citizens, and philosophers begin arguing that political apathy might be not just good for democracy but obligatory for most citizens, we require more than mere prejudice against apathy. We must consider whether there is something to be said for apathy, and if so, what the limits of it might be. Moreover, contemporary discussions of the ethics of democratic participation have largely neglected the classic works of the mid-twentieth century with respect to their arguments about apathy.

An important contribution of this chapter's analysis is its focus on mechanisms of collective action and social group identity. Much previous discussion of the ethics of democratic citizenship has relied on highly abstract and historically uninformed versions of the rational choice paradigm, in which all human action is seen as individually rational, and the relevance of history is minimized. This approach has systematically obscured the thick social ties that actually shape citizens' behavior and interaction. The approach taken here seeks to highlight the mechanisms by which apathy and its effects spread via social networks and shared social knowledge. This is an important advance because it helps to flesh out the precise social mechanisms by which some long-standing speculative arguments might operate in the world, perhaps opening the door to their being tested empirically or confirmed by observation. Indeed, where possible, empirical evidence of the collective phenomena I highlight is cited. This approach serves to move democratic ethics forward by setting aside deracinated rational actors in favor of socially conditioned flesh-and-blood human beings.

Why Might Apathy Be Good?

Political scientists and theorists have long been interested in political apathy, yet this interest has often taken the form of appreciation rather than criticism. Though this appreciation tends to be qualified, it presents a tradition of thought about apathy that stands in marked contrast to that pursued in this chapter and in democratic theory more generally over the past few decades.

A widespread view in post–World War II political science was that some amount of apathy is good for democratic stability. Bernard Berelson, Paul Lazarsfeld, and William McPhee, in their classic study *Voting*, argue that apathy among a substantial share of Americans contributes to the stability and flexibility of the political system. It does this, first, by promoting compromise. "Extreme interest," they write, "goes with extreme partisanship and might culminate in rigid fanaticism" and a general breakdown of democracy. Though compromise can be born of a "sophisticated awareness of costs and returns," more often it arises from indifference (Berelson, Lazarsfeld, and McPhee 1954, 314–15). Apathy among some citizens, then, allows for compromises to be struck because apathetic citizens are not wedded to intransigence on policy in the way extremely interested partisans are. Representatives know they can make compromises because not all of their supporters are strongly interested in the specifics of the result.

Additionally, Berelson et al. argue that apathy enables flexibility in responding to new phenomena and events. "Without [apathetic citizens]—if the decision were left only to the deeply concerned, well-integrated, consistently principled ideal citizens—the political system might easily prove too rigid to adapt to changing domestic and international conditions" (Berelson, Lazarsfeld, and McPhee 1954, 316). The point is similar to that regarding compromise. Apathy among some citizens allows representatives to try new things in response to emerging problems, even if the new response flies in the face of existing partisan orthodoxy. A politics without such citizens would leave representatives cowering before partisan constituents intolerant of novel ideas that stray beyond the established ideological fold.

Throughout, Berelson et al. (1954, 315) emphasize the need for a certain kind of balance in government and how apathy aids this salutary equilibrium. The balance is struck between two heterogeneous groups within the polity. Highly politically interested partisans help stabilize the political system through adherence to relatively stable ideologies, while persuadable apathetic citizens lend the system flexibility and the capacity to change. Each body of citizens serves as a counterweight to the other, checking the other's natural tendency to a deleterious extreme—avoiding rigidity in the one case and proteanism on the other. Since stability and flexibility are both essential features of any political system, political apathy thus serves a vital function as counterweight in an elemental political balance.

Samuel Huntington (1975) famously celebrates apathy on different grounds. He claims that it prevents the overload of the democratic system with demands it cannot fulfill. Preventing such "demand overload" is important, argues Huntington, because democracy cannot meet all the demands made of it by the groups who became politically mobilized in the 1960s and 1970s, when Huntington was writing. Such failure to meet demands undermines trust in the system, degrading its legitimacy. As a result, the capacity of government to act at all also degrades, which causes further failures to meet demands. This further undermines trust, in a vicious downward spiral. Declining trust in democratic institutions is a core feature of what Huntington calls the "democratic distemper," and apathy is a key prophylaxis against it, he claims. If many citizens are disengaged from politics, the thought is that their interests and desires could be safely ignored by the political system. The system could then concern itself with a smaller set of demands that it could actually meet. Though Huntington admits that the resulting exclusion constitutes a democratic cost, he judges the trade-off for stability worth it. On this account, then, as before, the key contribution of apathy is to the stability of democracy. The function of apathy is not, however, homeostatic balance as for Berelson et al., but rather to forestall the perverse results of wider political mobilization, particularly among the most politically marginalized, whose interests and demands are to be systematically sacrificed to the god of democratic stability.

A third moment of appreciation for apathy is found in Robert Dahl's idea that apathetic citizens constitute a salutary reservoir of "slack" in the political system. Dahl introduces the idea of slack by means of a story from mid-twentieth century New Haven city politics. A pair of investors wanted to build some cheap metal houses in a New Haven neighborhood, and those living there worried it would threaten the character of the neighborhood: a classic not-in-my-backyard, or NIMBY, scenario. The residents of the neighborhood were mostly working-class people, many of Italian and Russian Jewish origin, who did not habitually participate in politics. When a few key residents learned about the plans for the metal homes, they spread the news through the neighborhood and mobilized residents to pressure city officials to block the development. After many months of collective effort, they were ultimately successful. Yet this episode failed to mark the rise of an empowered community, since afterward the residents subsided back into political abeyance, in contrast to the expectations of many democratic theorists who often say that such empowering events trigger an enduring habit of participation (Dahl 1961, 197).

For Dahl, this scenario is a democratic triumph because it shows how nearly exclusive concern for one's own private interests is compatible with the democratic value of equal concern for the interests of all. Unlike Huntington, who seems willing to sacrifice the interests of marginalized groups to keep democracy stable, Dahl wants to find a way for citizens to be able to engross themselves in their private lives while also avoiding their political exploitation. Benjamin Constant (1819 [1988]), writing a century and a half before, recognized the same dilemma and saw it as insoluble; he thought the best one could do was to exhort one's fellow citizens *not* to completely lose themselves in their own concerns. Dahl seems to take this option off the table by naturalizing apathy, seeing it as the default political orientation in "liberal societies, [where] politics is a sideshow in the great circus of life" (Dahl 1961, 305). In liberal societies, nonpolitical life is thus the main attraction. By making apathy natural, Dahl sparks a need to find a way to accommodate it within a democratic frame. The concept of slack squares the circle. Citizens who usually spend their time on their private affairs can be mobilized when their interests are directly affected, avoiding the domination Constant feared, while also securing to them the private happiness privileged by a liberal modernity.

Slack thus makes apathy safe for democracy, or at least for a strongly representative and pluralist form of it. It allows citizens to generally use their limited resources of attention, time, and money as they please in private life while occasionally shifting some of them toward politics to achieve a concrete goal. For Dahl, the only goals with sufficient pull to play this role are self-interested ones. Citizens would normally become interested in politics not out of a sense of duty or dedication to the polity, but because their own interests are on the line. Together, these two features—allowing citizens to mostly devote themselves to their private pursuits and hitching citizen political mobilization to the powerful drive of self-interest—constitute the attractiveness of slack and open a democratically legible space for apathy.

The normative orientation of Dahl's idea of slack is less a concern for the stability of democracy than the ideal of equal representation. This marks a significant divergence with the more direct celebrations of apathy of Berelson et al. and Huntington, for whom stability is a far greater concern. Nonetheless, for all three, apathy is functional to democratic politics.

These views constitute some of the most influential ideas about apathy to come out of post–World War II political science. This post-war context is significant in part because, as I discuss below with respect to Hannah Arendt, these authors all looked back to the fall of democracies across Europe in the years prior to the Second World War and saw as the culprit not widespread political apathy but intense mass mobilization by fascist movements. The perception, right or wrong, that an excess of demotic energy aided the rise of totalitarian dictatorships helped shape the study of political systems for a generation and more. The mass apathy celebrated by many post-war studies of the American electorate was meant to highlight a different, better way to do democracy, one that promises to moderate the energy of the people and render them tractable to responsible political elites via limited, regularized electoral competition.

Recently, a different set of arguments for the value or justification of apathy has arisen. I want to look at three such arguments before moving on to the arguments for why apathy does not benefit democracy. These contemporary pro-apathy arguments illustrate, respectively, a communicative-functionalist approach, a moralistic approach, and an epistemic approach to justifying apathy.

In Annabelle Lever's argument against mandatory voting, she suggests that avoiding political engagement and participation of all kinds can be important because they "enable the weak, timid and unpopular to protest in ways that feel safe, and that require little co-ordination and few resources" (Lever 2010, 911). Though Lever is thinking here about the right to abstain from voting, her point suggests that refraining from political engagement of any kind is a cheap and easy way to protest, which puts it within reach of even the most marginalized members of society. For her, then, apathy as ignoring politics can serve as a form of protest, and one especially important for the weakest citizens. This is because this kind of apathy could show up in a number of ways—on surveys, in election returns, in popular uptake of government initiatives—which could signal to observers the government's (lack of) support among the people. Apathy might, for instance, effectively communicate discontent by rendering the government unable to muster voters or get citizens to abide by some new policy initiative. Apathy thus becomes publicly visible when it manifests itself in low turnout, or frustrated government plans. Such a signal is likely to be especially important in cases of oppression or democratic corruption when other forms of political expression are effectively blocked. Thus, apathy could have value as a form of protest, at least in some circumstances.

For Lever, then, apathy is potentially functional to democracy, but in a different way to that of post-war political scientists' views. According to her, democracy requires a robust system of political expression with a variety of means of communication, and it would be foolish to rule out any avenue, even one constituted by apathy. It is, by this account, a way of signaling that something is wrong, that someone is not happy with the job the government is doing, or perhaps even feels democracy in their polity is so problematic that engagement is pointless. Such a publicly visible escape valve for discontent is especially valuable in extreme cases, though its utility in other circumstances might be less. This renders Lever's argument more conditional and sensitive to circumstances than those so far discussed.

The second contemporary argument for apathy comes from Christopher Freiman (2021), and consists in the view that political apathy is morally superior to political engagement for most people most of the time because we can do more to help other people through private philanthropy than through politics (cf. [Brennan 2011]). Freiman argues that virtually all political participation is pointless because it doesn't change anything, but that philanthropy can directly save lives. As a result, political engagement is not just suboptimal but morally wrong when one can do more good for others through earning income in the market and using it to provide aid directly (Freiman 2021, 131–37).

Freiman's argument is narrowly moral in that it assumes that we all have a general duty to aid others that might provide a reason to do politics. Freiman's aim is to sever the connection between moral duty and political participation that others have sought to forge (see, e.g., Maskivker [2019]). In so doing, he generates a freestanding argument for the value of apathy, one that does not—and does not claim to—aid democracy in any specific way. Rather, it views democracy as instrumental to the moral aim of altruism. It is in this sense a moralistic argument for apathy, as opposed to the others that posit apathy as functional to democracy in one way or another.

The final argument for apathy comes from Brennan and is perhaps the most aggressively positive about a certain kind of apathy since it posits that not only is apathy often good for democracy but is, in fact, *morally obligatory* for many citizens most of the time. Using a long-standing libertarian view of voting, Brennan argues that to cast a ballot—or, indeed, to engage in any form of political participation aimed at affecting the state—is to attempt to impose coercion on others, via the policies that the government might enact. Participation is thus more morally laden than is often thought since the coercion of others is generally involved. In particular, Brennan argues that participation's coerciveness makes it morally incumbent upon all citizens to ensure that they vote responsibly, meaning that they do so in an informed way that furthers the common good

(Brennan 2011). If citizens are not informed about politics and if they lack the detailed information he thinks is necessary to identify the common good, as Brennan thinks is the case for most citizens, they must, as a matter of moral obligation, refrain from participating in politics (Brennan 2016). In those circumstances, such participation would irresponsibly impose on others the risk of the misuse of coercive power. According to Brennan, apathy by the uninformed is thus not only helpful for democracy, but a moral obligation for these citizens.

I must pause here to anticipate a point that will be made more fully later. Brennan's line of argument might be thought to render many of the arguments offered below moot since, without the information necessary to sort out just from unjust outcomes or even to correctly identify which electoral choice one's interest recommends, citizens cannot do what those arguments suppose they must. If citizens lack sufficient information to act responsibly, it seems to undermine democracy at the root.

Yet there are numerous elementary problems with this line of argument that render it for practical purposes specious, and I want to rehearse a few of them before leaving a promissory note for a fuller response later. First, to conclude that citizens lack the information they need to act responsibly presupposes a thick account of correct political choice, or even a comprehensive theory of justice, in addition to a reliable and comprehensive measure of what people know about politics. But not only is such a measure currently unavailable (Elliott 2020a, 393–94), there is no such publicly legible standard of correct decisions by which to judge whether people's information is sufficient to vote "well." Disagreement over such standards is not just endemic to politics, but arguably constitutive of it (Waldron 1999, 102). Efforts to impute correct voting invariably make very strong assumptions about what is rational for citizens to want (or about what kinds of identity determine one's views about politics), but this usurps the judgment of citizens who may weigh the issues at play in their political milieu differently. Giving equal respect to the judgment of citizens is a fundamental part of treating them as free and equal and, indeed, of democracy itself (Schwartzberg 2016, 2018).

Second, Brennan's line of argument supposes citizens must possess full or nearly full information about politics and the political world—as well as background social scientific knowledge—to make rational political choices. Yet people make basically rational decisions from highly incomplete information all the time, in the marketplace and in politics (Elliott 2019, 9). Often, in both contexts, they do so by using information shortcuts, a mechanism given no serious consideration by Brennan despite its obvious and empirically verified relevance to his argument (Elliott 2018a).

Third, Brennan assumes that the level of informedness of citizens is fixed, and thus that institutions must be adjusted to accommodate apparent public ignorance. Yet empirical evidence shows that the public's level of information varies with political institutions, such that citizens who live, for instance, in multiparty systems have more information than those that live in two-party ones because multiparty competition both fills the information environment with more information and raises the information level citizens need to make electoral decisions (Fortunato, Stevenson, and Vonnahme 2016). This evidence suggests that ignorance itself can be adjusted through institutional design. Here I lay down a promissory note for the argument to come in chapters 4, 5, and 6. There I will offer a series of institutional responses to concerns about citizen informedness that focus on the way certain institutions can cultivate an epistemic environment and habits of mind among citizens that help answer the challenge.

Thus, we find a wide spectrum of arguments that seem to show the political or moral value of apathy, at least some of the time. Apathy may (1) aid democratic stability, (2) add flexibility, (3) make self-interested apathy safe for democracy, (4) enable the easy expression of discontent in a way open to the most vulnerable, (5) enable us to focus on making a real difference for others, and (6) save democracy from the ignorant input of its least responsible citizens. We shall see in the remainder of this chapter that some of these arguments are at best incomplete while the advantages promised by others can be secured without the dangers posed by apathy. We will in the end be left without reasons to favor political apathy or endorse a right to it.

Why Apathy Is Bad I: Injustice and Complicity

So, why is it wrong to think citizens have a right to be apathetic about politics? What reasons require that they dedicate at least some of their moral economies to the politics of their democracy? In this section, I expound two arguments—one made by Tommie Shelby and the other by Eric Beerbohm—that establish an obligation not to be politically apathetic in common circumstances. These arguments are rooted in the value of fairness and justice. On Shelby and Beerbohm's views, citizens owe it to each other to mobilize politically so as to bring about a more just system when injustice reigns.

Drawing on the work of John Rawls, Shelby (2016) argues that individuals have a "natural duty" to help create just institutions where they do not currently exist. By framing this as a natural duty, Shelby means that it is not conditional on either the existence of fair institutions, which would make the duty conditional on such institutions already existing, or reciprocity from others, which requires others to contribute to trigger one's own obligation. The duty to bring about just institutions is thus not conditional. It is an obligation all must fulfill, regardless of circumstance.

Shelby's primary concern is with the "ghetto poor," a group partly defined by suffering from entrenched, systemic injustice. Due to this duty, the ghetto poor—along with others suffering such injustice—have a prima facie claim to the aid of other citizens in creating institutions that do not so victimize them. This is owed to them as a matter of fundamental entitlement—it is a claim of justice. It is also a claim of fairness. Although Shelby explicitly discounts justifying the argument on grounds of reciprocity, there is an important sense in which all of us would want there to be such an obligation in a world where we did not know if we would be the victims of systemic injustice. It is thus only fair to assist others in this project, as we would expect it for ourselves when we are the victims of injustice.

But what is the character of this assistance? Much of the time, it is political participation. Since we are talking about the justice of fundamental social and political institutions, changing those conditions means taking part in the processes that shape them, processes that partly constitute politics. The specific forms of participation called for are likely to vary widely with the context. Some injustices might be redeemed electorally, by electing candidates or parties firmly committed to using the power of office to redress them. Other forms of injustice, particularly entrenched types, may often require more than electoral participation. More demanding forms of activism may be required, even including civil disobedience, with all the personal cost that it entails.

Shelby's duty to aid raises important questions about just how demanding the duty is, yet I defer addressing these concerns until chapter 4. For the time being, we are interested solely in whether citizens can be obligated to do *anything* as citizens, as opposed to being apathetic toward politics. Here we have seen that one reason citizens cannot be apathetic is that they are subject to a duty to bring about just institutions where they do not exist. In conditions of injustice, this duty imposes expectations of political participation aimed at ending that injustice and installing a just set of institutions. Not only do we owe this to our fellow citizens as a matter of fundamental justice, but we ourselves would not want to belong to a polity without such a duty, since we might ourselves be subject to injustice and in need of such assistance.

Beerbohm also argues that we have an obligation to participate when our political institutions are unjust. This obligation comes from our complicity in the injustice of a democratic government that represents us and acts in our name. For Beerbohm, we are tied together with fellow citizens through the coercive institutions that act in the name of all of us and to which we contribute in myriad ways. Institutions like those of the state put us into complex relations with others, and these relations become morally freighted when the institutions enable or embody injustice. These complex, institutionally mediated relations between citizens involve all citizens morally in the actions of those institutions. By putting us in this position vis-à-vis others, our shared institutions also give rise to "position-relative reasons" to act, at least in circumstances of injustice (Beerbohm 2012, 76–77). Thus, when our democratic government—which represents us and acts in our name—does something unjust, we share the blame for it. Beerbohm argues that we are complicit.

This complicity cannot be offset by refraining from political participation. A common justification for not participating in elections, for example, is not wanting to grant a problematic political system, political party, or particular candidate legitimacy by even participating in the election that might empower them. Beerbohm argues that one cannot insulate oneself from shared responsibility for government injustice by not voting—or, in our terms, by being politically apathetic. This is because of the institutional ties binding citizens together. If our democratic state is unjust, and we do nothing about it, we are like someone who knows that a friend plans to rob a bank and prepares him breakfast that morning or puts gas in his getaway car. We provide support, to one degree or another, to the overall enterprise and knowingly do nothing to blunt its evil intent. This makes us accessory to the injustice. Even if we do not vote, we still support our institutions in myriad other ways, from paying taxes to obeying laws to allowing the state to infer we support its unjust actions via silent acquiescence. This last should not be taken lightly, as authoritarian governments throughout history have less often sought their populations' enthusiastic support than their passive resignation. Moreover, accepting the benefits made available by the state signals that one thinks "the government is worthy of a transactional relationship" (Beerbohm 2012, 72–73). Even making use of public services, from roads to parks to police, bestows a degree of valued recognition to the state when one takes advantage of its services in silence. Thus, because of our complex relationship to the coercive institutions of the polity, even our inaction serves to sponsor the activities of those institutions.

The only way to forestall our complicity with the state's injustice is through making clear our opposition, via public action. We must disrupt the impression that the people support the government's injustice and do our best, with others, to change its behavior. Moreover, as with Shelby, the "urgency" of our participation will vary with the "moral properties" of the institutions and situation we find ourselves in (Beerbohm 2012, 76–77). In other words, a more unjust situation, or one in which the moral stakes are especially grave, will call for greater participation from us. Our obligation calls for greater participation in proportion to the seriousness of the injustice. Such participation can, moreover, help to hearten others who feel the same way, further mobilizing opposition and making future democratic victory more likely.[4]

Freiman objects to this line of argument because he thinks private philanthropic efforts to remedy injustice are sufficient to discharge the complicity established by Beerbohm. Even if an injustice is caused by political means, we are not obliged to do politics to respond to it, he says, because we can take action on our own to directly address it (Freiman 2021, 99–101). A fatal problem with Freiman's argument, however, is that we must first *pay attention* to politics to learn what injustices there are and how the (democratic) state is implicated in them. Yet this is flatly inconsistent with Freiman's aim to explain why we can "ignore" politics. Indeed, the activities he associates with the habit of political engagement such as reading news articles and studying social science are precisely the ways that most people come to understand that there is a need for action, even private action (Freiman 2021, 135). He suggests that such attentive activities immorally subtract from the time you could spend generating income to contribute to private charity. But these activities are epistemically indispensable for remediating injustice of any kind. Freiman's argument thus cannot establish that private action, undertaken in ignorance of politics, is sufficient to discharge complicity.

---

4. Both arguments cry out for examination of how much participation they require. I must postpone this discussion until chapter 4.

Why Apathy Is Bad II: Equality

Many democratic theorists identify equality as the normative core of democracy. For these theorists, anything that systematically blocks political equality destroys the fundamental value of democracy.[5] In this section, I show how political inattention undermines political equality. When any citizen or group of citizens is apathetic toward politics, it creates compounding and enduring inequalities in political power in ways that make even approximating equality impossible. This generates an equality-based reason to deny a right to apathy.

The first way that inattention produces political inequality is by short-circuiting the representative mechanism of anticipated response. Because representatives know that their actions will be observed by the public, they expect that if they sufficiently displease the attentive public, they will not be reelected (Key 1961; Mansbridge 2003). In anticipation of such a response, they seek to serve the interests of this part of the public. Representation achieved this way does not rely upon the active participation of citizens, but merely upon *attention* along with an implied threat of future participation.

Inattention prevents this mechanism from operating and so hinders equal representation. Inattentive citizens are not represented because representatives come to know that they can neglect inattentive groups' interests without fear of electoral reprisal. Over time, representatives learn which groups they can safely ignore and those to which they must cater. This cements habits of neglect for the inattentive, including creating ignorance of inattentive groups' interests and concerns. These habits build self-reinforcing expectations among all involved that certain groups do not matter, blunting the motivation of traditionally apathetic and under-represented groups to contest their unequal status. This unfolding pattern of what we can call, following James Wilson (2019, 134–36), "deliberative neglect" gives rise to enduring political inequality.

The spread of common knowledge regarding who does and does not matter politically gives rise to a distinctive egalitarian harm on the view that all citizens must have, or be recognized as having, equal standing. On this view, when it becomes obvious to all members of society that some

---

5. I argue later that political equality is a distinctly inferior value to inclusion within a wider ideal of democratic equality. In this section, I treat political equality as tantamount to democratic equality.

groups are significantly more powerful than others due to variance in their levels of political attention, the possibility of relating to each other as equals evaporates. Such a state of affairs constitutes a violation of equal standing and thus political equality.

The second way political apathy generates political inequality is by degrading the civic capacities of the inattentive. By civic capacities, I mean the civic skills and knowledge needed to take part in politics. Civic skills include the embodied practical knowledge of how to go about participating in politics, including the mechanics of registering and turning out to vote, social connections with politically active groups and individuals, and, crucially, familiarity with the political landscape, its rules, and its key players (Verba, Schlozman, and Brady 1995). When we ignore politics and take no active part in it, these skills degrade, and with them goes our ability to engage in political participation. Those who lack civic skills through inattention face steep costs to engaging in ordinary forms of participation because they must (re)acquaint themselves with the basics of political life, such as who the major parties are and what they stand for and how to go about participation. Inattention breeds the decline of civic skills, which in turn brings about the inability to participate, which itself causes further degradation of civic skills, constituting a vicious cycle of disempowerment. Thus, apathy and inattention lead to enduring political inequality.

The degradation of civic skills and short-circuiting of anticipated response explain why Lever is wrong when she argues that the mere potential for political influence that comes with the right to vote is enough for the equitable protection of citizens' interests (Lever 2010, 906). Though she does not use this language, Lever banks on the phenomenon of anticipated response. She also assumes that citizens automatically know how to go about using their political rights. The arguments from a moment ago show that these assumptions are untenable. Merely possessing rights to participate is consistent with being effectively unable to use them, and this inability affects whether elected officials take the interests of apathetic citizens seriously. Political rights can no more secure meaningful equality on their own than can a car get us to an unfamiliar place without a map.

A third way that apathy creates inequality is through network or social contagion effects. A wealth of empirical evidence shows that behaviors, including political behaviors, spread through social networks like infectious disease (Bond et al. 2012; Christakis and Fowler 2013). Political disengagement would spread as follows. When one person is inattentive to politics, it makes others in that person's social network recognize inattention as a possible behavior. When it spreads through enough of a social network, it becomes a local norm of that group and so becomes reinforced by the ordinary but potent pressures of everyday social life. In the language of social choice, disengagement comes to constitute the social coordination point at which an equilibrium of nonengagement with politics is reached.

As I discuss in the next section, both social contagion effects and the short-circuiting of anticipated response are especially problematic because they imply that the harms of inattention are not limited to those who neglect politics. They extend also to those who share their interests, identities, and political principles through the diminution of that group's political voice. This might not be a problem if the proclivity to be inattentive were distributed equally across groups in society, since then all groups' voices would be equally diminished. But inattention is distributed unequally (Prior 2018), so it generates political inequality.

In all of these underappreciated ways, inattention and apathy create lasting patterns of unequal power and undermine equal standing. Democratic egalitarians therefore must deny that a right to apathy is consistent with democracy's core value. If democracy is to embody the ideal of political equality, it cannot be that citizens decide for themselves whether to give politics any of their time and attention.

Why Apathy Is Bad III: Harm

Much of the intuitive appeal of the right to apathy, and of prevailing liberal democratic practice in line with it, comes from nonparticipation not seeming to harm anyone. Indeed, to use J. S. Mill's language, it appears to be a form of self-regarding action, over which society has no legitimate power. Someone not engaging in politics seems to make a self-regarding choice not to exercise their political rights. Just as it is up to us whether to choose a religion or whether to exercise a right to get married, so too should it be up to us to decide whether to exercise our political rights.

Even if apathy were other-regarding, moreover, it does not initially seem to cause harm to others. It seems like the only real harm involved would be to the individual and his or her own interests by not defending them in the political arena. If individuals choose to accept that harm in order to spend their time doing other things, social opprobrium or legal compulsion would seem to be misplaced, just as it would be for any other harmless conduct of which we might disapprove. Only harm to others can justify interference in the individual's choices, according to both Mill and widespread liberal democratic intuitions.

I suspect that something approximating this analysis is behind the common sense that not participating in politics is perhaps foolish (rather than wrong), but not something for which people ought to be blamed. This reaction might be similar to that toward someone smoking. However, I argue that the understandable intuition that apathy harms no one is incorrect. In fact, it harms or risks harm to identifiable groups, up to and including the entire democratic polity. The sense that political apathy is harmless and of little consequence to others is thus faulty. I also argue, however, that even though apathy causes harm, it is *not* blameworthy because the mechanisms of this harm are sufficiently indirect to render them not at all obvious to people, and no one should be blamed for something they did unknowingly, at least not when the knowledge is obscure or hard to acquire. We shall see, moreover, that there are additional reasons not to treat apathy as blameworthy later. Apathy is best thought of as a democratic nuisance, like pollution, one collectively generated and requiring collective remedy.

Political apathy harms those in society that are similar to the person who is inattentive by ensuring underrepresentation of the group that they help comprise. I made a similar point in the last section showing how apathy creates inequality via unequal patterns of representation. The idea here is that apathy on the part of any single individual harms everyone belonging to groups to which the individual also belongs. The issue is thus not inequality but the harm that such unequal power causes. In other words, it is about the *outcome* of unequal power relations, not those relations themselves, which constituted the equality-based claim in the last section.

The harms at issue come in at least two forms. The first is familiar and consists in harming or burdening the ability of people to live well—what we often talk about in terms of harm to people's interests. Concrete examples of this kind of harm include enabling discrimination against certain groups, exploitation of certain groups' labor, depriving some communities of access to clean water or educational opportunities, or failing to prevent targeted fraud and economic predation against the group (Coates 2014). When groups are not politically empowered, they are left open to all of these sorts of serious mistreatment, among others, and each apathetic member of the group enables that mistreatment.[6]

---

6. Some critics of widespread active citizenship, such as Brennan and Freiman, allege that participation cannot empower anyone and does not matter because a single vote or other act

Another way of talking about this first kind of harm is in terms of the distribution of benefits and burdens that a democratic political system generates. Inattention prevents the *just* distribution of benefits and burdens by biasing the inputs into the democratic system. We can call this "aggregative distortion." The missing voices of the apathetic produce this aggregative distortion and ensure that, at best, goods necessary for living well are undersupplied to groups to which the apathetic belong, crippling their pursuit of happiness, and, at worst, opening them to oppression and victimization.

The second kind of harm caused by apathy involves the provision of goods that are vital for a particular group's pursuit of the good life as they see it, but not for others' pursuit. There are, in other words, some goods that are specific to particular groups' flourishing and which the state might or might not provide or protect. Most polities, for instance, do not tax churches, providing vital support to religious organizations that serve as cornerstones of the good life for many individuals. Another example of a group-specific good is sacred sites, such as ancestral burial grounds, and the ability to visit them. The city of Vallejo, California, for instance, planned to build a park on an ancient Ohlone Indian burial site in 2011. A group of American Indians from different tribes occupied the site for more than three months, eventually winning a cultural easement over the site that would preserve the integrity of the remains and associated artifacts. Though this example stands uncomfortably within my wider concern about small, intensely interested groups dominating politics, the point here is a minor one. Group-specific goods like this easement often depend upon collective action by the group to ensure their protection or provision. My point is that political apathy can acutely threaten such goods.

---

of political participation is not decisive (Brennan 2016; Freiman 2021). If that's so, participation couldn't protect any groups from abuse as I suggest. Yet this view is based on rotten microfoundations because the theory of voting and participation it draws from is an unmitigated failure in producing accurate predictions of voter behavior (Green and Shapiro 1994; Geys 2006b; Abizadeh 2021). A more accurate view would emphasize social group identity, civic skills, and institutional incentives as the key determining factors of participation. We vote, participate, etc. when people similar to us socially do so, not when it passes a cost-benefit analysis. When we center groups in this way, moreover, it allows us to recognize basic social facts about participation and power. It is no coincidence that the most powerful groups in society participate at the highest rates (Verba, Schlozman, and Brady 1995; Schlozman, Brady, and Verba 2018). Their participation helps cement and reproduce their group's power over time, showing the efficacy of participation after all.

Apathy does this by undermining the willingness and ability of members of the group to engage in collective action. Mustering members of groups for collective efforts is made more difficult by habitual apathy on the part of group members. This is because of the social contagion mechanism discussed above; insofar as members of the group socialize with one another, they will come to share similar views of politics and propensities to take part in collective efforts on behalf of the group. Apathy toward political affairs makes it harder for the group to mobilize politically and protect its group-specific goods and other interests in the wider society.

Contagion adds a social dimension to the harm of apathy that also amplifies its size. This is important because one response to this argument is to dismiss apathy's harms as too insignificant to merit moral concern. Yet the harm is not the imperceptible quantum it may appear to be. This is partly due to social contagion effects that serve to concentrate the harm on a smaller group, increasing its effective impact. The harm of one person's nonparticipation is not distributed across all of society, but mainly across those groups to which they belong. When even one person is apathetic, she ensures underrepresentation for all the groups to which she belongs. The small harm done to any individual is thus multiplied by the number of people in those specially affected groups. And since most individuals belong to multiple groups, the scale of the harm is probably not so small or insignificant when summed over all the individuals so harmed.

The mechanisms of contagion, aggregative distortion, and undermining collective action are sufficiently opaque to the ordinary citizen that they cannot reasonably be expected to know the harmful effects of their neglect of politics. Even if people have an inkling that similar others could use their help, this is not enough to render their absence blameworthy. Nonetheless, it does not erase the harm of apathy.

Why Apathy Is Bad IV: Stability

Political apathy also threatens democracy by creating a class of citizens who are not politically socialized. Politically non-socialized citizens are a menace to democracy because they may come crashing into the system with unrealistic expectations and a vulnerability to demagoguery, which can empower anti-democratic actors and threaten democratic stability.

Hannah Arendt offers a classic version of this claim. In *The Origins of Totalitarianism*, Arendt argues that totalitarian movements arise where there are masses of people who are not organized politically, belonging to neither political parties nor civil society groups. These masses are, moreover, politically neutral or uninterested, and usually do not participate in politics. The Nazis and European communist movements recruited members "from this mass of apparently indifferent people whom all other parties had given up as too apathetic or too stupid for their attention" (Arendt 1968, 311). Arendt's argument is that the social dislocation of this group attracted them to the totalizing political programs of the Nazis and Communists, reflecting a desire for belonging and meaning.

My claim is that the problem stems not from anomie, but rather a lack of political socialization. Political socialization is centrally about acclimatizing to the political system so as to understand its workings, its key players, and its rules, particularly its unwritten norms. Socialization decisively shapes one's expectations about others' behavior, as well as one's own, providing an acute sense of what is appropriate and what is out of bounds. It therefore captures a significant aspect of what I discussed above as civic skills—the embodied knowledge needed to effectively navigate politics. Yet it also adds a normative element, in that it includes a set of expectations regarding proper conduct within the system, in line with my view of democratic citizenship as an office.

The problem, then, is that ignorance of the political system's workings, born of unfamiliarity, can help fuel dissatisfaction with it in a way *distinct* from that of knowing about its workings and disliking them. Because Weimar was a new democracy and because the eventual supporters of the Nazis avoided engaging with its participatory institutions, they were effectively unsocialized to how a democratic system of government is supposed to work. This would make them unprepared for some of its ostensibly unattractive features, such as how electoral democracy requires compromise between groups/parties and how major decisions can take months or years to unfold. These are, indeed, some of the complaints that political cynics frequently have about democracy, expressed in terms of politicians selling out their principles and supporters and bickering instead of "getting things done" (Hibbing and Theiss-Morse 2002). Moreover, as discussed above, without citizens' active involvement, parties and representatives are strongly incentivized to learn to ignore and even sacrifice the concerns and interests of those who do not habitually participate, adding substance to the perception that the government does not care about people like them.

Citizens like these, who lack an understanding of how democracy works in their polity but also harboring antipathy toward it, provide an

electoral opportunity to unscrupulous politicians willing to violate constitutional norms. Such demagogues can exploit their ignorance to capture
power by promising action that violates the law or other long-standing
rules of the political game. A common approach for such politicians is to
scapegoat a social outgroup of some kind, such as Jews or immigrants, and
accuse mainstream parties and institutions of enabling this group's nefarious doings. Those who are innocent of how political decisions are actually
made are especially susceptible to the conspiratorial thinking such claims
often invoke. This serves to justify the demagogue's aims to revolution-
ize the state in order to purge those ensconced within the bowels of the
"establishment" who allow the nation's problems to fester. In the cases
Arendt is concerned about, this dynamic led to democratic collapse and,
later, the moral catastrophes of totalitarianism.

Sheri Berman (1997, 403) interprets Arendt's claim to mean that the
collapse or absence of intermediary institutions led to totalitarianism and
criticizes her on the grounds that this claim does not stand up to empirical
scrutiny. Berman convincingly shows that Weimar had a rich and thriving
civil society and that Nazi activists successfully co-opted much of it to
consolidate support for the party. But Berman emphasizes only one part
of Arendt's argument. Though Arendt might very well be wrong about
the extent of civil society in Weimar, equally important is her point that
the citizens who came to support the Nazis were largely *apolitical*, in the
sense of distancing themselves from the doings and institutions of national government.

Berman's own account of Wilhelmine and Weimar civil society supports Arendt—and thus, my point—when read this way. Berman records
that a great many civil society groups were organized and operated along
self-consciously apolitical lines. Most of these groups, she writes, "viewed
themselves as a sanctuary from traditional politics" (1997, 412). The groups
"were designed to foster certain values and lifestyles, rather than directly
engage the political process" (1997, 409). Berman characterizes the Prot-
estant middle class, from which the Nazis later derived pivotal support, as
an "increasingly alienated and fragmented constituency" in the 1920s, supporting Arendt's claim that Nazi support came from those estranged from
the political system (1997, 416).

We must note, however, that Berman does not take these groups at their
word; to her mind, they were hardly apolitical. Group members were "increasingly mobilized and politically active," largely in local government,
according to Berman (1997, 411–12). Moreover, individuals often sought

"political influence, social identity and economic advantage" through these civil society groups. Nonetheless, they "looked with disdain on parties and elections," which were, of course, the main political institutions of the day, and which determined who controlled the robust German state apparatus. This is why the key point still stands. Citizens unsocialized to the democratic political system constituted a threat to it since these citizens refrained from engaging with the political system's key institutions until the advent of the Nazis, and then flooded into it to aid their apotheosis.

The concern registered here is not limited to the context of the twentieth century. In the German national election of 2017, for instance, the Alternative für Deutschland (AfD), the extreme right neo-Nazi party, received over a third of its votes (35 percent) from those who did not vote in the previous election, far more than any other party (Research Group Elections eV 2017). The AfD is opposed to important features of the modern German constitutional order—such as constitutional protections for refugees and asylum seekers—that grew out of the experience of the Nazi era. In drawing support from nonvoters, the AfD could be benefiting from a reservoir of politically non-socialized citizens similar to those who helped fuel the rise of totalitarian movements in the twentieth century.

In response to this danger, individuals who wish to be apathetic toward politics could pledge to remain so, and perhaps agree to temporarily suspend their participation rights.[7] Such pledges could neutralize the threat that the spontaneous mobilization of unsocialized apathetics would pose to the political system. The problem with this solution is that no such pledge is credible, and no such system of disenfranchisement could be trusted to be faithfully administered. No one can credibly commit to stay apolitical over the long term. Times change and the issues on the political agenda change with them. What if these changes lead to gratuitous harm to the individual's interests? Or to an injustice that the individual simply cannot ignore? It is not difficult to imagine how a new issue might emerge that calls upon someone to take action. At that point, however, they may not be prepared to do so—or cannot do so—in a constructive way due to the degradation of their civic skills. The only solution is for them to remain at least somewhat engaged, or at least periodically active, to keep their civic skills serviceable.[8]

7. I am indebted to Jason Canon for raising this possibility and for a stimulating discussion of the point.

8. Another possibility would be to institutionalize the pledge not to participate via provisional disenfranchisement that is revocable after attending a "refresher" course on citizenship.

Thus, democracy is best preserved by maintaining a degree of connection to the political system on the part of all citizens. Regular contact with politics will help many citizens recognize that stereotypes of selfish politicians and pointless partisan gridlock are just that, stereotypes, useful as slogans to justify political apathy but not always robust enough to withstand scrutiny. Even if some become confirmed in their cynicism, exposure to politics at least converts thoughtless, inch-deep, sloganeering cynicism into a reflectively backed version. Such reflective cynics, I argue below, can be a useful force in democratic politics, even though thoughtless ones are indeed a threat.

The argument in this section inverts Huntington's worries about democratic overload triggering political instability. Where he worried that the rise of the "new social groups" of the 1970s would destabilize democracy by overloading the political system with demands, the argument here is that exclusion is potentially *more* disruptive of stability since it is effectively impossible for groups to remain durably passive in politics. Events always transpire to mobilize them. Far from apathy serving as a reliable guarantor of stability, it could just as often serve as political dynamite packed around the foundations of democracy, waiting only for a spark.

A better response is therefore to mobilize everyone and get them effectively heard and included in the political system. It is better to maintain a degree of connection with politics among everyone than to allow complete apathy by anyone because apathy invites the generation of a non-socialized mass of citizens that can destabilize democracy—perhaps opportunistically at the behest of a would-be despot. Whatever short-term disruption attends the initial process of including new groups, the cost

---

If one had not voted in ten years, say, we might require that they complete a civic education course or other resocialization program before resuming their political rights. Yet this would formalize the status of inactive citizen or subject, and such distinctions are not tenable. This is not only because no such system of disenfranchisement could be trusted to be faithfully administered, though that is also true, but also because formally disenfranchised citizens will not always remain apolitical. For example, the French instituted a rigid distinction between active and passive citizens during the early phases of the French Revolution to distinguish those with political rights from those without. The distinction proved absurd, however, as the "passive" *sans-culotte* showed just how passive their citizenship was during the Insurrection of 10 August 1792, during which they seized control of the national government. This admittedly extreme example reveals the deep logic of formally stripping citizens of participation rights, however provisionally—without formal outlets for expressing political dissent and settled habits of making use of them, circumstances can always transpire to politicize and mobilize excluded citizens into a destabilizing political force.

of their socialization is justified by the prospect of long-term democratic stability.

Thoughtless Reproduction of Political Apathy

Recall the distinctions I drew at the beginning of this chapter between apathy as I conceive it and how it is often understood. There I described thoughtless apathy, in which one is simply and naively unaware of politics, and consciously chosen or reflective forms of apathy. These two species of apathy are immensely different from an ethical perspective because an individual's preferences or patterns of behavior that have no particular justification deserve much less respect than ones the individual enters into knowingly and intentionally. Interference in the latter case is thus problematic in a way not present in the former. In particular, interference in the latter case bears directly on individuals' (political) judgment that politics is not worth their time. Yet democracy cannot legitimately draw boundaries of this kind around the political judgment of its citizens since it threatens to turn democracy into a partisan creed in a first-order political conflict—effectively telling citizens the only legitimate choice is one from among the existing political cleavages—contradicting the substantive openness that is necessary for democratic politics. There is, thus, a prima facie claim of respect owed to reflective forms of apathy on *democratic grounds*, since it may often be a legitimate exercise of political judgment. But this is not enough on its own to demonstrate that it is, in fact, such an exercise. There are compelling reasons to think many cases of what appears to be reflective apathy are neither genuinely chosen nor thoughtless but are, rather, problematically unreflective due to the social reproduction of apathy-supporting norms, discourses, and patterns of behavior.

Nina Eliasoph (1998) argues that political apathy is often sustained and expanded by cultural work that generates apathetic social scripts and norms. Her ethnographic study of political apathy focuses on socially active and involved citizens who participate in civil society to combat problems like drug addiction, yet who view problems like that of pollution from a naval base as not "close to home" despite being *literally near their homes*. Eliasoph explains this oddity as stemming from social patterns of speech, thought, and behavior that make tackling some problems thinkable (and *not* political) while rendering others out of reach (and political). Yet these patterns, and the apathy they selectively induce, are produced and reproduced by people in social interaction. The contours of what is politics and what is not politics, and so of political apathy itself, is thus not exogenous to politics but is often a product of essentially political processes wherein what makes a problem political is itself worked out.

Eliasoph's analysis emphasizes, moreover, that these processes are, in general, not consciously executed but go on behind citizens' backs even as those citizens themselves enact them. She argues that many issues reflecting difficult structural problems are articulated in political terms to put them out of reach of their efficacy, so as to prevent discouragement and preserve their agency. As she puts it, "many citizens want to care about *people*, but do not want to care about *politics*," and so they try to limit their concerns to issues to which they feel they can realistically make a difference, issues that are "small, local, and unpolitical" (Eliasoph 1998, 12–13). This drastic shrinking of one's sphere of public concern and explicit abandonment of politics complicates our story about apathy because citizens like these disclaim politics yet involve themselves deeply in the civic life of their community. Moreover, where those who embrace and propagate apathy in society do so (mostly) unknowingly and thus not autonomously, they nonetheless help innovate its scripts for new political moments via ongoing improvisational engagement with the stuff of politics, an engagement that itself comes to be hidden under an ever-shifting mélange of depoliticizing tropes.

From the normative perspective I bring to bear in this chapter, the significance of this analysis is that apathy may often be a product neither of simple thoughtlessness, as if it were a naturally occurring phenomenon outside the influence of human agency, nor of choice, with the moralizing implication that those who remain apathetic can be blamed for it or excusing it in the vein of tolerating a freely made choice. Rather, on this view, its origin is a heteronomous stew of anti-political cultural scripts, political cowardice, and bad faith. Together, they render political apathy a fascinating tapestry of these features along with false consciousness and, in particular, structural factors limiting individuals' real or perceived political efficacy.

In this situation, it becomes fraught to assume that one's affirmations of apathy are genuine. It raises the possibility of a form of unreflective apathy that is not thoughtless, since being able to cite apathy-supporting scripts entails paying enough attention to politics to learn such scripts yet is also not truly voluntary. Because citizens' assertions of apathy may reflect discursive strategies of avoidance that render certain issues and modes of engagement beyond the perceived agency of citizens to take on, we cannot be sure they are offered in the appropriate spirit of reflective endorsement. This suggests that any democratically defensible form of apathy must be entered into with an awareness of (or, less plausibly, an immunity to) the influence of these scripts.

Eliasoph's insights also weaken Lever's argument for the value of apathy insofar as there is no way to tell the difference between apathy borne of resistance and that of problematic unmindfulness of politics, or even acquiescence. It would be better to design a system that allowed us more opportunities to establish the difference between these orientations to politics, and this is a major part of my task in the rest of this book.

Toward an Ethics of Political Apathy

Is there any form of political apathy that might be consistent with the above arguments? Is ethical political apathy possible in a democracy? In this section, I consider whether there might be a democratically acceptable form of apathy distinct from how I have used that term but within the bounds of conventional usage. This is important since, to many, there seems to be ample reason to disengage from a politics beset by corruption or concerned with unimportant questions rather than vital ones. It is the impression that such opinions are often reasonable that can motivate a belief in the right to apathy. However, as we shall see, the arguments from earlier reveal—along with the complex nature of the sociocultural forces generating and reproducing apathy—at least two politically ethical forms of apathy. Both end up suggesting that the minimal extent of democratic citizenship consists in paying at least periodic attention to politics.

Let's begin by considering two challenges to justifying apathy that arise from the arguments above regarding harm and injustice. In both cases, others in society have a plausible claim on the individual not to be apathetic so as to avoid harming them or to provide aid against injustice. It is difficult to see how one can persist in affirming a right to be apathetic in the face of such demands.

There might nonetheless be special circumstances that occasionally neutralize these arguments, however rarely, and these might reveal the conditions for a democratically legible form of apathy. First, it might be that one belongs to a group that is not only adequately represented, but *overrepresented* in the halls of power. In that case, apathy might be excused as not so much harming the disproportionately powerful group but cutting them down to a democratically appropriate size. Cases of injustice present a somewhat harder question. If we assume that serious injustice is likely to exist in most imaginable societies, there may never be a time that one could be justifiably apathetic. Yet not all claims of injustice are equally justified, and it might be that in a given place and time, an individual rejects the prevailing claims for aid based on a reasonable political judgment that the claims are insufficient to oblige their help. So, although history suggests injustice persists in all times and places, certainty about what counts as injustice in any particular place and time often stems from hindsight bias. At the time, claims of injustice are almost always contested such that it may be reasonably unclear to ordinary citizens bereft of the leisure or materials to think deeply enough about such claims to conclude that their aid is required. This is just to say that it seems strange to blame citizens for failing to come to the aid of their fellow citizens against an injustice that the former cannot, for understandable reasons, recognize as such.

It is important to clarify that I am *not* saying here that the brute existence of disagreement about what justice entails justifies not acting, and thus apathy; that would be to negate Shelby and Beerbohm's arguments altogether. I understand their arguments to assume as common knowledge that injustice obtains, and to be concerned to show that the obligations that follow from such a conviction are more demanding than many conscientious citizens seem to realize. My point is that *without* the assumption of common knowledge, and so from *within* the conflicts over justice that define a particular place and time, there may occasionally be space for apathy among those who are reasonably unconvinced of the prevailing claims for aid against injustice. This point stands even if it is almost always the case that any adequately informed person would be convinced by the prevailing claims (as the enlightened of every age seem to believe about their own prejudices), since unless we believe that it is truly *always* obvious where justice lies, there will be some hard cases that open, perhaps, a finger's breadth of space for justifiable apathy.

Another condition of justifiable apathy is that it be adequately informed. This might seem obvious. Having enough information is necessary for all of the previous justifications; we must know whether our group is overrepresented, what the claims for aid against injustice in our society are, and have enough information to assess them, as well as to be on the lookout for problematic apathy-justifying social scripts and patterns of belief. This informedness condition may be the heaviest of them all, yet it is unavoidable. None of the other conditions can be met without adequate information. This condition alone might therefore be sufficient to render the set of justifiably apathetic citizens virtually empty, since some of this knowledge—such as the possibility of passively absorbing apathetic slogans—is surely obscure.

Moreover, the need to not only be informed at one point in time, but to *remain informed* about these issues over time necessitates a final condition: that one periodically check in on politics to ensure the facts that ground one's apathy, such as those about the representation of one's group and contemporary justice claims, remain current. This implies that political apathy in the strict sense of inattention to politics can only *ever* be punctuated; sustained political inattention is *absolutely inconsistent* with democracy. This point requires emphasis because it rules out an extremely common form of political apathy, one that includes millions of democratic citizens across the world. The inattention of these citizens toward politics will always be, at best, a fundamental hindrance to democracy, and a grave danger at worst. An adequate democratic minimum must therefore include at least periodic attention to politics. I discuss this requirement in depth in chapter 4.

Despite the difficulties of remaining informed and of fulfilling the other conditions of ethical political apathy, it is nonetheless conceivable that someone might meet all of them. Does that mean we have arrived at a democratically justifiable form of political apathy, one that might revive a husk of the right to apathy? We might think not since two other arguments against apathy, those based on equality and stability, have not been addressed. The harm and injustice arguments are special cases among the anti-apathy arguments since they involve others more acutely and directly than the equality and stability arguments. Yet the stability argument may also be answerable.

The requirement to be informed cuts against the worries of desocialization that are central to the stability argument because acquiring the information needed to justifiably meet the first three conditions would likely socialize one into the political system. Moreover, this reflective form of apathy can also serve the stabilizing function emphasized by Berelson et al. Since that argument is premised on a gradient of engagement, from intensely interested and ideological to less so—rather than the existence of completely apathetic citizens per se—this permissible form of apathy still preserves the productive dialectic constituted by the more and less interested. Indeed, complete apathy might actually block the stabilizing effect insofar as apathetic citizens fail to matter in elections or political life at all, leaving only the intensely interested ideologues on the proverbial field of political competition, and the instability likely to follow from it.

Reflective apathy is also required for making anything approximating Dahl's notion of slack serve the end of equal representation that he intended and avoiding another vector of instability. This is because surveillance of politics is required to make real the possibility of mobilization that constitutes slack. Dahl's NIMBY example of slack from New Haven is notable for how limited it is, illustrating how periodic political surveillance might generate more regular political mobilization, and thus better representation. He doesn't talk about all of the dogs that didn't bark—why, for instance, didn't the community mobilize to aid national Democrats in winning office so as to further the interests of working-class people like them? Or to aid Republicans opposing the spread of communism, since communism was on the march in the countries where many of the Italian and Jewish residents originated? Whatever their political views, the people in Dahl's New Haven neighborhood mobilized for a very narrow issue, even though they had many other problems that might be mitigated by political means. If members of the community remained at least occasionally attentive to politics, they might find other concerns that would mobilize them, expanding the areas of policy where their views and interests were adequately represented. Absent such cognitive engagement with the substance of politics—and the surveillance such engagement entails—there is little reason to think that the inattention of citizens constitutes a *salutary* slack in the system. It would instead threaten destabilization, for the reasons discussed in the last section. This leaves equality.

There may seem to be no getting around that apathy on the part of any citizen reduces political equality and gives rise to patterns of inequality and domination. But the same conditions discussed above suggest unique conditions where this might not be true. When an individual is part of an overrepresented group, for instance, their apathy may actually help restore equality via the mechanisms of anticipated response and social contagion, and so reduce the excessive influence of the group. Moreover, acquiring the information to be sure that aid against injustice is unneeded in one's own polity, or that one's group is in fact overrepresented, should help not only to socialize these citizens but also to help them build up the civic skills necessary for equality. Thus, the reflective form of apathy that also meets the other conditions outlined above, does seem to be compatible with democracy.

There is one other justifiable form of apathy—one that can eschew the five conditions just laid out—because it is temporary. This is the therapeutic Epicurean apathy advocated by Jeffrey Green (2016). Green argues that the stresses of democratic citizenship may occasionally require citizens to withdraw from the political arena and engross themselves in private life. Yet this retreat into one's own walled garden is meant not as a fundamental remaking of the citizen's relationship with politics so much as a restful yet limited reprieve. It is intended to recharge the citizens' civic batteries, as it were, so as to later rejoin the rough and tumble of the democratic contest, and to once again subject oneself to its inescapable stresses. That is, apathy here is prelude to actual democratic participation and active engagement.

Such temporary or periodic apathy is far from problematic. Indeed, one engaging in this kind of political sabbatical need not meet the stringent conditions outlined above since their apathy is time limited. Most harm or inequalities caused by their absence can be undone with their reappearance. Likewise, concerns about stability are moot since the citizen, in taking a break from the norm of political engagement, is already well socialized to the political system and so unlikely to be a systemic threat. Such a break might even enhance the individual's motivation to fight injustice because of the heightened contrast between one's repose and the manifest injustices suffered by others.

A temporary restful apathy can therefore be seen as an essential tool for democratic citizenship, and one that can help us to make sense of much of the conventional political apathy we see around us. The largest group of citizens who absent themselves from voting, for instance, are those who are politically interested and engaged, but just happen to vote irregularly (Doppelt and Shearer 1999). Moreover, some apathetic citizens were once politically engaged but had an experience that pushed them out of politics. Though I take issue with abstention later, it is possible that many of these citizens think of themselves as withdrawn into their garden for the duration of a particular (or particularly objectionable) political season.

An Objection: The Specificity Problem

There is an objection to the line of argument in this chapter that is worth addressing before closing. One might think that the chapter draws the sphere of democratic citizenship too narrowly, excluding forms of civically oriented or altruistic action other than political participation (or attention).

For example, Brennan and Freiman, in separate work, argue that every person has a duty to contribute sufficiently to the common good, but there is a division of labor that allows people to make different kinds of contributions, such as by earning money in the market to donate to life-saving charities (Brennan 2011; Freiman 2021). This leads to what is often called the particularity or specificity problem—how can we justify a duty to vote or make it obligatory to pay attention to politics when there are other, better ways of benefiting others (Maskivker 2019)?

This objection assumes, however, that the functions of citizenship fulfilled by participation are replaceable by or perfectly substitutable with these other activities. But this is not the case. Recall that when we view democratic citizenship as an office, we recognize that citizens play functional roles within democratic institutions. Citizens must fulfill these roles for institutions to meet the conditions of their own normative justification. In electoral democracies, citizens ignoring politics generates all the problems we have canvassed in this chapter, threatening associated justifications for democracy.

The point here is that some of these functions cannot be substituted with others, as Brennan and Freiman assume, because of the nature of the position of citizen and the role it plays in the wider institution. The state is a unique social organization because one cannot opt out of it—one may leave the jurisdiction of a particular state, but states are ubiquitous and presuppose preeminence in a particular territory. If I ignore it, it doesn't go away; its power doesn't evaporate or stop affecting me and shaping my life. Instead, all I have done by opting out is reduce by one the political significance of the groups to which I belong, as I argued earlier. And since the power of the state remains constant when some individuals and groups drop out of political relevance, that power now flows to those who are participating actively, with all the deleterious consequences I highlighted above.

None of this is true of the kind of altruistic behavior Brennan and Freiman recommend. My opting out of philanthropic endeavors doesn't hand power over to others; it reduces the amount of philanthropic activity there is. This constitutes a categorical difference. Because citizens play functional roles in democratic institutions, the absence of some materially affects the functioning of the institutions, generating skewed and biased outcomes. The same is not true of altruistic endeavors. They are thus different in kind and so altruistic efforts cannot substitute for political ones because political institutions operate differently.

Seeing democratic citizenship as a subset of altruistic behavior overlooks institutions and how they structure the expectations we have of one another in society. Democracy is how we do things together—how we decide upon and coordinate society-wide collective action. It is not just about "helping each other" in some simplistic sense, but also determining collective goals, constituting institutions of one kind rather than another, governing each other, regulating our relations and possessions, enforcing law, etc. It would be unhelpful and even meaningless to reduce all of these activities to mutual aid. The upshot is that we all have definite parts to play in the democratic process that cannot be ignored, nor can they be rendered protean and put at our discretion as a general duty to aid others.

My point here then is that the specificity problem is based on a confusion about the kind of thing political engagement is. It's not just a way to help others. In a democracy, it's part of the basic plumbing of society that we all must do our part, as democratic citizens, to maintain. So, while feeding hungry people is undoubtedly saintly, it doesn't keep democracy going. But that is what we are called upon to do as occupants of the office of democratic citizen.

Conclusion

In sum, we have seen four kinds of political apathy, two of which seem compatible with democracy. The incompatible forms are those that are thoughtless, meaning that one gives politics no serious attention, and unreflective, when one mouths apathetic slogans as clichés—that is, without thinking about them critically. The first form of apathy compatible with democracy is reflective rather than thoughtless, requiring informed consideration of the merits of political engagement. This form is severely hemmed in by five conditions: (1) it must be truly reflective and not the product of heteronomously adopting social scripts justifying apathy; (2) one must have plausible grounds for not caring about harm to one's group, such as that one's group is overrepresented; (3) one must reasonably reject all existing claims for aid against injustice; and (4) one must be and remain adequately informed to reach these conclusions by (5) periodically paying serious attention to politics. These conditions render even reflective apathy extremely unlikely to be ethical for most people most of the time. The second democratically defensible form of apathy is Green's temporary and therapeutic type. Because it is temporally limited and prelude to active citizenship, Green's form of apathy need not meet the other conditions of reflective apathy.

There are two essential implications of this argument. The first regards whether there is, after all, a right to apathy. The discussion here offers an equivocal answer. It suggests that there may be something like a right to apathy, but not in a form anyone would be likely to recognize. The limitations on apathy, captured in the five conditions discussed above, renders a right to it so constrained and conditional as to be virtually meaningless, at least according to conventional understandings of what apathy entails. It requires first considering the obligations we have to others who would be impacted by one's apathy, and so requires leaving behind naive and thoughtless forms of apathy. To some, this might seem tantamount to banishing it altogether. But this depends on what we mean by apathy. If we mean complete thoughtlessness about politics, then yes; this argument requires banishing apathy in this sense from our politics. If we mean instead having only a minute interest in politics paired with pessimistic assessments thereof, then no. Such political apathy or cynicism is, if periodically revisited by attending to politics and abiding by the other conditions, consistent with ethical democratic citizenship. Such a set of attitudes seems well within conventional usage regarding what counts as political apathy, even if it departs from my narrow definition. Though we have perhaps clarified much about a purported right to apathy, my main interest moving forward is in how considering such a right reveals the bedrock of democratic citizenship.

The temporary nature of Green's therapeutic apathy and the requirement that reflective apathy include periodic attention to politics suggests an essential temporal commonality that illuminates the minimum of democratic citizenship. Apathy in the strict sense of enduring or temporally unbounded inattention is ruled out. The only forms of apathy that democracy can countenance are those that are strictly limited in duration. One difference between these two forms lies in the default or norm regarding how time is politically valued (Cohen 2018). For the Epicurean, attention is the norm and apathy is the exception, while for the reflective apathetic the opposite is true. In both cases, finite temporal duration is essential. The flip side of this limitation, and the most important implication for the argument of the next chapter, is that democracy has a legitimate claim on *some* of our time, since only some of our time can be spent apathetically attending to other, nonpolitical parts of life. This is therefore another way of saying that politics makes legitimate demands on our time and attention. We saw in this chapter that the minimal extent of these demands is periodic political attention. In the next chapter, we shall see how far these demands can legitimately reach.

CHAPTER THREE

When Does Democracy Ask Too Much?

Realism and the Paradox of Empowerment

When, if ever, does democracy ask too much of its citizens? The last chapter concluded that there is a floor to democratic citizens' level of political engagement; this chapter considers whether there is a corresponding ceiling. Specifically, it asks whether it is possible for the participatory demands of a democratic regime, or a democratic theory, to go too far, and if so, why. I argue that democracy can ask too much because there are principled limits to its expectations of its citizens.

In arguing in favor of such limits, however, I take a different route than those who have argued for limiting democratic citizenship in the past. Whereas many realist critics of democracy have argued that we must moderate the demands — and aspirations — of democracy because citizens are *unable* to meet exacting standards of conduct, I shall argue instead that sufficiently exacting democratic standards violate *principled* limits to democratic citizenship, making them *wrong* rather than infeasible. I depart, therefore, from the arguments of realist critics from Joseph Schumpeter to Jason Brennan who have argued that democracy cannot work the way normative theory seems to require due to the findings of empirical social science. The merit of my approach is that it evades a decisive response to this realist critique, one that has led the scholarly debate into a fruitless impasse constituted by inconclusive speculation about what the empirical evidence shows.

Taking a principled approach to the question opens up a new horizon of inquiry that takes us beyond this impasse. I argue that there are reasons

(1) inherent in justice and (2) internal to democratic theory itself that impose limits on what citizens can be reasonably asked to do as participants in their democracy, and that these imply we should reduce participatory demands wherever possible. In the following sections, I first explain the impasse that much of democratic theory has fallen into. I then elaborate the two principled arguments for limits to democratic citizenship and explore their implications for democratic theory and the design of democratic institutions.

The Inconclusive Realist Critique

One of the most serious concerns about democracy over the past century has been that it expects too much of its citizens. It is argued that democracy, as conceived by political theorists, assumes citizens are able to behave in ways that empirical social science suggests they cannot. The conclusion usually drawn is that democratic theory requires thorough revision to better reflect the reality of citizens' limited time and cognitive and moral capacities. The basic strategy deployed in these arguments, however, is subject to severe difficulties, raising the question whether there are any less contingent reasons for limiting democracy's demands on its citizens.

Walter Lippmann, an influential public intellectual and among the first articulators of this realist line of argument in the modern period, illustrates the basic case well. Starting from the idea that democracy means the people direct what the government does, he argues that democracy requires more of citizens than they can possibly give. With no hint of irony or shame, Lippmann takes himself as an example of an above-average citizen, and admits that even he is utterly unable to meet democracy's demands of him:

> ... although public business is my main interest and I give most of my time to watching it, I cannot find time to do what is expected of me in the theory of democracy; that is, to know what is going on and to have an opinion worth expressing on every question which confronts a self-governing community. (Lippmann 1993, 10)

Lippmann's point is that for the people to take a meaningful role in directing the government's activities, citizens need to have informed opinions about the questions the community faces. But there are too many serious problems in modern societies for anyone to become meaningfully informed about them all. This makes it impossible for citizens to really direct the government, rendering democracy a mere word.

The basic argumentative strategy at work here has subsequently been deployed by many other realist critics of democracy. The strategy is to deduce democracy's requirements from democratic theory and then check, empirically (or quasi-empirically), whether citizens are actually behaving in accordance with those requirements. If they are not, it indicates that democratic reforms pursuant to those theories are perhaps not worth pursuing.

So, Joseph Schumpeter (1942 [1976]) famously argues that "classical democratic theory" makes unsustainable assumptions about the common good and about citizens' abilities, such that it must be rejected in favor of a more elite-centered model of electoral democracy. Berelson, Lazarsfeld, and McPhee (1954) of the influential Columbia school of political science conclude, in their seminal study *Voting*, that the widespread political indifference they observed suggests the need to revise democratic theory in line with how people actually behave.

More recent realist critics have reached similar conclusions using structurally identical reasoning. Christopher Achen and Larry Bartels (2016) argue that, in light of a bevy of empirical evidence, the "folk theory of democracy," in its many guises, must be rejected in favor of a new theory that is more amenable to the group affinities that powerfully shape citizens' political behavior and cognition. Diana Mutz (2006) finds that citizens' actual experience of disagreement generates enormous tensions between deliberative and participatory democracy, forcing choices between core democratic values like participation and toleration, which theorists have largely assumed are compatible. In political theory, Eric Beerbohm (2012, 141) seeks to provide a "more humane theory of citizenship" that incorporates the fixed cognitive limitations he takes empirical evidence to demonstrate. Ilya Somin (2013) argues too that the fixed problem of political ignorance renders all of the most popular theories of democracy epistemically untenable. Brennan (2016) also sees the evidence of political ignorance as damning for democracy, arguing that so few citizens are capable of responsible self-rule that we ought to look for ways to transcend democracy in favor some form of epistocracy, or rule by those with more knowledge.

For all their differences, these critiques share an argumentative method of appealing to empirical realities that are interpreted to delimit possibility horizons around democracy that exclude not just the optimistic theories or designs of reformers, but sometimes the democratic status quo as well. The facts, these critics suggest, preclude even rather modest democratic utopias. Yet this mode of normative argument is subject to a potent objection.

However terrible from the perspective of democratic theory citizens have been, all their faults are, in principle, *ameliorable*. This is because citizens' capacities are largely endogenous to the institutions they live under and the political culture in which they are raised. This means that citizens' capacities are not fixed but are, rather, cultivated (or allowed to atrophy) according to the specific political, social, and institutional conditions in which they find themselves. Carole Pateman (1970) offers a classic statement of this view in her argument that more demanding, participatory modes of social organization can generate their own support by cultivating habits of active citizenship. The implication is that the behavior observed empirically is a function of the cultural and institutional status quo, not humans' fixed underlying democratic capacities.

According to this objection, any judgments about what citizens are capable of vis-à-vis democracy will be flawed when based on inferences from empirical studies due to a version of the problem of induction: one cannot infer what is possible by only looking at what has happened. New institutions, including ones aimed at civic education and democratic socialization, could perhaps reshape citizens' capacities for the better. History and ethnographic studies show us, for example, the vast differences between ways of life today and that of the past, between our own ways and those of other peoples. All these suggest an immense plasticity to human capacities. Empirical studies under entirely different institutional arrangements might, the objection goes, reveal less morose results for democracy. Indeed, democratic theorists can point to numerous participatory and deliberative experiments to suggest possible effects of institutional reform on the population as a whole that are promising for reform (Wampler 2007; Warren and Pearse 2008; Fishkin 2009; Fournier, Van der Kolk, et al. 2011).

Adding to the strength of this argument is the fact that a great deal of the evidence these pessimistic conclusions are based on comes from surveys of Americans in the twentieth century. This is a fascinating time in American history, to be sure, but it depicts just one country—a country whose institutions leave much to be desired from a democratic perspective—during just one period in its history, during much of which it was racially authoritarian. It therefore makes even more sense to ask whether sweeping conclusions about the capacity of human beings (as opposed to Americans) to sustain democratic governments are reasonable on the basis of such narrow and contextually specific evidence.

However, as powerful as this overall objection may be, it is—for the most part—speculative. It is about what is possible and what can reasonably be inferred from existing evidence, questions very much open to interpretation. Scholars armed with data—in some cases, accumulated over the better part of a century—can scarcely be blamed if their skepticism persists. This leads to an impasse, one that has divided those interested in innovative democratic reform from those skeptical or dismissive of such efforts. Skeptics have in many cases believed that the evidence is on their side. Yet an honest appreciation of the meliorative objection ought to raise serious doubts about that.

Because this impasse stems from divergent interpretations of empirical evidence it raises the question whether there are *principled* reasons, as opposed to empirically contingent ones, for limiting democracy's participatory demands on citizens. Even if we grant that democratic capacities are almost infinitely expandable in the right conditions, is there anything to be said for wanting to mold democratic participation in ways that are *not* demanding on ordinary citizens? Are any such reasons consistent with, or expressive of, fundamental democratic principles?

I think the answer to these questions is that there are indeed principled reasons to limit democracy's demands on its citizens. Moreover, these reasons are distinct from the traditional realist argument that demanding forms of democracy are not possible in light of empirical reality; I do not accept that the facts are so clear. Instead, I argue there are at least two *principled* reasons to limit the demands of democracy on citizens that are not based on questionable inferences about the limits of their capacities.

The purpose of outlining these reasons is not to block all efforts at democratic reform. It is, rather, aimed at delineating side-constraints on such efforts and channeling them toward certain kinds of reforms that are responsive to the concerns the arguments highlight. The most important of these is a concern for expanding democratic inclusion through moderate expectations of participation, as discussed below.

Free Time and Democracy

The first principled reason to limit the participatory demands of democracy is that people have a fundamental right to control their time, which

generates a default, founded in justice, in favor of fewer demands. Here
I draw upon Julie Rose's argument that individuals are entitled to a fair
share of free time as a matter of basic distributive justice to argue that
democracy has definite limits to what it can expect of citizens. These are
limits based in justice, moreover, rather than feasibility or convenience.

Rose (2016, 4) makes a compelling case for free time as a fundamental
currency of distributive justice. By free time, Rose means time one can
spend at one's discretion, pursuing one's own ends, whatever they may
be. Free time is time not committed to meeting the various necessaries
of life—meaning not only necessary paid work, but also time spent providing for our own basic needs and those of dependents, such as cook-
ing and cleaning. Rose contrasts free time to leisure because leisure is
a specific good rather than an all-purpose one; it involves engaging in
intrinsically valuable activities like play or philosophical contemplation
and is specifically spent not doing paid work. Leisure in this sense is itself
a component of different conceptions of the good life and so is secured
by means of other all-purpose goods such as money, which are not themselves components of the good life but rather help secure things that are.
Free time, by contrast, is such an all-purpose good, to be used for whatever
furthers our conception of the good life. This could, for instance, include
doing paid work beyond what is necessary for subsistence, such as pursuing an entrepreneurial venture or moonlighting, but this is by definition
incompatible with leisure. Free time is thus not "a particular component
of particular conceptions of the good" but rather part of the fair share of
resources to which everyone is entitled (Rose 2016, 39). Rose contends
that free time in this sense constitutes a fundamental currency of distributive justice, meaning that it is to be considered one of the all-purpose
goods to which everyone is entitled a fair share.

Pivotal to Rose's case for free time as a fundamental currency of justice
is the non-substitutability of time and money. Many people assume that
the proliferating array of personal services mean that money can generally purchase time, and thus can substitute for it. If money were purely
substitutable for time in this way, we would not need to recognize time as
a discrete currency of distributive justice since arranging for a just distribution of financial resources would automatically secure a just distribution of free time. Yet Rose (2016, 77–89) argues persuasively that time
and money are not substitutable. Part of the reason for this is because
many personal basic needs simply cannot be hired out. No one can eat for
you; no one can exercise for you; no one can do physical or psychological
therapy for you; nobody can do your grooming in all the ways that are

necessary for adequate self-care (Rose 2016, 82). Though we may pay for many key services, money cannot fully substitute for time. Moreover, even if there are some time-consuming things that we could hire out, such as the care of a child, spouse, parent, or other dependent, Rose argues that there are numerous reasonable objections to buying such services on the market, such as that it degrades our intimate relationships, rendering it unreasonable to expect people to do so (Rose 2016, 83–84).

I want to add a key component to Rose's analysis that is currently missing yet opens the door to its application to democratic theory. Rose builds her account on a broadly Rawlsian foundation, using in particular the core notion of society as a fair system of social cooperation. For our purposes, this idea's most important use is in determining how much free time individuals are entitled to. To do so, Rose suggests that we must first determine how much time a society has to devote to the "shared burdens of social cooperation" (Rose 2016, 128). For Rose, these shared burdens are constituted by economic production and the provision of individuals' basic needs, such as care work. Yet, contrary to what Rose says, this cannot be all of the shared burdens necessary to social cooperation. This is because cooperation in complex societies also requires government, even if only to enforce the basic rules of cooperation. Where governments are authoritarian, this may not add much to the overall burdens of social cooperation because little or nothing is expected of individuals except obedience and taxes. Yet in a specifically democratic government, citizens must additionally participate in their own government. This implies that democratic citizens face additional burdens of participating in society's institutions of collective decision-making, adding to the shared burdens of social cooperation. My point here is not that authoritarianism has any advantage over democracy, but rather that Rose's analysis omits the democratic component of systems of social cooperation and in so doing obscures one key element of the shared burdens of supporting that system.

This matters because it implies that, all else equal, there is a general principle, grounded in justice, to reduce the burdens of democratic citizenship and participation wherever possible. No matter what principle we think is appropriate for the distribution of free time—egalitarian, prioritarian, sufficientarian, etc.—we should prefer to have more of it to distribute than less, other things equal, just as we would want more financial resources.[1] Since democratic government contributes to the burdens of

---

1. Rose explores the interesting tradeoffs between free time and economic growth, since we might think additional prosperity is worth having as much or more than additional free

social cooperation through requiring participation, there is a straightforward trade-off here between free time in the aggregate and democratic
participation. The upshot of Rose's argument that free time is a fundamental requisite of justice, then, is that free time cannot simply lose out
in this trade-off automatically. Just as we can design our institutions of
work and welfare to modulate the amount of free time individuals enjoy,
so too can we design our democratic institutions to depend on more or
less participatory input. Assembly-based democratic regimes could meet
more or less often, or be reformed into a representative form; electoral-
representative democracy could have more or less frequent elections for
more or fewer offices, etc. It is possible, then, that we should sometimes
be willing to reduce existing participatory demands, or forgo reforms that
would ratchet up those demands, in deference to the value of free time. If
the gains of added participation are low, for instance, or if the gains would
accrue mostly to those already advantaged in society, we might want to
forgo them. I address this latter possibility in the next section. There is
thus a defeasible principle of justice, not just convenience, for reducing
democracy's participatory demands.

To be sure, participation can vary not only in its amount, but also in
its mode or quality. Deliberative democracy was largely premised on the
notion that the aggregative democracy of elections includes too many
ill-considered preferences (Elster 1986, 112). Deliberation remains the
medicine of choice among democratic reformers for the ill of low-quality
democratic decision-making. Yet deliberation has been subject to its own
demandingness objection, on the grounds that it is a particularly time-
consuming step in collective decision procedures. Thinking about citizens'
right to free time, however, transforms this familiar objection. Rather than
it being simply one of efficiency or convenience, the problem becomes
much more serious. It is not just that deliberation is inconvenient because
it is temporally demanding—it is that citizens have a right *grounded in
justice* to the time that deliberation is consuming. They have a right to control how their time is spent, yet democratic institutions designed around
deliberation are laying claim to it instead. It could therefore be *wrong* to
build a democracy around time-consuming forms of participation such as
deliberation.

---

time in the aggregate. This question does not affect my point, however, since the demands of
democracy are not at issue in it.

This may seem a rather strong and implausible conclusion, but it accords with and clarifies two widespread intuitions about democracy. The first is the recognition that it is always better for democracy to make voting and other participation easier rather than harder. Though we could no doubt explain this view indirectly on grounds of inclusion—that raising the costs of participation deters many from engaging in it—there is also a straightforward sense that, if democracy is going to expect citizens to participate in it (as it must do to subsist), it has to make that participation as easy as possible out of respect for citizens' free time. Democracy disrespects citizens' entitlement to free time when it cavalierly lays claim to their time through expectations of participation and then makes it onerous to do. My democratic application of Rose's theory explains why, if democracy wants me to participate, the least it can do is make it easy.

The second intuition this argument helps us make sense of is that it is possible for democracy to ask too much of people, in the sense of too much participation, as this chapter sets out to illustrate. Everyone can recognize that this is true, and not just verbally. Just as parents can be too demanding of their children, or guests of their hosts, democracy can ask too much of its citizens. This is easy to say, but explaining it is more difficult. If we think democracy is as valuable as we routinely say, it seems like we should be willing to bear extreme burdens on its behalf, just as a child might go to great lengths to fulfill a beloved parent's expectations. In extraordinary times, this may even be the case for democracy. But in ordinary times, we all recognize that there are things other than democracy and politics that are worth our time. Rose's argument about free time, with my addendum regarding democracy, captures, explains, and clarifies this recognition, and puts it into a wider theoretical context that makes it useful for democratic theory.

One objection to this line of argument is that political participation has an intrinsic value that the argument neglects. Some struggle to imagine how anyone could live a fulfilling life without a fairly robust enjoyment of citizenship. For them, participation constitutes an intrinsically rewarding activity, one that enriches life by, among other things, serving as a means to social connectedness and making ideals like political equality tangible and meaningful.

If participation is intrinsically valuable—say, because it contributes something indispensable to a life well lived—then it might seem incorrect to think that a right to free time could compete with the claims of democracy. If we see participation—in the wide sense of agential engagement with the political realm—as itself a universal component of different ideas of the good life, but also see free time as a resource for these different ideas, then they wouldn't compete with each other. Rather, they would occupy distinct places within a life well lived, and the right to free time would not conflict with democracy's participatory demands.

Yet it turns out to be exceedingly difficult to explain why participation would have this kind of universal intrinsic worth. Ben Berger (2011, 130) considers the full panoply of canonical arguments for the kind of intrinsic worth that would make participation an essential component of the good life and concludes that all of them ultimately rely upon assertion rather than demonstration. The arguments offered fail to substantiate their claims. For example, some argue that civic friendship can provide a unique non-ethnic basis for political and social solidarity. This grants the participation embodying and sustaining this friendship intrinsic worth because it would be a constitutive element of a society in which human beings can flourish. Yet Berger (2011, 126) argues that these civic friendship arguments are flawed because they try to have it two ways at once; invoking the richness and depth of friendship to make civic friendship's power and importance plausible, while conceding when pushed that civic friendship is actually quite psychologically minimal, and so compatible with large pluralistic societies. Both of these claims cannot be sustained at the same time, however. Civic friendship must be thick if it is to solve the problem of solidarity, but it must be thin if it is to be applicable to modern societies. There is no obvious way around this double bind, and so civic friendship fails to explain why participation would have intrinsic worth for everyone.

To be sure, it is not Berger's (2011, 129) intention to show that participation lacks intrinsic worth altogether, nor is it mine. Rather, the point is that political engagement will only have intrinsic worth for *some*, not all. Only some ideas of the good and of the good life will be substantively and directly furthered by it.

For although participation might be an enjoyable pastime for some, it can be an unpleasant burden for others entered into only instrumentally, or out of duty. This antipathy need not, moreover, be a product of unfamiliarity with politics or negative stereotypes thereof, even if it often is. Political antipathy can also arise from negative experiences of intense political participation. Some try it out and find that it is not for them. They may find negative stereotypes confirmed, for instance, or, far from adding to their fulfillment in life, that it detracts from it, such as by introducing new fault lines in relations with friends, family, and neighbors. This discovery would not relieve them of obligations to participate, of course, if there are such obligations. But it does mean that we cannot blithely assume that participation has the same (positive) worth or can play the same role in everyone's conception of the good. There is, in other words, reasonable disagreement about the contribution of political involvement to the good, and to living well. The acceptance of pluralism about questions of this kind is, I take it, a principled cornerstone of any attractive political theory today.

If the intrinsic worth of participation is not universal, then it cannot be used as a legitimate basis for the design of fundamental democratic institutions since they must govern everyone, even those who do not agree that participation is intrinsically worthwhile. To them, the practices of democracy would themselves seem like an unjust burden on their free time, and reasonably so if they are multiplied endlessly out of a conviction of their intrinsic worth.

When we see the worth of participation in this light—from the realization that not everyone values it equally—it redoubles an essential point I made above. There, I argued that there was a clear trade-off between participation and free time in the aggregate because a system of social cooperation whose political system depends on more participatory input would have less free time to distribute. This generates, I concluded, a pressure, grounded in justice, to reduce participatory demands. Here we see an even stronger reason to keep a lid on the participatory demands of democracy. Reasonable disagreement about the contribution of political participation to a life well lived creates a further imperative to minimize participation's demands since it is not only that free time and participation compete, but rather that the value of participation is itself controversial. To build more and more of it into the social fabric would therefore amount to enforcing a certain (controversial) way of life, in contravention of fundamental principles of toleration and liberal justice.

It is important to be clear about what I am claiming and what I am not claiming in this section. I have tried to show that the right to free time generates a principled reason to limit democracy's participatory demands, not one based on considerations of convenience, cost, or perceived feasibility. The point here is not to deny that democratic participation has great worth, even intrinsic worth for many, as I said above. Nor is it to suggest anything about the current state of participation in actually existing democratic regimes—I am *emphatically not* suggesting that actual democracies ask too much of their citizens. The point is, rather, that the participatory demands of democracy are not just a matter of cost or convenience, but rather of justice. I am alleging that we must take the demands of democratic participation on the lives of ordinary people much more seriously than has been customary, particularly when we contemplate institutional reform. People are entitled in a fundamental way to control their time. Because democracy effectively lays claim to some of it through its participatory institutions, we must be prepared to think critically about the extent of democracy's claim. How demanding can democracy justifiably be if people are largely entitled to spend their time as they wish? This is the question that my argument makes not just salient, but imperative. We must also, as I will emphasize in the next section, keep in mind how the demandingness of participation is inextricably tied to who is excluded from sharing democratic power.

The Paradox of Empowerment

I just suggested that seeing participation as intrinsically valuable could lead one to advocate multiplying endlessly the institutional opportunities to participate. Many would see doing so as far from problematic, even positively good, regardless of why exactly they think participation is valuable. For what harm could there be in making more roads into the halls of power available for citizens who want to use them? In this section, I'll explain why more opportunities for participation do not necessarily improve democracy, and why democratic principle can itself recommend reducing participatory opportunities in some circumstances. In so doing, I'll explain the second principled reason to limit democracy's demands of participation: that increasing opportunities for greater participation may often perversely function to further empower existing elites and empowered groups rather than broadening access to power to marginalized groups.

The point here is that ratcheting up the participatory demands of democracy by opening new avenues of participation is not necessarily democratizing. This section aims to show that more opportunities to participate can sometimes harm democracy, and that some forms of participation can backfire democratically by reinforcing the power of currently powerful groups. This paradox constitutes the second principled reason to limit democracy's participatory demands. It suggests that we must design the participatory institutions of democracy with care and eschew the mistaken instinct to throw open the doors of power willy-nilly. There are ways of extending participation that serve no democratic purpose, or can even be anti-democratic, so we must be on the lookout for ways of shaping participation that expand the circle of democratic empowerment. In the end, I suggest that the least demanding forms of participation should be prioritized if we care about democratic equality.

Increasing opportunities for greater democratic participation often disproportionately empowers the forces supporting the status quo via the paradox of empowerment. The paradox of empowerment occurs when opportunities to participate serve to perversely disempower the already disempowered, intensifying their marginalization and further empowering the already powerful. Ironically, reducing the scope of democratic participation to its "cheapest" forms may improve democracy by opening it to more people. The paradox of empowerment thus shows that the result of limiting democratic expectations may be, counterintuitively, to promote fair representation and political equality.

The logic behind the paradox is simple: participation is costly. Taking part in democratic procedures requires incurring costs, if only opportunity costs. Yet not all forms of participation are equally costly—some are more costly than others. In particular, democratic innovations and modes of participation that have most interested political theorists in recent years—such as participation in associations and civil society groups (Cohen and Rogers 1995; Warren 2002), in social movements (Medearis 2015) and spontaneous collective action (Rosanvallon 2008), and, especially, in deliberative forums and mini-publics (Fung 2003)—are often particularly costly. Taking advantage of them requires significant resources and civic skills (Verba, Schlozman, and Brady 1995), as well as psychological "resources" like political interest and efficacy (Parvin 2018, 39), that may often be beyond what ordinary citizens have or can afford. They in particular require large amounts of time and energy, as well as physical mobility and temporal flexibility—the kinds of things that busy people in particular lack by definition. The paradox of empowerment thus occurs when especially costly or demanding forms of participation are opened up—as by democratic innovations—in an effort to empower ordinary citizens, and yet those opportunities are disproportionately exploited by those with the resources and other advantages needed to make use of them. This further empowers the already advantaged and provides them with further means to consolidate their advantages and power.

Despite the intuitive nature of the paradox of empowerment, it has drawn relatively scant attention from political theorists. The two most thorough discussions to date, those of Anne Phillips and of Michael Walzer, recognize the paradox at work in the intensely participatory contexts that emerged in the 1960s and 1970s and see it generating a real tension between participatory democracy and liberal or representative democracy (Phillips 1991, 120–46; Walzer 1970, 234–38). The tension lies between the former's tendency to generate inequality or "hierarchy" via the paradox of empowerment and the latter's tendency to encourage both equality and political passivity. Phillips and Walzer both suggest that this tension cannot be resolved but rather requires ongoing management or "adjustment," yet are unsure of what this would involve. I aim to precisely clarify this point by theorizing why and how democracy should be adjusted in response to the paradox of empowerment.

I know of only two other notable theoretical treatments of the paradox, one from Graham Smith discussed below, and the other by Daniel Innerarity. Innerarity's (2019, 4) discussion is very much to the point of the present one since he too is concerned that less advantaged citizens find it difficult to engage in forms of direct participation. He makes a persuasive case that, in light of the paradox of empowerment, democratic theory should be adjusted to emphasize the egalitarian potential of political mediation, as by representatives, over directly democratic forms of disintermediation. The present argument furthers and enriches this approach to reform with a deeper emphasis on institutions, but also widens the focus to encompass the overall question of politics' place in the lives of citizens.

The paradox of empowerment shows that new opportunities to participate do not always enhance democracy because it is not just a theoretical possibility. It is a reality, and one that may be more common than is often thought. The most obvious example illustrates the logic of the paradox in a fairly uncontroversial context: that of campaign finance. Allowing citizens to participate in the funding of political parties and campaigns as much as they want—by giving unlimited amounts of money to candidates or parties, for example—is widely seen simply as freedom for the wealthy to buy political influence. Most recognize that capping or even eliminating this form of political participation aids democratic equality by preventing the undue influence of those disproportionately well positioned to take advantage of it. This is a paradigmatic example of the paradox of empowerment in action since it shows how an avenue of popular participation—in this case, in elections, by lending (financial) strength to a favored side—does not actually empower the people in any meaningful sense, but rather strengthens those already powerful and advantaged in society. Yet it is far from the only real-world example.

In the 1990s, participation became a watchword in international development circles as a means to increase programs' effectiveness and combat the abuses of top-down strategies. Yet the results of many participatory development projects have exhibited the paradox of empowerment. New participatory institutions, as well as other opportunities for social empowerment such as employment quotas for low caste groups (Bajpai 2011), have often been dominated by the most advantaged members of local communities, including in many cases men, those of higher caste or social class, older people, and the wealthy (Gruber and Trickett 1987; Agrawal 2001; Agrawal and Gupta 2005). Nor is the paradox limited to contexts of developing countries. Although today social movements, civil society, and spontaneous collective action are widely celebrated as invaluable to democracy, they were also instrumental to the perpetuation of white supremacy and Jim Crow apartheid in the US South. The Massive Resistance movement against desegregation used all of these ostensibly democratic tools in the 1950s and 1960s to immense success in delaying desegregation (McMillen 1994). The paradox has also been observed in other established institutional settings like schools, where new participatory institutions including oversight boards are dominated by those with the greatest relevant advantages (Botchway 2001).

The paradox of empowerment is not, moreover, limited to these more traditional democratic institutions. Concrete examples of advantaged citizens arguably capturing control of innovative participatory institutions can be found in the three citizen assemblies on electoral reform held in British Columbia, Ontario, and the Netherlands between 2004 and 2007. These citizen assemblies were deliberative mini-publics convened to consider revisions to their respective polity's electoral system. Despite the use of sortition in the selection process for members, many social groups were underrepresented and others overrepresented, often dramatically. Younger citizens, visible minorities, blue collar workers, and citizens with lower educational attainment were severely underrepresented in the British Columbia Citizens' Assembly (James 2008, 112). For instance, 24.9 percent of British Columbians were visible minorities but only 11.9 percent of assembly members were. Similarly, those who did not graduate from high school made up 19.4 percent of the population of the province, but only 5.1 percent of the assembly.

Bias in educational attainment was enormous in all three citizen assemblies. Although those without college degrees made up 9 percent of the Dutch population, they only made up 1 percent of the Dutch citizens' assembly, while those with college degrees were 26 percent of the population and 57 percent of the assembly (Fournier, Van der Kolk, et al. 2011, 55). The Ontario case is even more striking since, province-wide, those without a college degree actually outnumber those with one (22 percent vs. 20 percent), yet those without degrees constituted just 2 percent of the assembly while degree-holders made up fully 44 percent of it (Fournier, Van der Kolk, et al. 2011, 55). It is impossible to know how this compositional bias might have affected the assemblies' deliberation, in part because of the insidious ways that such bias has been known to operate (Sanders 1997; Young 2000). For instance, would less educated assemblies have favored simpler electoral reform plans? We will never know. The point here is that those dedicated to democratic equality cannot dismiss the paradox of empowerment as a defect that doesn't apply to the newest democratic reform ideas, since we see it even in such carefully designed innovative institutions as these.

One might respond to these worries about unrepresentativeness with the simple technical trick of stratification. We might impose quotas, for example, that require that all age and racial groups or levels of education be represented proportionally to their numbers in society. Yet we cannot set a quota for every category of difference that may matter for making public decisions. Or, rather, we cannot do so while keeping the size of the assembly small. The size of the assembly imposes a strict limit on the amount of diversity the group can reflect. For example, every profession cannot be represented on an assembly of any manageable size, nor the diversity of opinion that exists within a given profession.

Imagine an assembly convened to consider local responses to climate change, including the management of forests and wilderness. Say that this assembly chances to have a wildland firefighter as a member. The firefighter's input might be considered invaluable on such an assembly due his familiarity with wilderness management. Yet perhaps this one firefighter has idiosyncratic views not common among his colleagues, such as favoring uncontrolled burning as a response to wildfires. Other assembly members might understandably defer to the firefighter in deliberation, in ignorance of the idiosyncrasy of his views, and this might substantively influence the assembly's conclusions. An obvious response to this scenario is to expand the size of the assembly to either improve the chances of getting another firefighter or setting a quota for the profession, to better represent the diversity of opinion within it. The problem presents itself immediately; we would have to grow deliberative assemblies to unmanageable sizes to account for all the possibly relevant kinds of diversity with quotas and stratification. Stratification is at best an imperfect fix that cannot represent every possibly relevant group in its diversity.

The upshot of all these examples of participatory backfire is that more opportunities for participation do not necessarily improve democracy, at least if improving democracy means anything like spreading power more equally in society. Sometimes, even often, efforts to empower citizens perversely backfire, handing additional tools of influence to those who are already advantaged and powerful. Those who do not, and cannot, put forth the effort required to use participatory institutions—above all, busy people—are thereby disempowered, their views and interests marginalized in the forums of democratic decision-making. The flip side of the paradox of empowerment is likewise counterintuitive. Just as more opportunities for participation can further empower the powerful, *limiting* avenues of participation to those that economize on citizens' resources, including their time and attention, could potentially shift power to the more disadvantaged. The key example is again campaign finance, where limiting or eliminating the ability of "everyone" to participate in this way enhances democracy by equalizing citizens' voices. It does so by economizing on the resources citizens might otherwise bring into politics, and that are unequally scarce in the wider public. In this case, the resource is money, but in many other cases, it would be time and attention, which busy people lack compared to the less busy or more politically dedicated.

It is vital to be clear about the nature of the claim being made here. I am not merely saying that sometimes participatory opportunities backfire. Rather, I am saying that *democratic principles* themselves recommend foreclosing some participatory opportunities. If we care about democratic equality and inclusion, this argument suggests we must take a more sober and considered view of proposed participatory innovations and reforms. Because of the paradox of empowerment, we know that some ostensibly democratic institutional reforms will reliably fail in the core task of democratic institutions, of rendering power more nearly equal. As the citizen assemblies suggest, this may even happen in the most unlikely places. The paradox therefore generates a reason, grounded in core democratic principles, for why we might want to limit or cap the participatory demands of democracy. When those demands serve to effectively reinforce existing social and political hierarchies instead of circulating power more widely in society, they ought to be curtailed. And they ought to be curtailed not just because they conflict with an entitlement to free time, but out of a commitment to democratic principles themselves. Sometimes, more participation is self-defeating of core democratic goals and so should be curtailed on democratic grounds. Just as limiting participation in campaign finance can strengthen democracy, so too, the reasoning goes, can limiting participation in other ways, at least potentially.

Note here the difference between the realist criticisms of participation discussed earlier and the reason we just discussed. I am not claiming that participation or deliberation should be limited because they are too difficult or costly to organize. Nor am I claiming that they lead to bad outcomes, and so should be rethought. Rather, the point is that democracy itself sometimes recommends limiting its own participatory demands, out of a concern to preserve its core value of equality. This is, therefore, a *principled* reason, stemming from democracy itself, to rethink democratic projects of reform and normative democratic theories calling for deeper engagement. Good democrats ought not, by this account, enthusiastically welcome every new participatory innovation just as such. They should instead first subject them to thorough scrutiny to assess whether, in the relevant context, it is likely to generate the paradox of empowerment.

Admitting that there is a reason grounded in democratic principle to limit democracy's participatory demands marks an important departure from one of the only other significant discussions of the paradox of empowerment, this one from Graham Smith. In analyzing democratic innovations, Smith (2009, 14–15) discusses the concern that participation might be too onerous on ordinary citizens under the heading of "efficiency." Note that the language of efficiency is of a piece with that of convenience and cost, which is frequently the language used to object to deliberative and participatory reforms. Yet Smith does not judge any of the great number of innovations he analyzes to be so inefficient as to impose an objectionable participatory burden on citizens. If we consider the high costs involved in some of these innovations, such as deliberative mini-publics, this might seem strange. The explanation is found in the difference between thinking of participatory burdens in terms of efficiency (or cost, convenience, etc.) and in terms of principle. When we see the time citizens spend on participation as something they are entitled to as a matter of justice rather than as something that might be used more or less efficiently by a democratic innovation (which is itself implicitly seen as entitled to citizens' time with no offsetting principled pressure to reduce its temporal footprint in citizens' lives), we become obligated to take a more stern and exacting view of that participation and the institutions calling for it.

One objection to this line of argument is that costly or demanding opportunities to participate may contain the *potential* for radical mass empowerment even if, much of the time, they do indeed serve to reinforce status quo patterns of power and privilege. This is surely an important point. Yet in designing or evaluating a democratic arrangement, we must consider not only the potential of participatory institutions but also how they are likely to function *systemically*. The logic of the paradox of empowerment and the examples cited above suggest that costly forms of participation are likely to systemically advantage traditionally powerful groups. This ought to move those concerned about democratizing power to appreciate the potential of concentrating it in participatory institutions with lower costs to participants, such as electoral ones. Elections remain the most inclusive participatory institution by a comically wide margin. More people vote than have even heard of a citizens' assembly, let alone than have actually participated in any deliberative institution (Elliott 2015, 215–16). The reason elections are so inclusive seems obvious enough; voting is almost incomparably less expensive than deliberative alternatives. I say more about elections in this vein in chapter 5.

Political theorists interested in more equitably sharing power should therefore turn their attention to the institutions of electoral democracy and help address the very real problems such institutions face. The emerging literature in political theory on political parties is just such a salutary development (Rosenblum 2008; Muirhead 2014; White and Ypi 2016), as is Jeremy Waldron's (2016) institution-focused "political political theory." The ongoing debate over mandatory voting also makes valuable contributions to exploring the conditions of a democracy that simultaneously respects citizens' free time and also distributes power widely (Birch 2009; Brennan and Hill 2014; Maskivker 2019; Chapman 2019; Umbers 2020). Due to the paradox of empowerment, such work does the most to clarify the institutional conditions of mass empowerment.

This is not to say that democratic innovations—emphasizing deliberation or otherwise—are useless or harmful to democracy. The paradox of empowerment is not immune to institutional design, as Michael Neblo's deliberative forums that reverse the usual biases in participation demonstrate (Neblo, Esterling, and Lazer 2018). Rather, the point is that democratic theory must take the entitlement to control one's time and the unique temporal limits of busy and marginalized citizens seriously in ways it has often not. To refrain from doing so not only threatens a moral harm but is also self-defeating of core democratic aims like equality and inclusion.

Objections from Demandingness and Injustice

Let us sum up the argument so far. The right to free time gives rise to a claim of justice against highly demanding democratic institutions and theories. The paradox of empowerment, moreover, shows why we would want limits of this kind as a matter of democratic principle and why un-demanding configurations of citizenship are likely to be more egalitarian than demanding ones in many cases. These two arguments constitute prin-cipled reasons to limit the participatory demands of democracy. In this section, I consider two objections to this argument.

One of the most straightforward objections is that the argument makes a fundamental error in criticizing the demandingness of democracy. In the philosophical debate on moral demandingness, Robert E. Goodin (2009) doubts that a difficult moral standard's demandingness can even consti-tute an objection to it. If a demanding course of action is truly what mo-rality requires after considering the first-order merits of the case, then that is what morality requires. The same might be said of democracy. If the conduct required by a democratic theory is necessary for democratic legitimacy, stability, justice, etc., then that is what is necessary, regardless of how difficult it might be. That citizens might struggle to accomplish it says more about the weakness or undemocratic character of the citizenry than about the standard. It merely means that many people fail to do their duty, or make poor democrats, which is something we perhaps already knew.

In reply, I cannot help myself to the response many would give to this sort of objection, which is essentially a kind of realist scoff. Maybe in prin-ciple we should not be concerned with the demandingness of a theory, a realist might say, but in the real world, it may determine whether people adopt it and use it to regulate their actions, affecting its ability to influence the world. This is precisely the type of attitude found in many of the re-alist criticisms of democracy discussed above. Since my approach is not realist in this way, however, this reply is closed to me. Luckily, it is not the only possible response. Though we might all indeed be bad democrats, it is also possible that there is an account of democracy that both makes good sense of our democratic commitments and is less demanding than accepted theories. Goodin's objection, taken literally, might forestall the search for such an account before it began. In one sense, my argument is precisely a call for such a search; indeed, one upshot is that such a search is imperative if we are to achieve the democratic promise of empowering the people, given the straitened circumstances of busy people and their entitlement to control their time.

Another objection to the argument is that these two principled reasons to limit the participatory demands of democracy might seem to prevent the sort of strenuous political activities needed to address entrenched injustice. The argument appeals to the means to live well, for instance, yet there are many who lack the means to live even a minimally decent life, often as a result of historic or systemic injustice. It is often the case, moreover, that we could, via demanding collective action, help remediate such injustice, and Tommie Shelby (2016) argues persuasively that we have a duty to do so. Is it appropriate to press the claim to free time in these circumstances? It might seem reasonable that a duty to remedy injustice might override a right to free time when the two are put into the balance against each other. At issue in this objection, then, is the question of how to square our obligations with our own desires, commitments, and life plans—which are advanced by means of free time.

This question has received a great deal of discussion in moral philosophy, in the debate over the demandingness of morality. Perhaps the central issue in this debate is the significance of the individual's own interests, projects, or commitments compared to the imperatives of morality, closely mirroring the tension between injustice and free time (Nagel 1986, 204; Scheffler 1992, 98–114). As a result, this literature supplies many possible standards for how to square our obligations with our ideas of the good. For instance, Peter Singer (2010, 18) suggests individuals have to sacrifice all the resources they can until they endanger something nearly as valuable as the life they could otherwise save through donating to life-saving charities. Analogized to politics, this would suggest comprehensive dedication of one's life to fighting for justice. The problem with this maximalist standard, as with many others in this literature, is that it fails to translate neatly into political terms since it tends not to integrate political institutions. Goodin (2009, 10) suggests that institutions can help us discharge moral duties and address moral demandingness through coordinating cooperation on complex tasks. In politics, institutions like the state are unavoidably present and so need not be built but only reoriented to address injustice.

For this reason, perhaps most promising as a standard for negotiating the demands of justice with the need for free time is one suggested in separate work by Kwame Anthony Appiah and Liam Murphy. Appiah and Murphy argue that we have done what morality requires when we have done our fair share, where "fair share" is the amount each individual would have to do to remedy injustice if everyone contributed (Murphy 2000; Appiah 2006, 164–65). This standard posits, counterfactually, that if everyone contributed to remedying injustice, the share of effort necessary from each person would be less. Even if everyone does not contribute, this standard helps to clarify what we can fairly expect of everyone. This standard works well with political institutions since institutions are, in one sense, mechanisms for sharing the burdens of complex collective tasks. When properly designed, such institutions would ideally make it such that fulfilling the basic expectations of citizenship is the same as doing one's share for justice. This fair share standard seems to make good sense in the political case since it limits individuals' contribution to their share of a collective effort to achieve justice if everyone (counterfactually) contributed to it coordinated by political institutions like the state. This supplies a response to the objection about injustice because it suggests that there is sufficient room in the lives of citizens for both obligations to promote justice and also for a right to free time.

With these objections answered, we can consider two broad implications of the argument I want to highlight. First, there is a metaphor of taxation we can now appreciate in light of both the right to free time and the paradox of empowerment. Together, these two arguments imply that demanding models of citizenship constitute a kind of "temporal poll tax" that effectively limits the power of busy and marginalized groups. Time-intensive forms of participation erect a cost barrier to taking part in democratic processes that is effectively exclusionary in a similar way to Jim Crow poll taxes. Both require citizens to shoulder a significant expense in order to exercise their right to participate in the democratic process. In the presence of unequal scarcity, particularly in temporal resources, this predictably disempowers those citizens whose time is scarcer. Though the temporal poll tax is without a doubt less heinous than those used to uphold white supremacy, it remains pernicious and anti-democratic. Preventing or abolishing it should be the project of all democrats.

The principled reasons to limit participatory demands together also supply a missing counterweight to the widespread assumption in democratic theory that more participation would always be better if only practical limitations could be overcome. Phillips (1991, 165), for example, laments that more participatory configurations of citizenship generate inequality via the paradox of empowerment and looks forward to a "future scenario" in which we can raise our expectations of participation. Yet if there are limits to democratic citizenship that are morally principled in character, as I argue, this sentiment is importantly mistaken. We must not expect participation over those limits even if doing so becomes feasible in the future. There are competing considerations—grounded in justice and democratic principle—to those that support expanding democratic participation endlessly. They cannot be legitimately ignored.

Conclusion

In this chapter, I argued that there are two principled reasons to limit democracy's participatory expectations of citizens. First, the right to free time generates a claim against highly demanding democratic institutions that is based in justice. Second, the paradox of empowerment illustrates how core democratic principles recommend limits on participatory expectations.

The paradox of empowerment also suggests, counterintuitively, that undemanding participatory institutions can often be more egalitarian than demanding ones. This means that the value of democratic equality often ought to exert a downward pressure on the expectations of citizenship built into participatory institutions, a normative pressure that is virtually always ignored. Thus, we see the chapter's original question of when democracy asks too much of its citizens at last answered; when it infringes on their right to free time by expanding its participatory expectations without regard to that right, and when it does so in ways that, paradoxically, end up detracting from democratic equality.

CHAPTER FOUR

The Citizen Minimum

Inclusion and Stand-By Citizenship

The last chapter concluded that it is essential to make democratic participation undemanding so as to widen empowerment in the context of unequal scarcity in the resources needed for democratic citizenship. One way of understanding this requirement is as one aim among others that must be balanced in designing democracy. This is, for example, the approach taken by Graham Smith (2009). He begins his study of democratic innovations by enumerating a series of six criteria against which he will assess these innovations. Among these is what I have called the paradox of empowerment (which he discusses under the heading of "efficiency"). Smith treats the concern raised by the paradox—that difficult types of participation are likely to effectively exclude many citizens—as just one dimension of concern regarding what we need out of democratic innovations.

If we see the need to make democracy undemanding as just one among other democratic necessities, we miss something essential about it. Making democracy undemanding is not only important for the reasons explained in the last chapter. It is also needed to realize democratic theory's first and most important priority: effective political inclusion. In this chapter, I make the case that we should *put inclusion first* in the design of democratic institutions due to its unique importance. This underscores the conclusion from the last chapter, about why we *must* make participation undemanding. I then elaborate a conception of inclusion that draws on arguments from earlier chapters to fill out an account of the democratic minimum that simultaneously serves as (1) a floor of democratic citizenship, (2) a reasonably undemanding standard of engagement, and (3) the criterion of what it means to be politically included. The first two sections of the chapter address inclusion and the latter three lay out the democratic minimum of stand-by citizenship.

The Priority of Inclusion

A central claim of this book is that if you want democracy to be egalitarian, you must make it undemanding. Yet democratic equality is a complex social and political ideal, with many different accounts of what this equality properly entails. In this section, I argue that democratic equality involves at least two contrasting ideals—inclusion and political equality—and that these are not only fundamentally distinct, but that inclusion should take priority in the practical task of designing and reforming democratic institutions. Disputes over competing accounts of political equality—such as that over relational egalitarianism, or James Lindley Wilson's (2019) equal authority view vs. equal power views—are usually downstream from this prior distinction. I argue inclusion, as distinguished from political equality, is more important both in principle and prudentially if one's aims include empowering marginalized groups and remedying injustices to which they are subject.

There is a common view among political theorists that inclusion is in some essential way an egalitarian idea such that political equality may seem to be the more fundamental ideal. Yet this view is mistaken. Though inclusion is indeed an egalitarian idea, *democratic* equality is not exhausted by the notion of *political* equality, meaning something like equal influence or authority in political decision-making. Inclusion and political equality are two distinct ideas of equality at work in politics, and both are probably best seen as expressions of a more fundamental idea of democratic equality.

My concern here is distinguishing these ideas rather than highlighting their commonalities because they bear distinct consequences for political action and reform, as we'll see. In distinguishing inclusion and political equality, however, I set myself at odds with one of the most prominent theorists of inclusion, Iris Marion Young, who subsumes inclusion into political equality. To grasp the importance of sharply distinguishing inclusion and political equality, and putting inclusion first, we must first consider Young's argument for assimilating the two ideas.

Young (2000, 24) argues that in "real political conflict" over exclusionary policies and institutions, political actors and movements "invariably appeal to ideals of political equality." For example, one of the aims of the civil rights movement in the United States was to combat the political disenfranchisement of Black Americans, yet the movement publicly presented this aim largely in terms of equality rather than inclusion. (We might quibble with the historicity of this generalization due to the variety of messages associated with such movements—the famous placard worn by protesters proclaiming "I AM A MAN" seems more about claiming an absolute worth as persons or dignity rather than equality per se, for example—but let us accept it for the sake of argument.) Young presents this historical regularity as a reason to assimilate inclusion to political equality *in political theory*.

Young's point seems to be that political theorists should follow activists and political movements in how the concepts central to their efforts are used. Yet the nobility of certain movements is no reason for political theorists to emulate mistakes they may make in applying concepts. It is important to remember that the imperatives of effective political messaging and sloganeering generate enormous pressures on political actors toward simplicity and efficacy such that nuance, and even accuracy, is often necessarily sacrificed. Political theorists should not be chained to choices dictated by such pressures. Though it is no doubt important that political theory not depart totally from popular usage, we must be free to distance ourselves from conventional use in studying political ideas where there is compelling reason to do so, as I shall now show there is in the case of inclusion and political equality.

The basic reason to distinguish inclusion and equality is because to assimilate them conflates two distinctly different questions. One addresses the issue of who is effectively admitted *into* the political realm and participates as a member of the citizen body. To this question, inclusion names a family of expansive answers. The other question addresses what the appropriate division of power ought to be *within* the political realm. Political equality denotes that all should have equal say, in some sense. Though there is more than a family resemblance between inclusion and political equality, it is far from obvious that the two answers naturally go together.

For instance, no less an advocate of progressive social reform than John Stuart Mill (1991) argued that everyone should be included in politics but that this did not imply that they should all have equal (voting) power within the political realm. Mill thus approved of inclusion but not political equality. The Athenian democracy illustrates the opposite case. Of all the

TABLE I **Regime types, by inclusion and political equality**

	Inclusive	Exclusionary
Politically equal	• Liberal democracy	• Ancient Athenian democracy • *Herrenvolk* democracy
Politically unequal	• Millian representative democracy • Democracy without campaign finance regulation	• Authoritarianism, oligarchy, monarchy, autocracy, etc.

residents of Athens, only free men who met certain requirements bore political rights. Those who did, however, enjoyed a degree of political equality practically unparalleled since. Democratic Athens thus embodied marked exclusion paired with striking political equality. These examples illustrate why I say debates over the exact interpretation of political equality are usually downstream from the question of inclusion; equality between equals does not exclude the possibility of a sizable group of excluded non-equals. Settling the question of what political equality entails does not necessarily tell us to whom that equality applies. We can see these alternatives illustrated in Table I.

I want to suggest that we should keep inclusion and equality distinct in order to keep legible these alternatives which are, today, increasingly live options. Epistocracy, or political arrangements that give more power to knowledgeable elites, has recently gained notable attention and plaudits from those exasperated by the seeming foolishness of their fellow citizens' political choices (Caplan 2007; Brennan 2016). Such arrangements generally remain inclusive but sacrifice political equality. More darkly, right populist movements across the world have charted a path in the tradition of ancient Athens, seeking to exclude disfavored groups— often immigrants and ethnic and racial minorities—from effective access to political power while aggressively promoting the power and welfare of favored groups. Such herrenvolk democracy, or a political order that is "democratic for the master race [herrenvolk] but tyrannical for subordinate groups" (Van den Berghe 1967), is emerging as one of the chief practical alternatives to what I have called in Table I, for lack of a better term, liberal democracy. By liberal democracy, I mean that family of regimes and political theories that favor highly expansive conceptions of who is included in democratic processes and also robust political equality. This includes many variants with different labels, including republicanism, deliberative democracy, etc., some of whose advocates might reject this categorization. Nothing turns on this terminology, however. It is simply a placeholder meaning simultaneously inclusion and political egalitarianism. Thus, it is important to keep inclusion and political equality separate so that we can better understand the real political divisions and live political options we find in the world.

We also want to maintain the distinction between inclusion and political equality because the two values are not created equal. Indeed, the central normative claim of this chapter is that inclusion must come *first* in the design and reform of democratic institutions. The first principled reason for the priority of inclusion is that it is simply more morally urgent, and thus important, than equality. This might seem counterintuitive to many readers due to the prominence of political equality as the core democratic value in much contemporary political theory and no small amount of actual political discourse. Yet the conclusion is unavoidable on reflection.

To be politically excluded is to be rendered a non-person as far as democracy is concerned. It is to be put outside the circle of those who rule, placed on par with *things* that are administered by the rulers. In different language, it is to be made a *subject*, one who is governed by others and seen as a passive object of policy (and perhaps, of exploitation), to be manipulated by the empowered class of rulers. This status has much in common with domination, or being subject to the arbitrary power of others, which the recent efflorescence of relational egalitarian and republican political theory has helped illuminate as a multifaceted moral, political, and social problem (Pettit 1997; Anderson 1999; Gourevitch 2015; Anderson 2017).

This harm is qualitatively different from that involved in political inequality. A citizen with a vote whose potency is reduced—but not eliminated—by the importance of, for example, money in politics is in a fundamentally different position due to the structural incentives embedded in elections. Exclusion means that one's concerns and interests matter not at all, and might possibly be targeted for exploitation, by those in power. Having a vote in a politically unequal democracy makes such harm or neglect by elected officials at least somewhat risky, since they may incur electoral sanction as a result. Having *some* say via elections is entirely different from having *no* say. The average citizen's interests may suffer neglect by those in power in an unequal democracy, but *excluded* persons are systemically vulnerable to active exploitation and having their interests positively sacrificed to those of regime insiders. The downside risk to exclusion is thus much worse than that of political inequality, giving it greater moral urgency.

There is also a non-instrumental harm involved in exclusion that is not present with inequality. This is a harm to one's status or standing in society. Being politically included in the sense of being enfranchised denotes a respect-conferring fundamental level of social standing. As Judith Shklar (1991, 2) argues, "the ballot has always been a certificate of full membership in society, and its value depends primarily on its capacity to confer a minimum of social dignity." The value of the franchise, she claims, is found in its membership-conferring quality. On this account, "the struggle for citizenship in America has . . . been overwhelmingly a demand for inclusion in the polity, an effort to break down excluding barriers to recognition, rather than an aspiration to civic participation as a deeply involving activity" (Shklar 1991, 3). Agitation for the franchise has thus been more about achieving a civic minimum of recognition than a crusade for democratic participation. According to Shklar, exclusion deprives individuals of the "minimum of social dignity," visiting on them not just second-class citizenship but something akin to the enslaved person's social death.

The American case after the end of the Civil War, as characterized by Shklar, makes the priority of inclusion over political equality come out starkly. The political system that the formerly enslaved people were admitted to during Reconstruction was a starkly unequal one, marked by corruption, clientelism, nativism, and classist elitism, to say nothing of the exclusion of women (Keyssar 2000, 61–76). Yet the formerly enslaved rightly saw their admission as marking a watershed moment for their standing in the polity. Though they would initially occupy the lowest rungs of the sociopolitical ladder, they were no longer entirely prevented from climbing it. They were at last given the minimal standing that would protect them from wanton harm and enable them to better their condition, at least for a tragically brief window of time.

If inclusion and political equality were even close neighbors in terms of their importance, we might hesitate to see the inclusion of the formerly enslaved as an improvement. Being admitted to a highly unequal democracy would seem to be a mixed blessing, even a Pyrrhic victory, if the value of equality rivaled that of inclusion. Yet this is not how we see the enfranchisement of the formerly enslaved. If we thought the value of equality and inclusion was nearly the same, we might be apt to see President Andrew Johnson's initial aims during Presidential Reconstruction— when he looked to break the enduring political and economic power of the planter aristocracy in the defeated South but also maintain white supremacy (Foner 2002, 183) — as a debatable prioritization of equality over inclusion. A reasonable person could agree with Johnson that excluding Black people but achieving true equality among White people was an attractive alternative if inclusion were in close competition with political equality. That we would utterly reject such an evaluation of Johnson's policy suggests we understand the political priority of inclusion implicitly. Johnson's seeming goal of an egalitarian "cracker" (or herrenvolk) democracy was strictly inferior to even a highly unequal democratic arrangement that included formerly enslaved people because of inclusion's unique importance.

This argument suggests a strict hierarchical ordering of the alternatives summarized in Table 1. Liberal democracy is to be preferred to all alternatives, and any alternative is to be preferred to authoritarianism. But between an unequal Millian representative democracy and an exclusionary but egalitarian Athenian democracy, we should strictly prefer Millian democracy due to the relative importance of inclusion. The ease of judging the Reconstruction case suggests, moreover, that the relative moral importance of inclusion is not really comparable to that of equality. Were it so, equality might substitute for inclusion at some margin, but that does not seem to be the case. This raises the important question: How should we understand their relation?

We do not need to posit anything as implausible as lexical priority to reflect the proper ordering of these values. I suggest, adapting Shklar (1984, 7), that we *put inclusion first* in the design and reform of democratic institutions. This means that, barring extenuating circumstances, conflicts between them should be resolved in favor of inclusion. It also means our plans for reform should always be formulated with inclusion in mind, even when the proximate aim is different — such as securing better deliberation, combating polarization, etc.

One might object that I draw the distinction between inclusion and political equality too sharply, and that instead they are properly understood as continuous with each other. Exclusion, for instance, might be thought to simply be the most extreme way of generating political inequality, just as having no financial income could be seen as defining one extreme of an unequal distribution of income in society. Using the analogy of economic inequality, we would not necessarily say that someone with no job is not a part of the labor market, for example, simply that they occupied one extreme end of it.

Recall that my claim is that inclusion and political equality are best understood as components of a wider ideal of democratic equality, but that each of them concern a substantially distinct political question. To see the significance of this distinction, consider again the difference it makes to matter not at all in formal decision-making processes compared to mattering only a little. When a group's members have no weight in decision processes at all, it doesn't matter how many members of the group are mobilized politically—one matters as little as a hundred, which matters as little as a million. Any number times zero equals zero. Excluded members of whatever number will always lack significance in decision processes (barring extralegal action). But if members of that group matter unequally—say as 50 percent of other citizens—then mass political mobilization could well make a difference. At this rate of inequality, a million becomes the equivalent of 500,000, a not inconsiderable number in many political contexts. To put it, as it were, mathematically: exclusion and inclusion are fundamentally different from inequality because of the unique properties of the number zero. I do not deny that one can *choose* to see inclusion and exclusion as continuous with political equality/inequality; there is nothing conceptually incoherent with doing so. My point is that there is a better way of looking at them, a way that does not obscure the unique features of exclusion and inclusion that mark them out for special concern.

Another possible objection is to the priority I assign to inclusion. One might posit a hypothetical wherein we secure perfect political equality by excluding a single person. Such a trade-off seems obviously attractive. But if we think such a trade-off is worth it, inclusion cannot have the kind of priority I claim for it. Yet this misconstrues the nature of my claim about inclusion's priority. Note that I said above *barring extenuating circumstances*, inclusion should win out in conflicts between it and political equality. I explicitly reject a strict form of Rawlsian lexical priority, wherein every jot and tittle of inclusion's requirements would have to be fulfilled before turning concern to equality. Rather, putting inclusion first means making it our first concern, one that *can* but need not always override others. It certainly should not be our only concern so long as it remains a concern at all, as in lexical priority. I do not deny that there might be circumstances where there is a trade-off to be made—these circumstances are just likely to be exceptional.

So, let us reconsider the hypothetical above. In the real world, what kind of individuals might be so important that excluding them from politics could bring about political equality? One imaginable candidate might be an absolute monarch standing in the way of establishing a representative democratic republic. Forcing that individual to abdicate and stripping him or her of political rights such as freedom of speech or the right to run for office to prevent them from returning to power might be a prudent way to establish and maintain a much more egalitarian political order. Yet it would come at a cost to inclusion in the former monarch's political exclusion. How would my principle of putting inclusion first guide our reasoning in such a circumstance?

I would say that putting inclusion first does not bar the ex-monarch's exclusion, and not just because replacing autocracy with democracy leads to overall gains in inclusion. Rather, putting inclusion first is a political principle, and so one that must be flexible to historical circumstances and our judgment of what is needful for the wider ideal of *democratic* equality in those circumstances. A revolutionary transition of the political order from autocracy to democracy is sufficiently exceptional that it is no embarrassment to the priority of inclusion for it to be relaxed in a limited way vis-à-vis former autocrats during such an unusual circumstance. It would still retain its value in guiding the distribution of ongoing efforts at institutional reform, for instance, pushing us to prioritize more inclusive arrangements.

The more common historical trade-off between inclusion and equality has concerned excluded groups much larger than a single person. Regimes where equality arguably won out over inclusion include colonial regimes wherein democracy is secured only to settler elites. In these cases, groups comprising from 10 to 90 percent or more of the population were stripped of political rights and thus politically excluded. Yet, ironically, there is often a culture of political equality in such herrenvolk democracies—see de Tocqueville's (2010, 89) insistence on Jacksonian America's "passion for equality" in the midst of African slavery.

Putting inclusion first is a political principle learned from examples like these. It is a rejection of the hypocritical sort of "passion for equality" that may be found among the enfranchised in these profoundly exclusionary contexts. That we can construct imaginary scenarios where inclusion should occasionally yield to equality leaves the principle of putting inclusion first undisturbed since it is constructed for the world we are acquainted with, not that of our distant imaginings. A proper challenge to the principle, then, would cite some actual historical cases in which equality came into conflict with inclusion and prioritizing equality made more sense on democratic grounds.

My reliance on seemingly distant history to illustrate the priority of inclusion may lead some to doubt its relevance today. Yet my comments suggest an important practical upshot of this argument to contemporary political disputes. As I write this, the issue of political inequality arising from economic inequality has reemerged as a central issue on the American, and indeed global, political agenda. Prominent politicians like Bernie Sanders and Elizabeth Warren rail against the power of wealthy interests and propose thoroughgoing reforms to address it. Even Donald Trump complained about the nefarious influence of moneyed elites in the 2016 campaign.

At the same time, numerous American states and local governments have erected new burdens on exercising the franchise. These governments, all controlled by the Republican Party, have designed these burdens along partisan lines to suppress voting by groups that tend to be electorally unfavorable to them. Such vote suppression seeks to push opposing partisans out of the electorate, and thus to effectively exclude them from sharing political power. The growth of inequality, on the one hand, and the reemergence of vote suppression, on the other, illustrate that inclusion and equality are both very much at issue in democracy today, at least in the United States.

These examples also suggest the *distinctness* of the problems that beset the realization of each value because each can give rise to markedly distinct policy agendas. For example, contemporary oligarchic tendencies in the US that threaten political equality seem to call for campaign finance regulation while combating exclusionary vote suppression likely requires rebuilding the bulwarks of the Voting Rights Act, among other turnout-promoting institutional reforms. It is thus not only that inclusion and political equality are conceptually distinct, but they also recommend radically different courses of action. Though of course these policies and institutional reforms might be packaged together legislatively, it should nonetheless be clear that they are themselves different and serve to advance democracy in distinct ways. These contemporary examples suggest the ongoing relevance of the lessons of history regarding the relative importance of these two values. Moreover, the argument suggests that the problem of vote suppression is qualitatively more important than that of combating the influence of wealth in politics.

This last point might seem surprising, and invites a natural response: Why can't we have both? Surely the wrongs involved in both inequality and exclusion are grave. Isn't insisting on the priority of inclusion to force a false choice? It is of course true that with infinite resources and time, we should insist on both, and there are of course parliamentary procedures such as legislative bundling that can make doing so sometimes trivially easy. Yet there are nonetheless situations when we are forced to choose. Relevant circumstances are not hard to imagine: the attention and dedication of leaders is finite, if not fickle; space on the political agenda is jealously contested; political capital is limited and ever dwindling. Practical limitations like these mean that there can always be trade-offs between pursuing equality and inclusion in actual politics. To deny that is to deny reality.

A more principled and abstract reason than this one is that political equality of the sort we would value today is put out of reach unless we put inclusion first. This is because if we equalize power *before* achieving inclusion, we end up with equality only between those who are already politically present. Citizens who are not present, for whatever reason, would be excluded from this equality and rendered categorically unequal to those who happen to be present, with all the implications of neglect, harm, and exploitation discussed in chapter 2.

Political equality that precedes inclusion results in the empowerment of a new elite made up of those who have the intrinsic motivation and the resources to engage in democratic politics. This elite is defined by self-selection and, above all, by pre-existing social and political advantages, including intrinsic motivation to participate in politics. Because all participation is costly, those with greater resources and predispositions to engage in politics will always be in a better position to take advantage of opportunities to participate. If, then, in pursuit of equality, we follow the recommendations of many political theorists and create numerous new pathways to power and influence for ordinary citizens who take it upon themselves to use them, these pathways would generally become captured by this group of already engaged citizens: another instance of the paradox of empowerment. Those who are currently excluded would not be empowered by these reforms—equality would belong to a kind of activist elite, generating an aristocracy of activists. An aristocracy of activists would resemble Athenian democracy or herrenvolk democracy in being egalitarian but exclusionary, yet in a context where exclusions are less legal and more determined by pre-existing social patterns of advantage.

Democratic theorists often seem to believe that there is a latent demand for deeper and more meaningful forms of democratic participation, and that, if instituted, citizens who currently do not involve themselves in politics will flock to new participatory institutions. I call this the "if you build it, they will come" hypothesis. This hypothesis achieves a neat trick since it finesses away the question of priority between inclusion and political equality by asserting that if you put equality first, you will actually solve the inclusion problem simultaneously.

One problem with this hypothesis is, like the hypothesis itself, empirical. There is little evidence that new forms of participation themselves draw in disconnected citizens. In fact, evidence from many deliberative experiments—in which subjects are invited to participate in deliberations about public issues—suggest that they often tend to attract relatively well-educated and engaged citizens, not those who are currently excluded, as we saw in the paradox of empowerment. Michael Neblo and coauthors have run deliberative forums that reverse this common bias, drawing in citizens who conventionally do not participate, and seem to mainly credit the forums' deliberative character (Neblo, Esterling, and Lazer 2018). More likely, however, is that the online design of the forums drastically reduced the costs of participation compared to the most celebrated instances of in-person deliberation. Thus, there are ways to design institutions to target excluded citizens and these need not take a deliberative form, as the success of lowering the costs of voting or making it mandatory demonstrate (Elliott 2017). The lesson is that prioritizing inclusion means designing institutions with the explicit aim of reaching excluded groups.

Another problem with the "if you build it, they will come" hypothesis comes down to political motivation—that is, disagreement about the value of politics as an activity. People vary in their interest in politics, as I have insisted all along. Some find it an essential part of their lives while others do not care about it at all. Building more egalitarian institutions could perhaps draw in those citizens who are not involved due to the unequal power of moneyed interests—of whom there are many, no doubt—but *not* those whose lack of involvement stems from their busyness and lack of intrinsic interest in politics. This latter group of citizens effectively exclude themselves, often due to the dynamics constructing inauthentic apathy that we discussed in chapter 2 or an artificially truncated political agenda, as I discuss in chapter 6. They would require a different sort of inducement to participate, likely one that stems from nonpolitical concerns or institutional reform. Thus, that busyness and intrinsic motivation varies from person to person almost certainly precludes the "if you build it" hypothesis from simultaneously solving the equality and inclusion problems since some will not come on their own.

Perhaps we should not care about these citizens. If they choose to absent themselves from even much more egalitarian institutions than we currently possess, we might think that we need not concern ourselves with them at all. If one is given a real opportunity to participate on equal terms and one does not take it up, we may think their subjection to the will of others is justified. I admit the possibility of this sort of response, yet I have never seen a substantive development of it. As it is, the notion simply fails to respond to the argument I have made so far. Those who are excluded—in whatever way that transpires—are subject to a degrading social status and made liable to exploitation. This is true whether exclusion is a product of de jure restrictions or de facto social patterns that determine one's resources for, and attitudes toward, political activity.

Inclusion Meaning What?

In the last section, we saw that inclusion must come first in democratic theory. But what does this priority entail? The previous discussion uses the idea of inclusion in quite general terms to mean an expansive family of answers to the question of who enters the political arena as a participant. In this section, I sketch the form of the idea of inclusion, while the next section addresses its substance.

Inclusion has at least two dimensions: (1) who *ought* to be included and (2) what it *takes* to be included. The former question has commanded much attention in recent years, especially in debates over global democracy. As problems have become more global, political theorists have sought ways to think about democratic politics beyond the confines of states. This debate has generated much fascinating work on competing principles for determining justifiable claims to inclusion, among other questions. The broad question of who ought to be included may seem to be the more interesting of these two, given its obvious normative weight and relevance to issues like migration that are increasingly important in actual politics. Yet I want to focus on the latter question, of what it takes for someone to be included in democratic politics. This question is both distinct from that about normative principles of inclusion and more important in ways that have not received sufficient attention.

Let's clarify first why it is a distinct question that cannot be reduced to the other. Consider the metaphor of a literal political arena, in which politics happens.[1] Being politically included is like having a ticket into the

---

1. This metaphor is consistent with seeing politics and democracy as expansive social ideals. It is also consistent with the feminist slogan that "the personal is the political," since even

arena. The question of who ought to be included is akin to asking how we should distribute those tickets—to the native-born, to all affected, to all subjected, etc. The latter question, that of effective inclusion, asks who *actually* makes their way into the political arena, ticket or no. Unless we assume everyone who gets a ticket will definitely use it, or that only those who are afforded one will manage to find their way in, these two questions will identify different groups. These questions are not therefore functionally the same and cannot be reduced to each other.

What it means to be included is also an intrinsically important inquiry because it illuminates cases that the other obscures. For example, asking what it takes to be included helps us understand hugely important cases of groups that were formally or informally excluded from politics *but intruded into it*, and thereby involved themselves in collective decision-making processes in difference-making ways. Using the arena metaphor, these would be groups who made their way into the arena without being afforded tickets. Consider, for instance, women's pivotal role in the reform movements of the late nineteenth and early twentieth centuries. From the abolition movement, to the temperance and prohibition movement, to a broad spectrum of progressive reforms, to women's suffrage itself, women played key roles in political struggles that succeeded in remaking politics in the United States and other western countries. The prohibition movement in particular was powered by women activists whose tireless work brought to fruition one of the most improbably successful (if retrospectively derided) political movements in American history (Okrent 2010, 12ff). Consider also the 2006 immigration demonstrations that brought hundreds of thousands of undocumented migrants into the streets across the United States to protest for humane immigration policies. These protests, and the mass mobilization that attended them, helped catapult immigration into the national spotlight, successfully scuttling a major anti-immigrant bill in Congress and "rendering Latino and immigrant voters a political force to be reckoned with . . . for years to come" (Zepeda-Millán 2017, 163). In both these cases, groups that were ostensibly excluded from participating in politics forced their own inclusion, informally.

---

if politics can be found anywhere in principle, this does not mean that literally everything is *always* necessarily politics. Saying politics can be anywhere is importantly different from saying it's everywhere all the time. Unless we adopt the latter view, which means that there is, even in principle, no such thing as private or nonpolitical social spaces, the metaphor of the political arena is applicable.

When we approach the concept of inclusion in terms of who *ought* to belong, we lose sight of these cases of "informal inclusion." These cases invite us to ask how these groups became politically active despite their formal exclusion. How is such effective, informal inclusion possible? What is at its root? The question of what it takes to be included helps illuminate this issue.

Significant cases of informal inclusion suggest that the question of what makes a group or individual included is at least as important, and perhaps even more so, than that of who ought to be included. The latter question has often been concerned with formal inclusion, meaning the possession of political rights, as well as supportive informal norms of inclusion, such as by not privileging "specific styles of expression" or setting the terms of discourse in ways that others cannot share (Young 2000, 53; Sanders 1997). Yet cases of groups who include themselves show that formal inclusion and supportive norms are *neither necessary nor sufficient* for democratic inclusion. This is a surprising claim. What I am saying is that when groups succeed in making themselves a part of political processes from which they are otherwise excluded, they show that the formal and informal rules structuring political exclusion are *irrelevant*—in a fundamental way—to whether citizens are actually a part of politics. Since groups have managed to make themselves matter for politics without such support, something else must lie at the root of inclusion. To be sure, this does not mean such rules are trivial or unimportant—indeed, this entire book is premised on the central importance of institutions—merely that, at the most basic conceptual level, they do not determine when someone is a real part of democratic politics.

There is a deep and consequential difference at work here between two approaches to doing political theory. The approach suggested by the question of what it *means* to be included is political and historical in nature, while that invited by the question of who *ought* to be included is more abstract and legalistic. This difference helps explain why the "who ought to belong" question obscures cases of informal inclusion.

Asking who ought to be included invites a quasi-legalistic methodological approach wherein candidates for inclusion seem to petition to have their credentials scrutinized at the bar of the appropriate principle. This approach lends the politics of inclusion a legalistic air, wherein barriers to inclusion are noted, adjudicated one by one, and judgment rendered upon them. We see this, for instance, in Lynn Sanders's (1997) critique of deliberation. Sanders highlights numerous ways that democratic deliberation is effectively exclusionary, such as in the denigration of testimonial forms of political expression in favor of discursive, exclusively reason-based ones. The implication is that Sanders has made a claim regarding a species of exclusion that can then be adjudicated as justified or not. Yet women re-formers and immigrants in 2006 did not wait for anyone to approve their participation—they showed that they were already a part of politics, what-ever anyone else thinks. No one gave them permission. When disenfran-chised women and undocumented migrants made themselves politically consequential, they showed that being a part of politics is very often a matter of neither law nor custom. They charted their own path to political influence, and in doing so offer us a lesson that there is something more fundamental to being a part of politics than others thinking you belong and affording you a ticket into the political arena, as it were, after an ad-judication process determining who belongs. What matters is *you* thinking that you belong.

This represents a *political* approach to inclusion, one that highlights the importance of mobilization. Whereas the question of who ought to belong invites the legalistic approach common to much political theory today, thinking about inclusion in terms of what it takes to be a real part of the political game invites a political approach. It moves us to ask: What makes groups matter in processes of collective decision-making? This is a question most democratic theorists can recognize as being essential to broadening democracy, which is of course a core aim of the present in-quiry. It is also a question that invites the answer: mobilization. By mobili-zation I mean primarily processes of consciousness changing which aim to persuade individuals and groups to make connections between their lives and politics, and to involve themselves in it. Lisa Disch (2021) has argued for a mobilization conception of representation that conveys part of the idea as I mean it.

To Disch, the proper task of representation is not to carry forward de-mands originating in a set field of social interests, but to *frame* the terms of conflict and *configure* the field of political contestation—which often involves determining who the players on the field are (2011, 108). Mobi-lization is about reaching out to individuals where they are to bring them into awareness of the significance of politics for their lives. Politics can do this by configuring the issues on the agenda and the way those issues are talked about to capture the interest of groups who would otherwise stay away. This is a key part of Disch's mobilization conception. Another im-portant piece of mobilization as I mean it lies not in making politics more enticing by reconfiguring its content, but rather in doing the shoe-leather work of reaching citizens where they are (literally), as by door-to-door organizing. García Bedolla and Michelson (2012) assess the effectiveness of a series of strategies for political mobilization and find lingering effects of some forms used in partisan competition that operated by transforming the awareness of people who were not politically involved. This suggests that mobilization can not only turn people out for elections but also change how they relate to politics itself.

So, what does it take to be a real part of democratic politics? What does it look like for excluded groups to manage to win entry into the political arena despite being denied a ticket? The answer to this question captures the essence of inclusion in the sense of what it means to be an effective part of democratic politics. It also conveys the minimum of democratic citizenship called for in chapter 2. I argue that what it takes to be a part of politics is, in the first instance, to see oneself as *already* part of politics.

Minimal Citizenship and the Substance of Inclusion

What does inclusion entail? What does it actually take to be included as a democratic citizen? This section pulls together numerous threads from other parts of the book to weave together an account of the minimum of democratic citizenship, a minimum that also qualifies one as effectively included in democratic politics. I call this minimal account "stand-by citizenship" following the empirical research of Erik Amnå and Joakim Ekman (2014). This minimum avoids apathy, per the argument of chapter 2 and is also moderate in its demands, fitting with chapter 3's imperative to make citizenship undemanding. Stand-by citizenship is a combination of two elements: critical attention and the civic skills needed for active participation. Together, these elements generate the third key feature: an upward flexibility that allows for more active participation when a citizen chooses to do so. Each of these elements is complex and requires explanation.

Let's begin with critical attention. Recall that the chief conclusion of chapter 2 was that there is no democratically acceptable form of citizenship that involves less than periodic attention to politics. The most apathetic any citizen can be about politics must still at least include giving some interest and attention to politics. This characteristic has been studied by political scientists under a variety of headings—political interest, political or public engagement, political awareness or attentiveness, political or ideological sophistication or level of conceptualization (Neuman 1986, 192). What these various labels are trying to capture is the idea of a citizen habitually paying attention to politics, and this is a key piece of the first element of democratic inclusion. To be politically included as a democratic citizen is, in the first instance, to be attentive to politics and the political world. It is to have the habit of paying attention to politics. When we see politics as involving us, even in the minimal sense of being of interest to us, we have found our way into the political arena, ticket or no.[2]

Yet attention is not enough on its own for any attractive form of democratic citizenship because it is consistent with a type of passivity that is incompatible with democracy. We see this in Jeffrey Green's (2010) account of a spectatorial or "ocular" conception of democratic citizenship. Green thinks that for most citizens most of the time, democratic citizenship does not resemble being an active self-governor but rather an *observer* of decision-making carried out by representatives and political elites of other kinds. Green is interested in empowering the people through their capacity to *watch* political decision-makers, drawing from Foucault's notion of the empowered gaze to model "ocular" power in place of the dominant paradigm of empowerment through "voice."

Green's citizen-spectators are thus politically passive in that they do not participate actively in politics. Yet they are not only passive with respect to conventional forms of political participation, but also with respect to their minds and judgment. "As a non-participant who only watches politics, the spectator does not decide, does not shape laws, and hence remains outside processes of collective authorship and self-legislation" (Green 2010, 8). Here Green reveals the passivity of citizen-spectators; they *only* watch. Yet they watch in a passive mode, not reflecting on what they see. The citizen-spectator "is not engaged in political discussion and debate, as the deliberative democrats presuppose, but rather watches politics as a spectator, looking neither to convince *nor to be convinced*

---

2. There is a temptation to dive into deep philosophical waters here. This is because inattention occupies a curious liminal space between the active consent that so much political philosophy emphasizes and the revolutionary or anarchistic rejection of political authority that forms its flip side. But what of simple disregard? What of indifference or apathy? How are such attitudes to be integrated into the grand drama of consent, obligation, and legitimacy found in the classic works of modern political thought? The questions raised by the idea of tacit consent are but a part of those regarding people who do not attend to their very existence. This is by no means an empty field of inquiry; Sean W. D. Gray (2021, forthcoming) has done important work on silence that grapples with some of the deeper questions. But I do not explore the issue further here.

by political arguments" (Green 2010, 65; emphasis added). Green's spec-
tators are not only nonparticipants; they do not even draw conclusions
about the debates they observe. They do not use their judgment to form
opinions about the things they hear in the political forum. Their faculties
of judgment are as passive as their bodies when it comes to politics. On
this reading, Green's view mirrors one of the great fears of spectatorial
and plebiscitarian conceptions of democracy—that they will lead to a passive, apathetic, and easily manipulated citizen body (Urbinati 2014). In
the light of both this concern and the argument against apathy I offered in
chapter 2, this passivity is a serious worry for democracy.

The passivity evident in Green's theory proves incompatible with even
a minimal standard of democratic citizenship, because citizens must be in
a position to render judgments at some interval, as in elections or other
opportunities to participate. Even on Green's account, citizens must be
able to sanction those subject to the people's gaze for that gaze to be empowered; a people that watches but cannot vote is not empowered in any
way. But to sanction presupposes forming a judgment that sanctioning is
called for based on some conclusion of one's own. It requires the exercise
of *judgment*. This is not to say that citizens must have opinions on every
conceivable topic, but they must bear formed opinions on at least some
political questions if they are to fulfill the most minimal demands of the
office of democratic citizen.

This need to form our own intentions and judgments suggests a necessary further condition of what it means to fill the office of democratic citizen. One must not simply pay attention to politics; one must also actively
exercise one's judgment through critically reflecting on what one sees.
This critical form of political attention—which I call "critical attention"—
constitutes the first and main component of minimal citizenship. The difference between critically attentive citizens and Green's citizen-spectators
is that while the latter are passive and inert in both their external and
internal engagement with politics, the former are, while often externally
passive, also *cognitively active*, subjecting what they learn about politics to
their critical judgment. Their political interest possesses a critical edge.

To illustrate this idea, consider the case of an audience member at a live
political debate. Under one description, we might fairly describe this person as watching the debate passively. She is passive in the sense that she is
not taking an active part in it, nor is she audibly making her presence and
opinions known from her seat in the audience. In short, she is externally
passive. But if she is critically attentive, she will also be listening and care-

fully considering the arguments put forward by the participants. She will weigh the cases put forward by them and judge which one has the most merit. She may, in other words, be deliberating internally as she seems to be watching passively. Such active listening and internal reflection involve the formation of opinions and the making of judgments. It requires exercising one's judgment and decision-making capacity, if only in making the decision as to which side, if any, is right or worthy of the listener's support. These processes of weighing, judging, and deciding constitute "internal deliberation," and are a minimally necessary piece of what it means to be a democratic citizen for reasons I'll discuss in the next section.

On its own, however, critical attention is not a satisfactory minimum of citizenship. I move on now to the second component of stand-by citizenship: the civic skills necessary for active participation. Recall the discussion of Hannah Arendt and Sheri Berman from chapter 2. There, the concern was that unsocialized citizens constitute a threat to democratic stability since they lack the embodied knowledge necessary to engage constructively with democratic institutions. Critically attentive citizens who only ever watch and *never* participate might likewise see their capacities for actual participation wither and die, rendering them incapable of participating constructively. This is why we must add to critical attention a measure of "civic skills," in the celebrated sense emphasized in Verba, Schlozman, and Brady's (1995) motivational resources model of participation.

Verba et al.'s resources model explains political participation (or nonparticipation) as a function of possessing certain resources. These include not just economic resources, but also informational and motivational resources. A key informational resource is the embodied knowledge of how to participate—the nuts-and-bolts questions of how and when to register, how and when to vote, who the candidates and parties are and what they stand for, when and where there are public meetings, etc. These resources are important because they help supply reasonable expectations regarding how the political system works and what to expect from it, as well as the practical know-how for participating in politics. This may sound like a tall order, but it is less demanding than one might expect since it is knowledge that is often gained socially, as a product of habit or unconscious absorption from those around us, as well as incidentally through actual participation. Being in the habit of participating thus keeps civic skills like embodied knowledge from disintegrating.

The single most powerful motivational resource for participation seems to be none other than our old friend, political interest. Verba et al. find that political interest is the most potent determinant of political participation of virtually every kind, giving it unparalleled empirical importance as a precursor of actual participation (Verba, Schlozman, and Brady 1995). This point cannot be emphasized enough. More important than one's race, than one's income, than one's level of education or socioeconomic status for taking part in politics is whether one is in the habit of paying attention to it. In some ways, this is obvious—of course two people with similar backgrounds, but who differ on their attentiveness to politics will participate at different rates—yet it is not always a part of the public stories we tell about how and why people do or do not participate in politics. This book is partly an effort to encourage more widespread recognition of political interest's importance. Moreover, this importance reinforces the point I made above, that political interest is the taproot of democratic citizenship—with it, all things are possible; without it, there's nothing to be done. It is thus essential that we maintain the resources needed to participate, particularly those like political interest and embodied knowledge that are in important ways under our control. Only with such resources can we actively participate in a constructive way should the occasion call for it.

Thus, we have the main elements of stand-by citizenship: critical attention and the civic skills needed for participation. Yet there is one final element of stand-by citizenship that these two give rise to: its "upward flexibility." Recall that we eliminated thoroughgoing apathy from the set of permissible forms of democratic citizenship in chapter 2. Here we see that this kind of apathy is inconsistent with stand-by citizenship due to the presence of critical attention. This sets a floor beneath the citizen's level of engagement. Moreover, stand-by citizenship does not itself impose any *ceiling* on engagement. Stand-by citizenship makes us poised for participation, like an arrow drawn back on a bowstring, tensed for action. We may remain in that state of preparedness indefinitely, or launch ourselves into the political arena, as far and as intensely as we choose. In this conception, the sky's the limit.

This is what it means to say that stand-by citizenship is upwardly flexible. It is flexible in being consistent with a wide variety of modes and intensities of democratic engagement, from watchful passivity to heart-and-soul devotion. This upward flexibility also lends stand-by citizenship its name since fulfilling its conditions makes us "stand by" for participation, prepared for it. When we are presented with a cause worth mobilizing for, we stop standing by and *step in*, into the political arena as an active participant. But this flexibility is strictly limited to an "upward" trajectory; we may engage *beyond* stand-by citizenship, but we cannot engage *less* than it. It thus defines the floor of democratic citizenship.

The upward flexibility of the conception helps insulate it from the accusation that it is too minimal. Unless one thinks it is always impermissible to be merely critically attentive (and also prepared for active participation) and so that one must *always* be actively participating, it is difficult to see how the conception could be too minimal. Sometimes adequate surveillance of politics reveals a political world in good working order, in which things are generally going well or in which problems are comparatively minor and already in good hands. Or, if we recall the democratically legible forms of apathy from chapter 2, such surveillance might reveal a politics in which people who share our opinions or demographic characteristics are unjustly overrepresented, justifying our inactivity so as to partly remedy that imbalance. In such moments, involved forms of participation are not necessarily called for beyond what might be necessary to maintain civic skills. Participation is, by this account, precisely what an individual judges would be appropriate in their circumstances, and those circumstances might sometimes call for their passivity. Requiring more than that—participation for its own sake, for example—seems potentially pointless as well as unduly demanding.

Stand-by citizenship's upward flexibility also has the merit of helping us make sense of moral, or rather, political, saints, who sacrifice more of themselves to political causes than most others (Wolf 1982). Recall the discussion from chapter 3 of disadvantaged citizens who undertake intense mobilization and political engagement despite many of them having plausible claims to opt out on hardship grounds, such as Black Americans during the civil rights movement. If ordinary citizens mostly stand by, heroic citizens step up, even throw themselves in to costly or dangerous political activity. Until now, we have lacked conceptual tools for adequately distinguishing these types of citizens. Though the language of heroism, perhaps a bit worn with overuse, is always to hand, we also often lament our own failure to do more to address the injustices of our day and may even feel guilty for not doing so. Yet there is an important difference between those who assiduously note the outrages of their day and engage in the available low-cost forms of participation to combat them and those who are blithely unaware of them at all. Stand-by citizenship does an excellent job of preserving and clarifying these distinctions because it supplies an exact standard that benchmarks the point where basic citizenship becomes extraordinary citizenship, as well as where blameworthy anti-citizenship begins.

Thus, we have arrived at our minimal conception of citizenship and inclusion. To be included as a democratic citizen at the most fundamental level is to be critically attentive to politics and to possess a set of civic skills requisite to participate constructively in politics. This is the least we ought to expect from democratic citizens. Notice that it is a considerable distance from thoughtless apathy, putting the account in line with the conclusions of chapter 2 that condemn apathy. Yet it is also amenable to being undemanding, in line with chapter 3, insofar as its achievement and maintenance calls primarily for paying politics periodic attention, and occasionally participating actively, perhaps by voting, so as to keep one's civic skills from degrading. This is also a considerable distance from ideals of engaged, participatory citizenship favored by many democratic theorists and reformers today, although it leaves room for them through the upward flexibility of the conception. Its undemandingness and flexibility also seems easily compatible with granting citizens wide discretionary control over their time and attention. In the next section, we'll see how this conception ultimately delivers the solution to this book's central problem of how to address unequal busyness while promoting core democratic values.

Democratic Credentials of Stand-By Citizenship

Stand-by citizenship is an attractive account of the minimum of democratic citizenship for two related reasons. The first is that it clearly defines the conceptually necessary root of all political participation; without it, citizens could not be said to meaningfully take part in the democratic process. This indicates that it is nonsensical to claim that democratic citizenship could involve anything less. The second reason is that, at least sometimes, stand-by citizenship is *sufficient* for fulfilling the role of democratic citizen. This implies that any more demanding account of the minimum of democratic citizenship will be excessive since there would be times when it would require action or engagement that is not democratically necessary under the circumstances. These reasons are related in that they together uniquely identify stand-by citizenship as the golden mean of democratic citizenship—not too little and not too much.

So, in what sense is stand-by citizenship the necessary root of political participation? Simply put: no form of meaningful political participation is possible without critical attention, the core element of stand-by citizenship. Consider that political participation is a species of intentional action, so it must therefore begin with an intention. Forming an intention regarding politics must begin in turn from cognitive engagement with politics. How else could an intention regarding politics be formed? One cannot intend to act politically without first paying attention to politics and thinking about it. Such attention and thought are thus necessary for animating acts of participation toward any political goal whatsoever.[3] Intention requires attention, so political participation requires stand-by citizenship.

Attention is also central to other foundational theoretical building blocks of democratic politics. Forming an intention regarding what government should be doing or who should be running it, for instance, also requires attending to politics, as does articulating one's political preferences and interests. Determining who one is and what one stands for politically likewise requires critical attention. Nor can we consent to (or reject) the legitimacy of our state without attending to the content of politics. Since every theory of democracy, no matter how minimal, depends on these ideas in one way or another—and also enshrines an important place for political participation, even if only in selecting leaders—this argument means that stand-by citizenship is strictly necessary for any account of democracy. Stand-by citizenship is thus highly ecumenical, constituting an orientation toward politics that no theory of democracy can do without.

Critical attention is particularly important to deliberative democracy. The normative core of deliberative democracy is an account of legitimacy, providing that decisions and institutional arrangements are legitimate insofar as everyone subject to them has reasons to think them so. Naturally, much rides on the nature of this receipt, and oceans of ink have been spilled debating what kinds of reasons are admissible for this purpose. Common to much of this work has been a focus on speech, or the "supply" of political communications, focusing on what kinds of reasons ought to be offered and in what modes. Other work has turned to the "demand" side, emphasizing the importance of practices of listening and the uptake of deliberation (Scudder 2020; Goodin and Dryzek 2006). This emerging body of work suggests that speech is at best half of the relation

---

3. One might, of course, interfere with or impinge upon politics without being aware of it, as it were mechanically, just as an inconveniently placed billiard ball might interfere with a shot. Yet we would not call such interference participation any more than we would say the tear gas canister lobbed at protesters itself participates in politics.

needed for successful deliberation, since someone must be listening for communication—and so interpersonal justification—to succeed.

Critical attention embodies habits of listening because it entails both paying attention and critical reflection. Paying attention to politics implies taking in the arguments and information spinning around the political ether and critically reflecting on them involves precisely the kind of processing that is required for a message to truly be heard. Critical attention, and the minimum standard of stand-by citizenship it helps constitute, is thus integral for citizens to participate in the practices of mutual justification that constitute deliberative democracy and undergird its legitimacy, especially when we recognize the essential role of listening for deliberation.

The notion that stand-by citizenship constitutes a necessary democratic minimum of citizen engagement might be more palatable than my next contention, which is that it is also sometimes a *sufficient* level of engagement as well. This idea may seem uncongenial to those durably interested in revivifying (or, perhaps, incepting) a robust participatory spirit in the democratic peoples of the world. How could critical attention and merely being prepared for participation possibly be enough for an attractive democracy? Surely more actual participation is what democracy needs. Recall the points I made above about how the upward flexibility of the conception insulates it from the accusation that it is too minimal. There I discussed two cases in which participation beyond stand-by citizenship is unnecessary, thus illustrating that stand-by citizenship can be a sufficient level of engagement in at least some circumstances. First, there are times when our attentive surveillance of politics shows us that our politics is in good working order, meaning that things could not be much improved, or that the problems that exist are minor and not important enough to justify intervention. Intensive participation at these times can seem unnecessary. Second, our surveillance of politics could sometimes reveal that people like us, sharing our views and interests, are influential in politics far beyond their numbers and desert. In such conditions, our own political passivity might be called for to help reverse that disparity. Though maintaining one's ability to participate remains essential through the upkeep of civic skills, in both of these cases stand-by citizenship provides a sufficient degree of engagement, since it enables citizens to be aware of the state of things in our polity and recognize if these conditions obtain.

An important objection to the line of argument in this chapter asks why we would want a minimum account of citizenship in the first place. This account may sound like that of a democratic mechanic, treating democracy like an engine that can be tuned up. But, one might object, democracy is instead a community and so more akin to a living thing that can flourish or languish than a machine with functional necessities. To someone with such a perspective, my language may suggest a flawed framework for thinking about democracy. What is needed if we think of democracy this other way is an account of democratic excellence, or of its flourishing. One might adapt the old saw that "one should live, not just survive" to democracy, and insist that democracy should "live" fully—flourish—not just persist and so that democratic flourishing requires pursuing a vision of the democratic ideal.

Here we run into a fundamental position of this book. The point of democracy for busy people is that many citizens are not in a position to fulfill an aggressive vision of democratic flourishing. What, then, should be our response? Setting aside the plurality of, and disagreement surrounding, these visions of democratic flourishing, we might persist in chasing one of them, even at the cost of leaving busy people like my mother behind. But this is why I argued above for the priority of inclusion. I do not think an attractive vision for democracy would embrace intense, meaningful participation for a few while effectively leaving many out. When we reduce the demands of a standard, we expand its universality and its inclusiveness. When we build it up into something grand and noble, we also tend to increase its demandingness and constrict, sometimes drastically, who can be a part of it. It is my position in this book that we must sometimes be willing to ratchet down our theoretical expectations of democratic flourishing if we are to avoid excluding busy people.

Nonetheless, it remains the case that stand-by citizenship is not all we might wish to see from democratic citizens. There might be other, more demanding ideals of citizenship that we expect citizens to live up to in order to realize some particular vision of democratic flourishing. It is not my intention to reject such projects out of hand. Indeed, one of the great strengths of stand-by citizenship is precisely its compatibility with more demanding accounts, via its upward flexibility, provided that they respect the right to free time and keep in mind the paradox of empowerment. Nor do I claim that stand-by citizenship resolves all the major problems besetting democracy today, though I see it playing a role in responding to the rise of anti-democratic populism insofar as such projects draw pivotal support from the less politically interested (Elliott 2020b, 99–100). I do not even claim that stand-by citizens are automatically good citizens, all things considered. They might make any number of errors in their political

decision-making and support any number of distasteful candidates or issues. Stand-by citizenship is not a cure-all for the challenges democracy
faces today, and it would be an important misunderstanding of the idea
to think it is advanced as a salve to them. It is rather the *precondition* to
any more spelled out vision of democratic flourishing. Where there are
tensions between it and such a vision — like one expecting complete devotion to democratic participation — this should invite us to reconsider the
wisdom of the vision, since it will likely be sacrificing democratic equality
to some other, less vital end.

What Difference Would Stand-By Citizenship Make and How Could We Tell?

What would stand-by citizenship change in democracies that embraced it?
This is a vital question that is easily misunderstood. Democratic theorists
and reformers often do not clearly spell out what pattern of participation
their favored form of democracy would entail. In his invaluable study of
democratic participation, Ben Berger (2011) uses the phrase "more and
widespread participation" to capture the goals of many democratic theorists, but this phrase is ambiguous. Does it mean "more" participation in
a quantitative sense or in terms of its quality or intensity? Does "widespread" participation mean participation coming from an ever more inclusive public, or does a large and representative one that falls significantly
short of universality qualify?

   The ambiguity in Berger's formulation, and in those of other theorists,
affords the opportunity to clarify exactly what difference stand-by citizenship promises to make. It does *not* propose to standardize the level of
participation of citizens to that of the basic level of stand-by citizenship;
it does not expect those engaged more deeply in democratic life to give
up their participation and drop down to the citizen minimum. This would
contradict its upward flexibility. Rather than leveling down, the aim is to
convert those falling below the level of engagement it specifies so as to
eliminate impermissible forms of political apathy.

   Stand-by citizenship aims to bring the reach of political engagement to
universal scope, in line with the principle of putting inclusion first. Everyone should be at least somewhat politically engaged. But this would not
necessarily raise the level or amount of participation of all citizens. A democracy that embraced it might see no change at all in the amount of par-

ticipation or engagement of a great many citizens, since it is probably the case in most established democracies that a majority of citizens are not disconnected from politics in the relevant way. This is an important point because when many scholars regard the problems of political apathy that preoccupy me, they often do so armed with a predisposition to want to see the overall average *level* of political engagement go up. Everyone should do ever more, on this view, with the possible exception of the most active of the activist elite, to whose level of engagement we ought to be aspiring.

This secular increase view of political engagement is quite different to what I suggest. Stand-by citizenship is a sufficientarian or threshold conception (with the added element of upward flexibility) and so it seeks to bring everyone off the bottom rung of the ladder of political engagement — or, perhaps more accurately, to bring people off the ground of apoliticality and onto the bottommost rung of the ladder of engagement. The idea implies no additional pressure to further involve oneself in politics unless doing so seems worthwhile to the individual. Once the population of impermissibly apathetic citizens is minimized through mobilization, education, and socialization, no further institutional or policy interventions are justified by the idea of stand-by citizenship. Further participation is, in other words, entirely left up to individual discretion and judgment. The focus of stand-by citizenship is thus on those totally or mostly disconnected from politics; its aim is *not* to secularly increase the amount of participation found in democracies today, but to bring those outside of the empowered circle of engaged citizens inside it.

One possible objection to the idea of stand-by citizenship stems from the problem of voting well. This problem arises from the libertarian view of voting, which sees it as an action undertaken by (isolated) individuals imposing coercion on others through authorizing state action. Because of these high stakes, it is argued that citizens are under an obligation to properly inform themselves about public affairs before voting, so as to avoid the negative impact of their voting badly (Maskivker 2019).[4] If stand-by citizenship requires citizens to participate at least sometimes, as it arguably does in order to keep up one's civic skills, then it may seem to objectionably require participation without including an obligation to become adequately informed.

---

4. This argument is ironic coming from scholars like Jason Brennan, who simultaneously emphasize that a single vote does not matter due to the size of electorates. If single votes don't matter, why should we hold voters to such high epistemic standards?

An important part of the reason I do not dwell on this supposed problem of voting well is because it is a phony problem premised upon several conceptual mistakes. I discussed some of these in chapter 2. For instance, there is no publicly legible standard for correct voting against which to substantiate that the problem even exists. What one person views as a substantively incorrect vote indicating blameworthy ignorance another will view as a justified one based on a different standard of correctness. There is no way to establish one standard that transcends such disagreement without destroying democracy. Another reason to dismiss the problem is that information is not fixed. The experience of participation can itself serve to induce learning, such that even if initial votes are ill-informed, they set the stage for better informed votes later (Shineman 2018).

What I want to emphasize here is that the problem of voting well assumes an artificially restricted and inaccurate picture of the decision situation citizens find themselves in. Citizens are not isolated atoms, floating alone through democratic space and forced to shift for themselves in the task of becoming informed, as this view implicitly assumes. Citizens are instead embedded in a rich ecosystem of institutions that can, in certain situations, operate to enrich the information environment and directly help citizens to learn what they need to know to make political decisions. That institutional context also shapes what sorts of decisions ordinary citizens are called on to make—electing representatives or voting directly on policy as in direct democracy, for example—further affecting the kind and amount of information they might need. I contend that, in the right institutional environment, citizens being critically attentive to politics is sufficient to resolve the underlying concerns of the supposed problem of voting well. The rest of this book focuses on institutional arrangements that help make participation not just accessible to ordinary, busy people, but also cognitively tractable to them, responding to the fundamental concern behind the problem of voting well.

Before turning to examine the institutions of a democracy for busy people, we must finally consider how we would know whether citizens are meeting the standard of stand-by citizenship. What measures are likely to indicate its presence? This may seem tricky because it is a phenomenological orientation toward politics and so is not directly observable. Yet a great deal of survey research seeks to measure internal dispositions like critical attention, so its tools are likely to be quite helpful. There are three metrics—two measuring attitudes or mental states and one measuring behavior—that can, used together, suggest how widespread stand-by citizenship is in a given polity.

The first is interest in politics. It is measured with questions like this from the American National Election Studies (ANES 2021):

> Some people seem to follow what's going on in government and public affairs most of the time, whether there is an election going on or not. Others aren't that interested. Would you say you follow what's going on in government and public affairs most of the time, some of the time, only now and then, or hardly at all?

Newer questions expand the number of response categories beyond these four and construct indexes of multiple questions to better control for measurement error (Shani 2012). Political interest provides the most direct measurement of stand-by citizenship since political attention forms the innermost core of the concept. Yet it remains an imperfect measure. It does not, for instance, capture the critical edge that we saw was vital to differentiate the conception from passive spectatorship. Nonetheless, attentiveness is closer to critical attention than apathy, and affords the ever-present possibility of being "mugged by reality" into taking a more critical view.

The second metric of stand-by citizenship is political information or knowledge. Political information surveys seek to gauge the amount of information an individual can recall about politics, primarily by use of factual questions about public affairs and current events. For my purposes, I am *not* interested in these questions as indicators of what people know about politics—these questions cannot actually do that, for reasons I elaborate elsewhere (Elliott 2019, 2020a, 393–94)—but rather of how much *attention* they are giving to politics and, even to some extent, how critical that attention is. Information questions are an attractive measure of critical attention because they capture "political learning that has actually occurred—political ideas that the individual has encountered, understood, and stored in his head" (Zaller 1992, 335). It thus gauges not just self-reported attention, but actual uptake of political content, indicating undeniably that actual attention has been paid and also that the content has been processed.

This latter point illustrates why political information also provides leverage on the criticality of the individual's attention—they not only watched passively but were cognitively active and reflective enough to retain the information. Conventional political interest questions on their own cannot do this. Yet in raising the bar in this way, political information questions are likely to undercount stand-by citizens. Where political interest questions will count some as stand-by citizens who are not because their attention is passive, in what scientists call a type I error, political information questions will fail to identify some stand-by citizens who cannot correctly answer knowledge questions for reasons unrelated to their cognitive engagement, making a type II error.

Turnout is the final metric of stand-by citizenship I suggest. Turnout is a good indicator of stand-by citizenship because it maintains the prepared- ness for further participation that is a necessary part of it and because it demonstrates a moment of paying attention to politics. As an actual exercise of political participation, voting necessitates paying attention to politics, as discussed above, thereby indicating that virtually everyone who votes is at least a stand-by citizen. Like political information, it likely undercounts those who are stand-by citizens since some nonvoters will qualify (a type II error). This is why I insist on using all three measure- ments in concert in order to gauge stand-by citizenship.

Conclusion

This chapter has sought to establish the priority of inclusion within the wider ideal of democratic equality and has elaborated a minimum stan- dard of democratic citizenship that fits with the arguments of the previous chapters and also with the imperative of putting inclusion first. Inclusion enjoys priority because its absence—exclusion—is categorically worse than political inequality. It thus identifies a more fundamental element of the wider ideal of democratic equality than the more familiar idea of political equality. Since we would not trade exclusion for equality, we must acknowledge that inclusion should come first in the design of democratic institutions, meaning that it should usually override political equality or other democratic principles and values when they conflict.

I also focused on a dimension of inclusion that has been overlooked. In centering what it takes to be included, rather than who ought to be, I foreground the practices or orientations constitutive of democratic citi- zenship. This allows us to bypass familiar debates about the principled scope of inclusion and consider instead cases of informal inclusion, where groups who were formally excluded from political rights nonetheless in- truded as agents into politics. These cases indicate, I argue, that neither formal inclusion nor supportive social norms are necessary for inclusion. Rather, what it takes to be included is, in the first instance, to see oneself as implicated in politics, as being concerned with and impacted by it. This constitutes a political approach to inclusion, one that takes groups seriously as political agents and avoids the paternalistic adjudication of claims for inclusion.

I pair this insight about the fundamental nature of inclusion with chapter 2's conclusion that one must at least pay attention to politics to avoid being impermissibly apathetic toward politics in sketching the ideal of stand-by citizenship. Stand-by citizenship constitutes the ecumenical bare minimum of citizenship expected of any democratic citizen. This citizenship minimum highlights the foundations of democratic citizenship on which any other more robust conception must be built, and so is compatible with numerous democratic ideals. In addition to paying politics attention, stand-by citizens' attention is properly critical. Another important part of stand-by citizenship is that citizens should possess the basic civic skills needed to step productively into active political involvement should the need arise.

Stand-by citizenship comes to constitute, then, a basic goal of any democracy, especially a democracy for busy people. No citizen can justifiably fall below the level of engagement it specifies, per the argument here about inclusion and the argument of chapter 2 regarding apathy. The task now is to consider how to build the institutions of a democracy of stand-by citizens, institutions that put inclusion first and so serve to empower busy people.

PART II

Democratic Institutions for Busy People

CHAPTER FIVE

How to Democratize Elections

Annual Elections and Mandatory Voting

The preceding three chapters explored the ethics of democratic citizenship, seeking to illuminate its minimum, its maximum, and a standard that avoids both excess and apathy. Along the way, we came across several principles that ought to guide the arrangement of democracy's participatory institutions. This chapter begins part II of the book, in which I more deeply explore what institutions are likely to be useful in a democracy for busy people. Most of this chapter concerns elections, but before focusing on them specifically, I want to collect the design principles we have so far discussed. The following list translates the normative arguments from chapters 2, 3, and 4 into institutional design principles for a democracy for busy people:

- Political participation must be simple, easy, and undemanding, in line with chapter 3's requirement of leaving citizens to control their time. This helps to prevent the paradox of empowerment, and thus promotes democratic equality.
- There must be institutions that reach citizens where they are, in line with chapter 2's injunction against apathy and chapter 4's goal of inclusion. Since apathetic citizens by definition lack the motivational resources required to engage actively with politics, this principle prevents anyone from being left out of democratic engagement entirely.
- In line with chapter 4's injunction to put inclusion first, institutions should seek to encourage stand-by citizenship, particularly among citizens who might otherwise be impermissibly apathetic.
- In addition to making participation easy, we should also concentrate power in the institutions in which it is the cheapest and easiest to participate. This

ensures that power is concentrated in the most accessible forms of participation, where stand-by citizens can most easily step in and affect governance.

- This principle also involves a corollary, which indicates that we should seek to attenuate the influence of intense forms of voluntary participation, at least where it occurs without authorization from a broad public.

Institutions designed with these principles in mind will help to put stand-by citizens in a situation where they can take active part in democracy while also helping democracy navigate the reefs of unequal busyness. It also realizes the core ideal of democratic equality in circumstances of enduring unequal busyness, in line with the priority of inclusion within that ideal. In the next three chapters, I'll explore how well elections, political parties, and randomly selected deliberative institutions, or minipublics, conform to these principles.

I focus on these three institutions because they span the spectrum of democratic reform, from parties and elections that few think imaginatively about reforming, to deliberative innovations that are very much at the forefront today. We shall see, however, that elections and parties, in suitable conditions, have the most to offer a democracy for busy people.

Democratizing Elections

Elections are the neglected misfits of democratic theory today. When democratic theorists and philosophers are not ignoring elections, they are often developing elaborate critiques of them and looking for institutional ways to bypass them. We see this, for instance, in the work of Hélène Landemore and Alexander Guerrero. Landemore (2020), following Bernard Manin, argues that elections have an ineradicable oligarchic or aristocratic bias and so deserve to be supplanted by randomly selected deliberative institutions. Guerrero (2014) sees elections as failing to secure either equal responsiveness or substantively good policy, due largely to the ignorance of voters, and so favors replacing them with lottocratically selected issue-specific assemblies.

Yet even as theorists elaborate these critiques, elections persist as the institutional mainstays of every democratic country in the world, and there is little visible prospect of their displacement any time soon. This gap between theory and practice is curious. While one should never underestimate the power of path dependence or status quo bias, the disparity invites a reconsideration of elections as democratic institutions—not in the fashionable spirit of critique, but rather one of appreciation. Is there anything to be said in elections' favor?

My purpose is not to offer a general defense of elections, nor do I aim to rebut all the critiques offered of them. Rather, I want to register an important line of praise for elections stemming from their uniquely good fit with the principles for a democracy for busy people. I also offer at least the beginning of a response to some recent critiques of elections. Elections are the most inclusive democratic institution we know of by a substantial margin, and this provides them a powerful democratic pedigree when we appreciate inclusion's priority among democratic values. I also suggest that there are ways to further democratize elections through reforms that help to cultivate stand-by citizenship and improve democratic responsiveness. The discussion of these reforms constitutes the bulk of this chapter. Since failures in responsiveness have been a key criticism of elections in recent years, this agenda of reform helps bolster elections against emerging skepticism.

In the end, I suspect that elections are guilty of nothing so much as being passé; they are familiar and fail to fire the imaginations of those who dream of better worlds. Yet their prosaic advantages are so dramatic that we should nonetheless concentrate on ways to mend rather than subvert them. No alternative I am aware of seems even remotely as promising for a democracy for busy people. Indeed, as we shall see in chapter 7, the most successful instances of deliberative institutional innovations have arguably succeeded precisely because of their integration with the electoral system.

Let me offer a word to clarify what I mean by elections, so as to set the scope of the chapter. I am concerned here exclusively with elections for representatives; I do not address direct democracy in this chapter. I do, however, make a few comments about the prospect of liquid or delegative democracy, which is often seen as a kind of direct democracy, in chapter 6. In chapter 7, I discuss deliberation's role in fixing some of the defects of direct democracy. Though direct democratic elections share some of the features that make elections attractive—specifically having to do with the accessibility of voting—they lack others that are even more important, such as an integral connection with political parties that make the choices facing voters cognitively tractable. This will be explained more fully in chapter 7.

The next section lays out the core advantages of elections from the perspective of a democracy for busy people. The third section discusses specific arrangements in the administration and structuring of elections that fit best within its principles. The following section explores how mandatory voting can help cultivate stand-by citizenship and improve responsiveness. The final section, "Annual Elections and Responsiveness," discusses how annual elections can reshape the relationship between constituent and representative in ways that powerfully incentivize responsiveness, particularly to society's more busy and disadvantaged members.

The Core Advantages of Elections

From the perspective of a democracy for busy people, elections are almost uniquely well suited to constitute its central participatory institutions. This is because they are closely consistent with almost all of the design principles elaborated above. The ways in which elections match those principles constitute elections' core advantages in a democracy that puts inclusion first.

The first of those principles requires that political participation be simple, easy, and undemanding to leave citizens with as much time under their control as possible. Electoral participation, in modern forms at least, is the quintessential example of participation that is simple, easy, and undemanding. In the paradigmatic case, democratic governments make available a place to vote that is close to each citizen's home, open a temporal window of—at least—a long day in which to come and provide the ballot and a way to mark it. Moreover, and as I argue at length in the next chapter, the choices on the ballot have been filtered and simplified by the party system so as to leave citizens with a fairly simple set of choices. These choices, in turn, become the focus of media coverage, partly because of their small number and high stakes. When parties and candidates are forced to compete with each other, moreover, they do all they can to besiege potential supporters with persuasive messages before they cast their ballots, attempting to answer the voter's implicit question of who they should vote for with reasons and information that flow into the media environment. This further simplifies the act of voting and alleviates the cognitive burden of doing so. We know, moreover, of many other ways to make voting even simpler, easier, and less demanding than this paradigmatic case, and I discuss some of these in the next section.

One of the design principles of a democracy for busy people is to seek institutions that reach citizens where they are, in order to make contact with apathetic citizens who lack the innate motivational resources to take the first step toward political socialization. Though elections in themselves do not necessarily reach people where they are, they do get *very close* to where people are, precisely because they are so easy to access. When well designed, the vote ought to be no more than an arm's span away. Institutions like mandatory voting, discussed in the next section, can help elections to close the last mile. Through the medium of law, mandatory voting brings elections right to every citizen's front door. Political parties, moreover, can take us not only *to* the citizen's door, but *through* it, to actively encourage participation and make active appeals for support, as discussed in the next chapter. When we consider these institutions together as the inseparable package they ought to be, then elections do indeed reach people where they are.

An underappreciated function of elections helps them to encourage stand-by citizenship, in line with another of the principles of a democracy for busy people. Elections promote stand-by citizenship by generating a large, society-wide event that simulates media coverage and widespread public discussion. This event focuses and concentrates society's attention, collectively, on politics, granting even the most pluralistic society a unifying focal point (Chapman 2022). For a time, politics is everywhere, and not necessarily in the poisonous way recent American polarization has revealed (Talisse 2019). Rather, every person's social circle[1] should include people who are talking and thinking about it. This generates, by the mechanism of social contagion discussed in chapter 2, a substantial social pressure for each individual to think and talk about it. This pressure is intensified by institutions like mandatory voting, which extends the reach of elections into all parts of society through the law. Since that kind of attentive focus on politics is the key element of stand-by citizenship, elections can generate a social environment that discourages apathetic inattention and encourages stand-by citizenship.

One of the most straightforward design principles in a democracy for busy people is to concentrate power in the least demanding modes and institutions of participation. A corollary to this principle is to reduce the influence that can be gained through more demanding modes of participation

---

1. In a well-functioning democracy for busy people, there should be exceedingly few people who find themselves in social milieu where politics is a foreign country. Institutions like mandatory voting and political parties help to extend the reach of elections.

in proportion to the rise of the cost of that participation. Elections—
whether for representatives or in direct democracy—are uniquely compatible with both of these principles.

This is, first, because the decisive power is put in the hands of those
whose participation is the least costly. In elections, the ultimate decision
belongs to the voters, and voting is, as we have seen, extremely cheap and
easy. It is, indeed, likely the least expensive form of participation, though,
as I'll discuss in the next chapter, there are many hidden costs to voting
that parties often invisibly help to defray. For now, the brute fact of voting
being inexpensive and yet also decisively powerful makes democracies
that center elections much more likely than conceivable alternatives to
empower busy people and avoid the pathologies of inequality generated
by more demanding modes of participation.

It is worth lingering on this point for a moment since it forms one of
the essential yet, for some, uncomfortable truths about electoral democracy. Critics of elections sometimes overlook that their alternatives, based
usually on deliberation and sortition, often do not decide things authoritatively, as do elections. Yet we saw in chapter 2 that those who participate
in politics authoritatively, as in voting, matter in a categorically different
way to those who don't. The authoritative power found in elections forces
centers of power to bend to mass publics in ways that non-authoritative
deliberative institutions never can. Those who decry the aristocratic bias
of representative democracy ignore the massed power reposed in elections at their own peril. Or, rather, at the peril of bringing, through their
own preferred innovations, democratic politics one step forward and two
steps back.

Another basic feature of the vote furthers a different principle of democracy for busy people. Because everyone has one and only one vote that is
weighted equally with everyone else's, elections effectively cap the influence
of those who would take every opportunity to participate in politics and
thereby enhance their influence. This feature embodies the principle that we
should seek to attenuate the influence of intense participation. Because elections effectively impose a participatory "ceiling" constituted by the single
vote, they further this principle.

Nonetheless, elections include many other roles for citizens beside that
of voters, such as volunteers or donors, and through these roles, some citizens could secure for themselves unequal power. If we focus on these features of elections, it might seem to call into question elections' consistency
with the principle of attenuating the power of intense forms of volun-

tary participation. Yet this is not the case. There are, at least in the United States, millions of citizens who volunteer their time and effort to contact, organize, and mobilize their fellow citizens (or at least their co-partisans). These campaign efforts are, as Eitan Hersh (2020) has argued, exercises in power. Those who participate in these ways attempt to multiply their power in the polity by increasing their influence over other citizens. The most effective ways of doing so, according to Hersh, are likely not through phone banking once every four years but rather through taking an active part in the quotidian business of one's community and becoming someone that others rely on and view favorably as a positive community member. When one is recognized as a positive presence in one's community, one's efforts to contact and mobilize one's neighbors are more likely to be effective, and thus powerful.

These forms of campaign participation are, in addition to being about power, quite costly and effortful. Not everyone can do them. Those citizens with more time, more education, more interest in politics, etc., are far more likely to engage in them. This makes campaign participation a possible vector for the paradox of empowerment via elections.

Yet the influence citizens derive in this way is much more diffuse and uncertain than that of a vote, offsetting the danger of promoting political inequality. A vote is certain where a phone call, or conversation with a neighbor, is not. There is no way to be sure that the influence we believe we exercise over others through these campaign efforts decisively changes their minds, or otherwise alters their behavior.[2] Indeed, most of these efforts likely *are* wasted insofar as empirical evidence finds small (though real) marginal effects for such strategies in the aggregate (Green and Gerber 2019). The reduced certainty of these more difficult forms of participation thus offsets the opportunity opened by them for some citizens to gather more power into their hands at the expense of others. This serves to attenuate the power of those who are intensely interested and motivated to participate, in line with the corollary principle mentioned above. Elections thus do not, via this route, give disproportionate power to political busybodies.

Elections, therefore, are a powerful instance of the principle of concentrating power where participation costs are low. Moreover, the greater uncertainty of more involved forms of electoral participation—like campaign

---

2. There is fascinating experimental field research showing the differential effects of different campaign strategies, (see, e.g., Green and Gerber [2019]). Yet these are aggregate effects—the efforts of any given participant may affect precisely nothing.

volunteerism—alleviates the concern that elections will concentrate power in the hands of the traditionally advantaged.

This last point, that elections avoid concentrating power in the hands of the traditionally advantaged, will strike many as ironic since elections are often thought to precisely empower an elite made up of the wealthy, who participate not by phone banking or knocking on doors but by cutting huge checks to parties and candidates. In countries like the United States representatives are, in addition, usually themselves much wealthier than the average citizen. This all seems in line with the ancient Greek belief that elections are inherently aristocratic or oligarchic (Manin 1997).

Yet an elected elite is markedly different from those empowered through other means, such as interest group pluralism. Pluralism enjoyed a long season in mid-twentieth century political science as probably the single most influential theory of democratic politics. Its attraction stemmed in part from its seeming to combine a realistic understanding of the political process with a passable democratic pedigree via James Madison (Dahl 1961, 1956 [2006]; Easton 1965). What made it democratic was that groups—presumed to spring up spontaneously like mushrooms, as Hobbes said of human beings—would make their own voices heard through organized political pressure campaigns. The example of slack in mid-twentieth century New Haven discussed in chapter 2 is just such a campaign. Research from the better part of a century confirms, however, that pluralistic empowerment is far from equal, since it ends up giving disproportionate influence to better financed and organized groups, above all to the wealthy and business interests (Schattschneider 1960; Schlozman, Brady, and Verba 2018).

Pluralism is, in effect, the inverse of elections, when understood this way. Where elections empower the disadvantaged members of the polity by making the least effortful participation the most powerful, pluralism empowers the most advantaged by multiplying the power that their resources and additional effort can secure. Pluralism, therefore, empowers the incumbent elite, while elections allow for at least the possibility of empowering a non-oligarchic elite. Indeed, even the greatest critic of unrestricted, oligarchic campaign finance would have to agree that so long as votes remain the decisive factor in elections, the influence of money within them will necessarily be less than absolute.

My point here is not that money in politics is unproblematic; as an advocate of elections, I deplore its corrupting influence. Indeed, its presence besmirches the reputation of elections themselves, eclipsing claims like my own about their inclusive power. I simply have little to add in this place to the scholarship of people like Lawrence Lessig (2011) among many others who likewise deplore money's distorting influence and suggest various promising ways to reduce or eliminate it. I agree that elections where wealthy citizens can spend unlimited sums influencing elected officials and public opinion are compromised in important ways. This is not, however, a reason to abandon elections. As Dimitri Landa and Ryan Pevnick (2021) argue, money in politics would remain a serious problem even with randomly chosen deliberative forums, which are the main alternative to elections today. They argue that such forums could also be targeted for capture by wealthy interests through strategies such as offering post-service inducements to those who help safeguard their interests in office or incepting public opinion with congenial ideologies, thereby shaping the ideas of the pool of those who might be chosen to serve. The problem of money in politics thus stretches far beyond elections and demands coordination on strategies that will address the problem directly rather than displacing elections and so losing the champagne with the cork.

There are of course other objections to elections than those mentioned here. But, as I said above, it is not my intention to answer them all since I do not aim to provide a systematic defense of elections. Rather, I have tried in this section to highlight some of the core advantages of elections when we center the imperatives of a democracy for busy people. These advantages turn out to be very great and are not easily duplicated by alternative institutional forms. If there is any general response offered here to criticisms of elections, it is to insist on certainty that a given defect is intrinsic to elections rather than parochial to some specific institutional arrangement or state of affairs. The United States' campaign finance regime, for instance, is unusually privatized and unregulated compared to that of many other advanced democracies, largely as a product of a series of highly contingent jurisprudential decisions by the US Supreme Court. Before concluding that the inclusionary power of elections is to be sacrificed in pursuit of a radical fix for elections' democratic defects, true friends of democracy should seek patches to this venerable Ship of Theseus, lest we be stranded on rough seas in an untested vessel.

Elections in a Democracy for Busy People

Elections have much to offer to a democracy for busy people, but its design principles do not recommend all electoral arrangements without discrimination. Some ways of doing elections are better than others by its lights. So, how could we reform elections to better help them conform to and further a democracy for busy people? My aim in this section is to provide a unifying framework for a set of electoral arrangements that can powerfully improve democratic inclusion where they are lacking. When we put inclusion first, we can recognize this set as constituting the basic plumbing of a democracy that empowers busy people.

As we have seen in the recent efforts at vote suppression in the United States, there are ways of administering elections that can generate costs big and small, visible and invisible. These costs then burden different groups of citizens unequally, harming inclusion. Voter ID laws, for example, may only allow some types of identification for voting which not all citizens have and so effectively exclude them. For instance, they might allow gun carry permits to count but not student IDs, even when they are issued by state universities (Herd and Moynihan 2018, 56). And to get the right forms of identification, documents are often required that not everyone has access to, such as original birth records. Poorer people, older people, and people of color often face insuperable barriers to locating such documents, effectively neutralizing their entitlement to the franchise. A democracy for busy people must see such seemingly minor administrative burdens as of decisive importance since they constitute the mobilization of institutions against inclusion.

This is not simply through their effect on voting. It extends also into the subtle capillaries of civic welcoming. Inclusive institutions generate a welcoming and supportive environment for the exercise of democratic citizenship. I insist on "welcoming" here, because, as I have highlighted, the citizen body is in need of ever recurring invitations to join the political arena since some people are just maturing into political awareness out of adolescence, while others are just awakening to the wider world from long-standing apolitical habit, and still others are restarting their political interest after a period of quiescence.

What do welcoming electoral institutions that recursively invite citizens in look like? First, they make it as easy as possible for people to participate, and—even more essentially—make it easy to find out *how* to participate. They make what software designers call the "user interface" of democratic participation dead easy to navigate and manipulate. The metaphor of a website is quite useful here. Most websites have what is called a "front end," which is user-facing and comprises the interface that users encounter, as well as a "back end," which is largely hidden from users' view and enables the front-end but is, at the best of times, complex and robust to the widely varying ways users will attempt to manipulate the front-end. This latter criterion of robustness is crucial because it is what makes an interface functional to people in widely varying circumstances—making it key to inclusion. The institutions of democratic participation in a democracy for busy people should seek to make the front-end of citizen participation as accessible and foolproof as possible, shifting as many burdens into the technical back end as possible. In this metaphor, the back end would be constituted by election administration procedures, as well as the authorities tasked with implementing them. They ought to take upon themselves as much of the brute effort involved with participation as possible.

This is all quite abstract, so what might all of this mean in practice? Let us start with two simple examples. Extending the voting period over several days, as over a weekend or with early voting, widens the temporal window for voters to vote and enhances their temporal flexibility in doing so. This especially aids those with limited temporal flexibility like busy people by allowing them to shift when they vote to a time that best fits with the rest of their commitments. This affords them greater control over their time and makes voting less difficult. Mail voting works similarly to empower those with limited temporal flexibility. There is evidence that mail voting particularly helps those who lack stable habits of voting to succeed in doing so, such as younger voters and other low-propensity voting groups, a key goal for a welcoming set of democratic institutions (Bonica et al. 2021). In addition, it allows for those with limited physical mobility or who live far from a polling place to access the ballot. Mail voting also gives people the leisure to examine the ballot and do their own research about the options on it, particularly those they had not thought much about previously, such as ballot initiatives or minor offices. It thus expands temporal flexibility on yet another dimension by extending the time citizens spend, as it were, in the voting booth. This can help prevent citizens from feeling rushed in making decisions and allows for more thorough internal deliberation.

There are few electoral institutions more amenable to inclusionary back-end engineering than voter registration, yet its history is rife with abuse and manipulation with the aim of depriving citizens of the chance to vote. For instance, registration was introduced in many places in the US by reformers in the early twentieth century who sought to thereby keep immigrants and other perceived undesirables, like the poor, from voting (Piven and Cloward 1988; Keyssar 2000, 151–59). The brute fact of having to register effectively doubles the burden of casting a ballot since it means having to make another decision—not just whether to vote and then who to vote for, but also whether to get registered—and expend additional effort dedicated to getting registered, in addition to making the trip to the polls on Election Day. Moreover, registration deadlines precede Election Day by widely varying amounts from jurisdiction to jurisdiction and may be changed with little notice, creating a further cognitive tax on participation since citizens must keep track not only of Election Day—for which there are numerous signs in the wider social environment—but also the registration cutoff date, which is all but socially invisible. One reason for this social invisibility is that registration deadlines often vary by state, meaning that there is no single date around which to coordinate polity-wide expectations, public education campaigns, and organizational efforts, as are created by Election Day itself. Adding a registration requirement and mandating that citizens be the ones who discharge this responsibility thereby presents citizens an unnecessarily daunting environment for democratic participation.

Aggressive purging of the voter rolls has also been used to reduce voting by supposedly undesirable citizens, such as felons. For example, in the run up to the notorious election of 2000, many jurisdictions in Florida removed names from the rolls that matched or were similar to those of felons, without taking any serious steps to ensure that those so purged were in fact felons (Berman 2015). This led to the disenfranchisement of 12,000 Floridians (Herd and Moynihan 2018, 52–53), particularly those of color whose names tended to be similar to those of felons.

A democracy for busy people would view proper registration practices as vital to a "user-friendly"—and so inclusive—interface for democracy. In addition to the above, doing so would require, in the context of the United States, removing elected officials from the chain of command in election administration. Elected officials must not be in a position to arrange for aggressive purges of voter rolls or any other partisan effort to disenfranchise citizens or tamper with election results. This is a matter of not just institutional design, but *constitutional* design, since in many states independently elected Secretaries of State are vested with immense and even final power over election certification and administration by the state constitution.

Another simple step taken in many democracies around the world is to switch the default regarding whose responsibility it is to place names on the voter roll in the first place. Whereas in democracies like the United States it is the responsibility of citizens to ensure their names appear on the voter rolls before Election Day, it could instead be made the responsibility of election administrators. Governments generally have all the information already at hand regarding who lives where and could put that information to work for citizens by registering them to vote automatically.

Better still than automatic voter registration—or rather, ideally paired with it—is same-day voter registration. This institution allows citizens to register to vote on Election Day if they are not already registered, and then immediately cast a ballot. Same-day registration ought to be considered a marquee best-practices institution for election administration since it effectively neutralizes most other efforts to manipulate registration for partisan purposes. Purges of the voter roll are all but useless when citizens can register the day of, for instance. Both of these latter rules, regarding automatic voter registration and same-day voter registration, concern the technical rules of elections rather than electoral administration, as with removing elected officials from the chain of command. Together, they help render voting much more tractable for busy citizens by streamlining democracy's front-end and shifting burdens to the back end.

Another important kind of pro-busy citizen reform has to do with the timing of elections. Political scientists often speak of "low-salience" elections to describe off-year or off-cycle elections, in which there are only state and local offices on the ballot, as well as many initiatives and referenda. I want to emphasize that the salience of elections is very much a matter of *timing*, and so of institutional design. No election is inherently low salience—some are *made* that way. One can make an election low salience, meaning not widely noticed, by moving it away from a traditionally recognized national election day, such as the United States' Tuesday after the first Monday in November.

Low-salience elections are ripe for the paradox of empowerment. By multiplying the number of election days there are in a year and distributing offices across them, those in power can shape the electorate in ways that structurally disempower less engaged citizens. There is clear evidence that asking citizens to vote frequently, in the sense of several times a year, causes voter fatigue and depresses turnout drastically, particularly among the poor and less politically engaged people (Boyd 1986; Rallings, Thrasher, and Borisyuk 2003; Garmann 2017). Aligning state and local elections with national ones does not merely increase turnout, moreover, but it also improves the representativeness of the electorate. Consolidating elections, then, is a major step forward for busy citizens, whose budget of time and attention for politics is exhausted before others'.

Just as registration deadlines are easy to miss because they lack social salience, elections in odd months of the year that elect only state or local offices fail to generate what Emilee Chapman (2022) has emphasized as the social focus created by general elections. Instead of being widely inclusive, such low-salience elections predictably turn out only intensely interested groups. Perhaps the best example of this are elections for local school boards, which are often scheduled to be low salience, ensuring that local teacher unions in particular are able to have disproportionate influence on the outcome because they energize and turn out their members who come to compose a significant proportion of the diminished electorate (Allen and Plank 2005, 519). Whatever one thinks of teacher unions, it is clear from all we have seen that no group should be able to instrumentalize elections to their own narrow benefit in this way. The power they derive from such arrangements is built upon the exclusion of other citizens, particularly busy ones. Thus, low-salience elections have been used to concentrate power in the hands of organized groups, to the detriment of busy citizens (Anzia 2014).

Such elections would, therefore, be durably eliminated in a democracy for busy people. This could be accomplished by consolidating elections, such as by a requirement that all elections be gathered into no more than one annual Election Day. Governments — or rather the factions that control them in a given moment — will always have incentive to engage in manipulating the electoral calendar, so the exclusion of such methods must be established as a constitutive basic rule of democracy. Such a rule would likely need to be constitutionalized or otherwise entrenched to prevent governments from manipulating election timing. This might be a challenge in federal systems where authority over elections is decentralized, like the United States. Yet this is not the only challenge created by federalism for a democracy for busy people.

Almost anything that simplifies the task of voting is a win for inclusion. This includes clarifying the lines of accountability in democratic systems. When it is easy to identify who is responsible for a given policy outcome, it is a huge win for busy citizens. Multiple veto points, overlapping fields of jurisdiction, and federalism create cognitively challenging conditions for citizens to make sense of because they make it effectively impossible to determine who is responsible for various policy outputs or the persistence of public problems. The centralization of power serves to make it accountable to ordinary people who do not have the time or resources to monitor every nook and cranny of their institutional milieu for abuse or malfeasance, and to trace its origins back through the institutional thicket. When the buck doesn't stop anywhere, or if no one can easily tell where this particular buck stops, accountability becomes impossible for the vast majority of citizens who are busy living their lives. Centralizing power and simplifying the lines of accountability and authority in democratic regimes is therefore a major contributor to a democracy for busy people.

There are of course numerous other concerns of institutional design that properly enter consideration over arrangements like federalism and veto points. Federalism, for instance, is rare among the world's democracies, yet is almost ubiquitous among the world's largest and most diverse countries (Taylor et al. 2015, 91). This is at least partly because federalism can help countries to "hold together" when they are composed of numerous ethnic, religious, linguistic, or national groups, as large countries often are (Stepan 2001, 320). Federalism tends to spawn veto points, moreover, since a common feature of federalist systems is second legislative chambers that represent the subnational units and share power in setting national policies. In cases where the very existence of the polity may lie in the balance, concerns about democratic inclusion may easily fall by the wayside. Nonetheless, insofar as we care about democracy, we must not let such issues entirely obscure the importance of having a political system that is simple enough in its structure of authority to be understandable to ordinary citizens who do not make politics their lives.

This line of thought also indicts a common American practice known as the long ballot. The long ballot is a key part of an approach to democratic design that attempts to centralize power in the hands of voters rather than other actors in the wider democratic system, such as political parties. It works by making more offices directly elected, as well as through direct democracy. Giving voters more items to decide upon in this way lengthens the ballot, hence "long ballot." The result of the long ballot however is a perversion of its supposed aim of popular control. As some progressive reformers argued in the early twentieth century, the long ballot overburdens citizens who cannot give enough attention to the multiplicity of choices they are thereby saddled with to make intelligent choices (Hirschhorn 1986). Overburdened voters simply leave vast tracts of the ballot blank (called "roll-off"), empowering intense policy demanders, such as interest groups and political machines, who can thereby win with the support of their activist or clientelist supporters within effectively smaller electorates.

The long ballot might seem like a challenging case for a democracy for busy people because its aim is precisely to take power out of the hands of activist elites, who would otherwise control offices and policy, and put them into voters' hands. Yet the long ballot fails to accomplish its aim because of the finitude of the people's attention—they're busy. This is precisely the kind of concern that the argument of this book seeks to highlight. Centralizing power into fewer high profile electoral contests actually boosts inclusion by making it easier and more cognitively tractable for ordinary citizens to provide authoritative input into the political process and so represents a superior approach to democratic institutional design when we put inclusion first.

The concerns I raised and reforms I suggested in this section are far from unfamiliar to most political scientists. Nor are they alien to actual well-functioning democracies. Nonetheless, many democracies have only some of them while others lack almost all of them. What I hope to have done is to unite these reforms in a common framework with a consistent political vision—a democracy inclusive of those who lack the time or interest to engage deeply in politics. This vision illustrates why this suite of institutions is so vital. It is not, as often discussed, simply a matter of convenience. Simplifying democracy's "user interface" as much as possible is an imperative of inclusion, which is the most basic requirement of democracy. My account makes clear, then, as a matter of democratic theory why reforms like these are of the highest importance.

Mandatory Voting as a Tutelary Institution

Mandatory voting is likely to be a powerful means for cultivating stand-by citizenship, and thus to help build a democracy for busy people. This is not directly because of its undoubted power to induce turnout (Hirczy 1994; Blais 2006, 112–13; Birch 2009, 96), but rather because of its ability to reach every citizen where they are and nudge them, especially the least engaged, into sparing a thought for politics. I thus focus on mandatory voting as a "tutelary institution" that can help induce the kind of cognitive political engagement characteristic of stand-by citizenship. Mandatory voting is also a powerful way to improve democracy's responsiveness, particularly to busy and disadvantaged citizens, though I shall say only a little about this thoroughly discussed point.

I must briefly clarify what I mean by mandatory voting. For my purposes, mandatory voting is a strictly enforced legal requirement that every eligible voter attend a polling place or submit a mail-in ballot during an election, on pain of a small monetary fine unless an adequate excuse, including conscientious objection, is provided. Now, this does not describe all actually existing regimes of mandatory voting. Many are not enforced at all, and others use more draconian sanctions, or lack robust excuse mechanisms (Birch 2009, 20–39). It also assumes background conditions in which turning out to vote is made as easy as possible, such as by consolidating elections to only one per year, holding elections on holidays or weekends, allowing no-excuse absentee voting, using same-day and automatic registration, etc. This particular model of mandatory voting largely follows Lisa Hill's (2004) blueprint for a best-practices mandatory voting regime based on Australia's system and has numerous advantages vis-à-vis plausible or real-world alternatives that I detail elsewhere (Elliott 2017, 657–59). Most important for our purposes is that mandatory voting on this model can be counted on to be highly effective at inducing turnout while remaining reasonably undemanding on ordinary citizens.

It is obvious enough what it would mean to advocate mandatory voting to improve turnout; requiring people to turn out tends to get them to vote, and this improves responsiveness to them and their interests. Mandatory voting thereby secures more nearly equal turnout across social groups, and it is argued that this systematically reduces inequalities in responsiveness to groups who tend not to vote without the mandate (Lijphart 1997). Some version of this argument is probably the most widely prevailing one in favor of mandatory voting in the existing literature (Engelen 2007; Hill 2014; Chapman 2019; Umbers 2020). I want to suggest that it is no accident that critiques of elections as unresponsive are based on the assumption that voting is not legally mandated, since that is the status quo in most existing democracies. If the arguments of the advocates of mandatory voting are right, then the lack of responsiveness observed by critics like Landemore and Guerrero is likely a function of the lack of mandatory voting, at least to some extent. Should it be instituted, a more equal responsiveness would be realized. A substantial amount of empirical evidence supports this supposition. Numerous high-quality studies have shown that mandatory voting demonstrably favors policies benefiting the groups that do not otherwise participate in elections (Mueller and Stratmann 2003; Fowler 2013; Bechtel, Hangartner, and Schmid 2015). This suggests that mandatory voting does indeed help close the responsiveness gap that so concerns scholars like Guerrero.

So much for mandatory voting and responsiveness. But what does it mean to advocate mandatory voting as a tutelary institution? This is a much less common notion and is my main interest in what follows. Ben Saunders (2010) provides an initial idea of what it means when he argues for mandatory voting for first-time voters. He argues that compelling first-time voters to vote helps them to learn what voting is like and motivates them to gain the knowledge they need to participate in the future. The aim of his unique suggestion is to help citizens make an *informed* decision about whether to vote (very much in keeping with the spirit of stand-by citizenship). Here mandatory first-time voting acts as a means to inform citizens about voting and to gain the background knowledge involved in active citizenship.

In a similar vein, I have argued for mandatory voting as a nudge toward political engagement (Elliott 2017). That argument applies to voting Thaler and Sunstein's (2008) concept of nudging as a means of structuring decisional defaults to favor certain outcomes. I argue that mandatory voting can encourage—but not require—cognitive political engagement and that this is justified and democratically attractive. I conclude that we ought to set the default for voting to "vote" rather than "abstain," and that only mandatory voting can do so. The goal here, though, is not directly to boost turnout but rather to nudge citizens toward thinking about politics and taking an interest in it. Making voting mandatory—not just for first-time voters, as for Saunders, but for all national elections—provides a recurring reminder that politics is ongoing and potentially impacts one's concerns and interests, and so may be worth one's focused attention. Most recently, Andrei Poama and Tom Theuns (2019, 805–6) have argued for mandating voting for felons, partly on the grounds that doing so will help teach them democratic values and socialize (or re-socialize) them into the political system. In all of these arguments, mandatory voting serves to educate or socialize citizens into pro-democratic habits, most prominently cognitive political engagement.

It is important to mark the distinction between this relatively novel justification for mandatory voting and the most common alternatives to bring out some of its core attributes. Probably the most influential justification for mandatory voting is that of Arend Lijphart (1997), who argues for mandatory voting on the grounds that it would promote more equal representation by enhancing the turnout of marginalized groups. Versions of Lijphart's argument have been endorsed by numerous scholars and politicians at one time or another. Promoting equal representation is not the direct concern emphasized by the view of mandatory voting as a tutelary institution. The concern is instead a necessary precondition thereof: universal political attention. Without such attention, as we have seen, there is little reason to expect equality in any meaningful sense.

A more novel and sophisticated argument is that of Chapman (2019), who argues for mandatory voting on the basis that it approximates a moment of universal political participation, which publicly instantiates political equality. Such shared moments of equality are essential for making real and publicly affirming this fundamental democratic principle. What distinguishes Chapman's argument from the tutelary view of mandatory voting is that hers is an intrinsic justification, one fulfilled by the bare functioning of mandatory voting. The tutelary view is by contrast instrumental, in that mandatory voting is seen as a means to promote stand-by citizenship, and so would presumably be defeated by empirical evidence showing it could not do so. Another common justification of mandatory voting is that it prevents free riding of nonvoters on voters' contributions to democracy, as Lachlan Umbers (2020) has argued. There are some affinities between viewing mandatory voting as a tutelary institution and as a commitment device against free riding. Both are oriented against apathy rather than directly for equality. Yet Umbers (2020, 1309n6) fails to explain what the exact contribution nonvoters fail to provide is, acknowledging that the free riding argument could be compatible with numerous forms of political engagement other than turnout. The tutelary argument specifies that the minimum required from citizens is stand-by citizenship and argues for mandatory voting as a uniquely good tool for promoting it.

Emphasizing mandatory voting's tutelary power to encourage political engagement may seem an odd angle from which to argue for it. As we have seen, doing so flies in the face of much of the literature on mandatory voting. Though I share the common aim to promote equality with mandatory voting, the route must be somewhat more circuitous when our concern is to do so in the context of unequal busyness.

Recall that stand-by citizenship, as the minimum of democratic citizenship, is most concerned with preventing apathy. Mandatory voting seems especially well placed to prevent apathy because it nudges everyone to give politics some thought. I say, and insist on, "nudge" here because of course one is always entitled to disregard politics after due reflection, even where turning out to vote is legally mandated. As in Saunders's argument for mandatory first-time voting, the idea is that legally requiring turnout provides a real opportunity to reflect on the value of political engagement. But my proposal differs in that it makes voting mandatory for all elections, which encourages this reflection to recur periodically, to be renewed or rejected in the face of new political and social developments.

Bearing in mind the instrumental nature of the tutelary argument, we might ask, can mandatory voting actually encourage the sort of critical cognitive political engagement and readiness for participation that constitutes stand-by citizenship? What evidence is there that mandatory voting even has this tutelary power? Suggestive evidence comes from comparative studies of political knowledge. Numerous analyses have found that countries with compulsory voting have higher political knowledge levels and greater general political engagement, especially among the least educated and low-propensity voters (Gordon and Segura 1997; Berggren 2001; Sheppard 2015).[3] This latter finding is especially key. Mandatory voting does not have uniform effects across the population—it does not raise the political awareness of every member of the population by one unit, for instance. Instead, it has a unique influence (what social scientists call a heterogeneous effect) on those with low levels of education. According to Miguel Carreras (2016), in mandatory voting states, those with the lowest levels of education "make efforts to obtain political information by paying more attention to political news and by discussing about politics more frequently" while everyone else's levels of attention remain unchanged. Mandatory voting thus seems to be especially well suited to promoting the minimal kind of citizenship represented by stand-by citizenship without necessarily boosting the wider politicization of the population. It targets those most likely to fall off the bottom rung of the ladder of political engagement and motivates them to learn more. This will almost certainly serve to reduce the share of the population engaging in impermissible forms of political apathy. In sum, though these studies differ about some findings, all agree that mandatory voting substantially reduces the share of the population that knows nothing about politics at all.

Cross-sectional evidence like this is strengthened when there is a plausible mechanism that explains it, and in this case, there are several. The most straightforward is that when citizens expect to have to vote due to

---

3. Some might doubt these findings by reference to experimental studies that seem to suggest that those who "feel" compelled to vote via mandatory voting are less generally informed about politics compared to those who would vote anyway (Selb and Lachat 2009; Singh and Roy 2018). But these are lab experiments conducted entirely with subjects living in mandatory voting (MV) states. In addition to questions of external validity, even the authors of these studies themselves admit that their findings say nothing about comparisons between MV and non-MV states, which is the question here.

the legal requirement, they figure that they might as well expend at least some effort on searching for information that can help them in this task. Here some combination of the sunk cost fallacy and a likely belief in the duty to vote (Elliott 2017, 660–61) seem to motivate information search efforts. Another mechanism comes from Berggren (2001, 543) who argues that background features of the institutional context induce the generation and dissemination of free information that attentive citizens can then pick up. Once citizens are mobilized by the legal requirement, parties and other groups in society invest in attempts to educate and persuade them. In this case, mandatory voting both helps to make citizens attentive *and* motivates other political actors to win them over by supplying them with information in expectation of their greater propensity to participate. These two effects combine to generate improved political knowledge by those at the lowest end of the attentional spectrum.

Mandatory voting thus works hand in glove with party competition to generate even greater epistemic and attentive gains for both citizens and democracy. Mandatory voting induces demand for information which parties, prodded by competitive pressures, are in turn induced to supply.

In addition to cross-sectional data, there is also experimental evidence suggesting that electoral mobilization akin to mandatory voting induces political engagement. This comes from an impressive field experiment conducted by Victoria Shineman (2018) in San Francisco where she provided subjects with information and a cleverly designed financial incentive that simulated the effect of a fine as in mandatory voting. Shineman found strong evidence of information gains stemming from this mobilization, offering further evidence that the mechanisms described do in fact operate to boost engagement.[4]

Shane Singh offers an important qualification to this line of evidence. He finds that among those dissatisfied with democracy, mandatory voting can actually have demobilizing effects by reducing knowledge and interest in politics (Singh 2021, 93–94). The findings I have so far discussed have mostly looked at the effect of mandatory voting homogenously, as applying to all groups in the same way, while Singh looks for heterogeneous

---

4. Loewen, Milner, and Hicks (2008) also conducted a field experiment that they take to cast doubt on mandatory voting's power to induce information gain. Yet their incentive took the form of a payment rather than a virtual fine, as Shineman's did, offering a poor to nonexistent comparison with mandatory voting. Moreover, the treatment seems to have failed even to induce turnout, which the authors themselves acknowledge raises doubts about the validity of their conclusions.

effects that are conditional on having negative attitudes toward democracy (Singh 2021, 65). For this group of citizens, mandatory voting seems to intensify their disengagement. Recall, though, that democracy for busy people allows for reflective forms of apathy and disengagement. So long as citizens periodically check in on politics—which mandatory voting encourages them to do—it is not a problem for them to be dissatisfied with democracy and generally not engaged with politics. Singh's results could simply be the result of the exercise of their political judgment. It just so happens that for those unhappy with democracy reflection about politics may sometimes confirm and strengthen their existing attitudes. The intensification effects Singh finds, then, could be consistent with mandatory voting discharging its tutelary function of encouraging citizens to reflect on active citizenship. Some just conclude it is not worth it.

Bearing Singh's qualification in mind, there still seems to be reason to think mandatory voting is the most powerful way to promote stand-by citizenship.[5] This is because, due to mandatory voting's operation through the law (and assuming a developed state apparatus), it can reach every single citizen. This complete social penetration is profoundly important because, unlike many other forms of democratic reform, it does not rely upon citizens having *any* native civic motivations or knowledge. It reaches people where they are and can jar them out of political passivity, even if this nudge confirms some citizens in their cynicism about politics. At least they are no longer the thoughtless, passive subjects of others.

This universal reach is a power that virtually no other proposed democratic reforms can match. Those reforms emphasizing deliberation in small, randomly selected groups, for instance, always exclude virtually all citizens since lotteries, by design, select small groups. As a settled institution extending over long periods of time, moreover, mandatory voting can serve to socialize new generations of citizens into the political system, motivating them to learn the basics of what they need to know to navigate politics.

---

5. Making this our explicit aim helps to insulate the argument from the objection that this motivation is potentially self-defeating. Jon Elster argues that institutions cannot be justified on the basis of their side-effects because actors will lack sufficient subjective motivation to engage the institution on its own terms (Elster 1986). One cannot, in other words, justify mandatory voting on the basis of generating more political knowledge since the knowledge is a side effect of turnout, and the turnout itself needs to be justified not just normatively but also *motivationally*. Yet recall the aim here is not directly to stimulate turnout but rather political interest, which is not vulnerable to motivational self-defeat as is turnout since it is pre-decisional and mostly pre-reflective.

Assuming, then, that mandatory voting can serve as a tutelary institution, how well does it abide by our design principles for a democracy for busy people? It seems likely to be highly consistent with them. First, as just discussed, it has a unique ability to reach citizens where they are because it operates through the legal system. This ensures a more equal level of political engagement that leaves no one off the ladder of political involvement entirely. Mandatory voting provides a nudge to engagement and offers an obvious next step by also encouraging voting. Second, mandatory voting is undemanding of citizens because it is easy to meet the legal demand. One can vote, or only turn out and not vote, or offer an excuse, such as conscientious objection or illness. But all of these are likely to focus one's attention on politics one way or another, at least for a time. Finally, as an electoral institution, it utilizes elections' unique structure of concentrating power in the least demanding forms of participation. Mandatory voting is thus one of the most promising and important democratic institutions for anyone sharing the concerns that animate this book.

A serious concern one might have about this tutelary argument for mandatory voting is that it is paternalistic. By assuming that citizens need to be taught and reminded of their democratic duties, one might think we thereby treat them like naughty or forgetful children, in need of the meddling of a nanny state. One response to this concern would be to adopt Saunders's suggestion that we only make voting mandatory for first-time voters. This suggestion works reasonably well with the widespread understanding of young adults as needful of instruction in the finer points of "adulting," and thus mandatory voting is not a serious infringement of their emerging autonomy. We might think older adults must be excluded from this reminder out of respect for their presumably mature autonomy.

Yet there are two reasons to see this argument as flawed. First-time voters are not only young adults in the last days of adolescence—they also include those who grew to adulthood without political connection or involvement, or else migrated to the polity. These adults are in the same position vis-à-vis politics and voting as younger people just coming of age. This means there is less reason to see first-time voters as uniquely young. It also forces us to consider whether the issue is first-time voting per se, or a developmental story anchored to the period of young adulthood. It seems to me that the former makes the best sense of Saunders's case since it emphasizes learning about the basics of citizenship by doing them, rather than the relative permissibility of coercive interference in the lives of youth on the cusp of legal adulthood.

This does not seem to help us, however, with the paternalism accusation, since it brings us to a position where mandatory voting is precisely aimed at young and old without discrimination. The targets are differentiated not on the basis of age, but on their degree of connectedness to the political realm. This means adults are targeted for coercive persuasion, which seems to squarely trigger the concern about paternalism. Yet there is a powerful response to this paternalism objection.

Democratic states have the existential right to promote democratic habits among their citizens. This is necessary in order to secure those citizens the fair value of their basic political liberties (Elliott 2018b). Because, as I argued in chapter 2, democratic equality is eroded when only some people are attentive to politics, it undermines the value of others' political liberties when democracy is indifferent to this. Since citizens' political liberties, when adequately provided for and protected, constitute the existential character of the state as a democratic one, democratic states have the right to take steps to secure those liberties through promoting democratic habits like political interest. So long as the interventions democratic states undertake in this regard do not violate other vital democratic values, such as the integrity of the person or freedom of conscience, they are justified (Elliott 2018b, 88–89).

If democracy as a regime is to mean anything, then, it must be able to take steps to shore up its foundations in the habits of citizens. One may call this paternalistic, but only after explaining why individuals should be allowed to overthrow democracy, insofar as they are concerned, by evading even the minimum requirements of democratic citizenship.

Annual Elections and Responsiveness

Time is a powerful democratic resource. This is not for the banal reason that time is important for every human endeavor, but rather because the neglect of time as a resource for democracy has blinded us to a set of tools that allow us to manipulate time for democratic ends (Schwartzberg 2014, 183ff). Knowing that we have these tools is important because it enriches the institutional toolbox we have for dealing with the challenges of contemporary electoral-representative democracies, such as elections' failure to respond adequately to the views and interests of citizens. As mentioned above, critics like Landemore and Guerrero take these failures to recommend wholesale institutional renovation, abandoning elections in favor of largely untested institutions like deliberative mini-publics, liquid democracy, and other randomly selected "lottocratic" institutions. Advocates of these reforms often frame them as the only alternative to the intolerably unresponsive electoral-representative democratic form. These innovations are exciting and many show real promise for enhancing democracy. Yet they are not the only arrows in the quiver of democratic reform. In what follows, I suggest that time, in the form of annual terms in office, offers a neglected path for reform that can transform the relationship between representatives and constituents in radical and unexpected ways. My ultimate intention here is not to argue for annual elections as a concrete institutional proposal per se, but rather to illustrate how different reforms, such as those manipulating time, can transform elections in ways that negate the most powerful contemporary critiques thereof.

I am concerned here with what Elizabeth Cohen (2018) has recently called "the political value of time." Cohen argues that time is a constitutive element of the architecture of all democratic regimes in ways that are essential for the achievement of justice. Time is, for instance, a currency of justice, as when people are assigned different prison terms for similar crimes. Time can also be engineered into democratic processes to encourage democratic deliberation and informed will formation. Time's political value, therefore, consists in the myriad ways it effectuates democracy, citizenship, and political justice.

The specific sort of time Cohen is concerned with is durational time, as measured by a clock or calendar. This differs from other kinds of time, such as cyclical time, which measures time based on natural cycles like the seasons or days and nights, or eschatological time, which periodizes time in an unfolding pattern culminating in the eschaton (end times). Durational time, unlike these other kinds, is scientifically demarcated, liable to mechanical tracking, and, above all, publicly available. It thus does not require a priestly or scholastic class to interpret or track, as tracking the progress of heavenly bodies would during most historical periods, and so is open and available to all, at least in principle.

Building from Cohen's work, I am interested in what we might call "electoral time," or the ways durational time is used in electoral politics. Elections constitute a specific kind of "temporal boundary," according to Cohen. Temporal boundaries divide time into different (mundane) periods, such as before and after the enactment of a law or constitution. Whereas a single-moment boundary fixed at a particular point in time, like the founding of a sovereign state or the beginning of a monarch's reign, mark out a single specific moment as special and result in changes that affect all that comes after it, repeated temporal boundaries periodically recur across time, dividing it into periods that might be regularized. Because the repeated temporal boundary perpetually and periodically repeats itself, it thereby disperses power across many points in time (2018, 58–60). These boundaries therefore allow for new perspectives to emerge, new information to be taken into account in subsequent moments, and open the possibility for new decisions to be made or new officials to come to power. Moreover, as we move through time, the legitimacy of decisions made in the past become more and more democratically tenuous, as the consent legitimizing them expires. Repeated boundaries allow for consent to be renewed, and new decisions or even reaffirmations of past ones to reflect contemporary sensibilities and new considerations.

Elections are the quintessential example of repeated temporal boundaries. Their repetition forges the cyclic relationship between representatives and constituents theorized as essential for the representative relationship by Nadia Urbinati (2006). Urbinati sees representation as a dynamic practice of deliberative exchange between representatives and the represented, a two-way conveyor belt of information, persuasion, grievance, and demand. Elections power that conveyor belt by giving representatives an invincible incentive to check in with their constituents, if only to improve their chances at reelection.

This temporal analysis of elections unlocks a distinctively democratic characteristic of elections that has been obscured in recent years. Critiques of electoral-representative democracy often invoke Manin's (1997) argument that elections are intrinsically oligarchic or aristocratic because they tend to select the richest or best, rather than ordinary citizens. Manin contrasts this with the largely obscure (at least when he was writing) institution of sortition—or random selection—which the ancient Athenian democracy used to staff most public offices, resulting in the literal empowerment of humble ordinary citizens who were randomly chosen to fill important offices. Cohen's analysis allows us to see that elections do, in fact, have at least this one ironclad democratic credential: that they distribute power across time, placing it into a greater number of hands. In this way, the dead hand of history, or an electorate long since transformed, does not rule aftercomers, who are instead afforded the opportunity—through a new election—to choose their own rulers, policies, or even perhaps constitution.[6]

---

6. To be sure, sortition can recur as well, as it did annually in ancient Athens. I do not claim in what follows that manipulating the duration of a term in office is a tool unique to election, merely that doing so has not been explored as a way to democratically improve *elected* governments specifically.

A key reason to see elections as democratic, then, is that they disperse power across time. Whereas a dictatorial coup fixes power for an *indefinite* period, elections fix power for a *limited* period, cementing, in the fundamental institutions of government, an ever-present possibility for changing direction later. Putting power into more hands, over time, grants elections an undeniable democratic quality.

Thinking of elections as recurrent temporal boundaries reveals a new variable for reforming electoral-representative democracy, one that has not received any recent consideration and yet responds to some of the deepest worries about elections today. This variable is the length of term in office. I argue that manipulating the duration of this period can profoundly transform representation and the relationship between elected representative and constituent in ways that powerfully improve responsiveness.

The basic logic is straightforward. Longer durations between elections mean fewer opportunities to change political direction. This concentrates more power in the hands of representatives because they get to hold power for a longer period of time. It also reduces their accountability, for reasons I'll expand on below. In addition, longer terms reduce the incentive, which Urbinati argues is vital for democratic representation, that representatives might otherwise have for maintaining healthy deliberative practices involving their constituents. Indeed, overall, long terms threaten to weaken the representative relationship altogether. As the length of the duration between elections is extended further and further, the closer the recurrent temporal boundary comes to a single-moment fixed temporal boundary. At the vanishing point of recurrence, democracy transitions into dictatorship or some other authoritarian regime, as the last election becomes the *final* election. At every point along the way, the connection between the representative and the represented grows weaker and more attenuated. Shorter durations between elections, by contrast, reduce the power of representatives, strengthen their incentives to be deliberatively linked to their constituents, and increase their accountability.

Shorter terms make representatives more dependent upon their constituents by cutting down the slack that can otherwise grow within the representative relationship. By "slack," I mean something similar to the notion of slack discussed in chapter 2. Recall that the idea came from Dahl (1961), who theorized that politically passive citizens constitute slack in the political system that might be taken in when citizen mobilization was needed to safeguard the interests of those citizens. In that instance, slack was a way for ordinary citizens to enjoy their private lives without endangering their interests. Dahl's account thus focuses on the perspective of the passive group, rather than that of representatives. Here we shift focus to the representative to see slack differently. From the perspective of the representative, slack indicates a kind of discretion or freedom that those active in directing the political system enjoy vis-à-vis the passive group of citizens. The politically active elite can govern as they like absent the latter group's mobilization. The duration of an elected representative's term grants them a supply of discretion consisting in formal independence from external check or control. The focus is thus not on the people generating the slack through their passivity, but rather the representatives enjoying it.

Slack in this latter sense is automatically generated in proportion to the duration of an elected official's term in office—the longer the term, the more slack there is. Dahl saw slack as good because it makes quotidian political passivity safe for democracy. When we center the representative, however, slack takes on a different hue, as the central concern shifts to power and accountability. Instead of serving democracy, slack attenuates it by freeing representatives from accountability to those they are supposed to serve.

Manin (1997, 203–4) argues that it is constitutive of representative government that representatives enjoy partial autonomy in making decisions and exercising power. Yet the degree of this partial autonomy—exactly how partial it is—is essential for determining the balance of power between representatives and constituents. To put it simply: longer terms increase the power of representatives vis-à-vis constituents; shorter terms reduce it. I do not think that those who criticize representative government as essentially nondemocratic, or even anti-democratic, properly appreciate the enormous differences that manipulating the length of term can make.

A very long term in office essentially insulates elected representatives from electoral accountability for the vast majority of what they do. Achen and Bartels (2016, 149–58) find that the public's ability to hold representatives accountable on the most important issue for most people—economic performance—extends back no further than about six months. Representatives' performance for the entire rest of their tenure has no substantial effect on their electoral support. It seems then that we can divide the term of office between an electorally accountable period crowded temporally close to the next election and the rest of it as a period of unaccountable power. Achen and Bartels even suggest an absolute scale for the accountable period—about six months. The longer the term beyond that period, then, the more temporally extended becomes the period of unaccountable power. To put it even more strongly: the longer the term, the *larger* the amount of unaccountable power there is. The result is that the autonomy of representatives becomes less partial and more complete the longer the term.

This principle linking long terms with unaccountable power casts in a new light one of the most powerful arguments in favor of longer terms in office. This is the argument that representatives need time insulated from the pressures and distractions of campaigning to concentrate on governing. When we recognize that the longer the term, the more unaccountable power is created, this time spent away from the public's scrutiny appears less clearly as the responsible discharging of one's responsibilities as an elected official and perhaps more as a turning away from the people to the enjoyment of an unchecked power. The argument thus takes on more of the flavor of technocratic high-handedness than we might otherwise notice.

A longer term in office not only serves to empower the representative, but also trains the public in passivity. Part of the argument that long terms allow representatives to get into the real business of governing is that it generates a salutary break in campaigning. Yet, as I argued above, one of the things that campaigns do is focus the attention of the *public* on matters political, stimulating cognitive engagement with politics and, depending on the party environment and electoral rules, combating citizen passivity. More frequent elections therefore train the people to be more frequently politically engaged, neutralizing one of representative government's greatest weaknesses from a participatory point of view. When we space them further out to accommodate representatives getting familiar with their office and its responsibilities, we do so at the cost of demobilizing the electorate. Such demobilization helps boost the amount of unaccountable power there is in the political system, as inattentive citizens check out, detracting from democracy and endangering the interests of citizens and of the public. This, then, seems to constitute a sharp trade-off between providing space for representatives to govern and maintaining the interested engagement of the citizenry in ways that empower them against representatives.

I want to suggest annual elections as establishing an attractive balance between time spent in deliberative contact with constituents and time spent governing. As Achen and Bartels' findings suggest, retrospective voting seems to generate a sharp accountability period of roughly six months, while the other six months of the year, representatives enjoy greater independence from electorally consequential public scrutiny. If the primary concern about elected officials today is that they are insufficiently responsive to the public and are too willing to govern in contempt of their constituents' interests, then cutting short the temporal leash of their independence is a natural response.

Some might be skeptical that annual elections could have this effect, so I want to highlight one particularly salient historical example in which annual elections seem to have forged a sufficiently robust electoral connection that they could induce governments to make policy that was not only wildly at odds with the interests of the immensely powerful moneyed elite, but also in deep tension with a key element of the hegemonic ideology of the day. I refer to the rage for paper money in the Revolutionary-era American republic.

The conventional story of the drafting and ratification of the Constitution of 1789 casts it as a dramatic act of high statecraft made necessary by the rolling disasters of governance under the Articles of Confederation and the Revolutionary-era state governments. A key part of this story emphasizes the democratic excesses of the state governments, evident above all in their issuance of paper money (see, e.g., Bessette [1994]). The significance of the issue of paper money, and other debt relief efforts, in this crucial period cannot be overstated. For many of the most prominent men who gathered in Philadelphia for the Constitutional Convention, paper money was the quintessential disastrous policy demanded by irrational mobs and enacted by overly democratic state governments. These gentlemen hoped the new, more powerful federal government would be able to stymie these policies. For instance, the Virginia Plan's famous (or infamous) veto over state laws, which James Madison fought desperately for at the convention, was directed principally at laws allowing for paper money and other popular forms of debt relief (Klarman 2016, 132–33). (Of course, the Constitution would eschew such a veto in favor of simply banning the offending policies by name; more on that below.)

Yet this familiar story of excessive democracy producing bad policy presents a highly incomplete and, indeed, partisan picture of paper money's significance in the context of 1785–1787, and one that in particular ignores the class politics of the issue. Historian Michael Klarman offers a retelling of the Constitution's origin that properly contextualizes paper money in its place and time and avoids the classist parochialization that generations have imbibed about the issue due in part to naively reading only the wealthy men who had both a personal and ideological interest in opposing it.

The first element of this revised story is the context of social and economic catastrophe that prevailed in the new United States as a result of severing ties with Great Britain. Following the patriot victory in the Revolutionary War, Britain cut economic ties with its former colonies and also forbade trade between them and all other British possessions, particularly those in the Caribbean. Yet trade with the rest of the British empire was the economic lifeblood of the former colonies, whose economies had originally developed as export-oriented cogs in the vast economic enterprise the empire comprised. Trade was, in other words, the raison d'être for the colonies' very existence. Britain's move therefore effectively destroyed the fledgling nation's economy, which shrank, in terms of per capita gross national product, roughly *50 percent* (Klarman 2016, 75). This number represents a gobsmacking economic collapse, one rivaled in American history only by the Great Depression of the 1930s.

This economic collapse helped trigger, in turn, a monetary and fiscal crisis that ended up causing nothing less than social collapse in some parts of the country. Cut off from traditional British sources of credit, American traders now had to fulfill all foreign contracts in hard specie, meaning gold and silver coin. Similarly, the state and national governments that had borrowed from abroad during the war now faced having to repay their foreign loans in specie. This led to a form of capital flight, as gold and silver migrated abroad, creating a critical shortage of currency in the United States. "Shortage of currency" is a curious idea to people today, who live in the post-gold standard era of fiat money, since central banks can simply create new money to forestall currency shortages before they occur. But in the era before such innovations, a country—like the US in the 1780s— could literally *run out of money*, meaning that there was none available for loans or ordinary economic exchanges, forcing exchange to halt or resort to barter. Despite the currency shortage, state governments, pinched by war debts and the need to fund the national government, raised taxes and generally demanded tax payments in specie (Klarman 2016, 75–76). Farmers were doubly unable to meet these and other debt payments. Not only was there no specie to be found at any price, but they lacked anything that could readily be converted into money. As a result, states took the only thing of value these farmers had: their land. Thousands and thousands of farmers were dispossessed of their farms for taxes and debt. In some parts of Pennsylvania, Klarman reports, 60 to 70 percent of farms were seized for nonpayment of taxes. Moreover, some parts of the state jailed as much as 10 percent of their overall population for nonpayment of debt (Klarman 2016, 76). There is hardly a better term for a majority of farmers, in an agrarian society, losing their land and for one in ten residents to be incarcerated than social collapse.

Paper money, and other debt relief measures, were the solution that many state governments turned to in this crisis. Seven of the original thirteen states enacted paper money laws between 1785 and 1786, and a further four states got within a hair's breadth of doing so (Klarman 2016, 77). Paper money directly addressed the currency shortage, and could, through legal tender laws that forced creditors to accept it at face value, also address the ruinous indebtedness of many in those hard times. And it is here that class politics enters the story. For a variety of reasons—such as state governments using it to buy staple crops like tobacco at double the prevailing price—paper money tended to depreciate quickly. This meant, in particular, that debtors could pay off their debts to their creditors at the face value of increasingly worthless paper money. The distributional consequences of this are similar to those of inflation, as real wealth is effectively transferred from those who have it to those who don't. Those with money to lend are paid back only a fraction of what they lent, while debtors pay back only a fraction of what they borrowed. The distributional politics follow naturally; the poor love and demand these policies while the rich oppose them bitterly.

These are the class politics of paper money that the conventional story of the Constitution's origin effaces. The protagonists of that story are exclusively rich men who saw their own fortunes and those of their class endangered by these relief policies. And we see that they were able to write their view not just into the law, but to etch it into the Constitution itself through the provisions of Article 1, Section 10 that forbade states from coining money, emitting paper money in the form of bills of credit, or from making anything legal tender other than gold or silver. These provisions stoppered all the efforts state governments had been making to respond to the economic and monetary crises.

The most important part of this story for our purposes is the reason *why* the state governments passed the paper money and debt relief legislation: because the policies were popular. The Revolutionary-era state governments were highly responsive to the needs and interests of ordinary citizens, particularly those in the direst straits (Klarman 2016, 76–77). Even the critics of these regimes acknowledged that they were responding to

what the people demanded; few alleged the governments were malfunc-
tioning or falling prey to capture or quotidian corruption. They were functioning as their constitutional design would predict. Though there were
several features of the state constitutions that made their regimes highly
democratic—such as an inclusive franchise, clear lines of accountability,
weak courts and executives, and in some states, unicameralism—the feature most frequently credited for generating the state governments' democratic responsiveness is annual terms in office (Klarman 2016, 76–77). All
but one of the Revolutionary-era state governments elected at least the
lower house of the legislature annually[7] (Lutz 1979). It is not hard to see
why annual elections would powerfully spur responsiveness to the poor
who constituted the majority. When the Rhode Island legislature, which
held elections every six months, overwhelmingly failed to pass debt relief
legislation, the next election, held only a month after the failure, brought
nearly complete turnover among the legislators, and the new members
promptly passed one of the most aggressive debt relief packages in the
country (Bessette 1994, 11). The frequency of elections meant that those
who opposed popular measures could not survive in office. Needs strong
enough to drive electorates, such as economic desperation, prompt timely
action from office holders when elections are frequent.

In passing these laws, then, elected representatives were responding to
the needs and demands of the majority of citizens, particularly the most eco-
nomically disadvantaged. In so doing, moreover, they powerfully defied
what many critics of elections today claim is the ineluctable aristocratic
or oligarchic bias of elections. Because we see so many millionaires in the
US Congress, for instance, elections seem to be structurally designed to
ensure the protection of the interests of the rich, it is sometimes said. This
is, at least, under the institutional arrangements we are familiar with, in
which fixed, multi-year terms of office are the norm.[8]

Annual elections in the early American republic, however, brought people to power who favored what served the interests of the poor majority
even at sharp cost to the interests of the wealthy. Nor was this a trivial issue,
on which the elite might be thought willing to compromise. They firmly opposed paper money and debtor relief laws and saw such policies striking

7. Connecticut and Rhode Island had elections every six months (Klarman 2016, 173).

8. For the purposes of this discussion, I bracket parliamentary arrangements where snap
elections called by governments or votes of no confidence that trigger new elections can cut
short the terms of legislators and governments. These arrangements call for a distinct analysis
that is beyond the scope of this discussion.

at the heart of their core interests. This firmness was not, moreover, purely a function of self-interest. In pursuing these policies, the elected American legislatures also flew in the face of a key aspect the prevailing political ideology of the time: the belief that property rights are sacred and inviolable, and so that governments' overriding commitment is to the preservation of property. Pursuing paper money and debt relief thus took a willingness to defy not only the wealthy but the natural law itself. The annually elected assemblies nonetheless delivered these policies as best they could, in recognition of dire necessity. If elections really empowered the wealthy in the irresistible way many critics seem to suggest, we would not have expected such radically redistributive policies to come to fruition. The fact that a majority of states did so, and most of the others came close, also means that this victory was repeated numerous times across different contexts, further suggesting that it was not a fluke. Passing legislation through several distinct elected legislatures is a difficult achievement, and each one represented a victory of the interests of the many over those of the few.

For the point I am concerned with here, the wisdom of the specific policies of paper money, legal tender laws, etc. is beside the point. Even if paper money and debt relief policies were ultimately disastrous to the goal of widespread prosperity, the point I am making is about institutional design and responsiveness, not monetary policy. Though responsiveness is surely not all that we want out of our democratic institutions (Sabl 2015), that is one of the main grounds on which critics have targeted elections. Those who want more responsiveness out of democratic government, then, need not see replacing elections with some novel alternative as the only path. They might instead shorten terms in office to reduce the amount of unaccountable power in the political system and rein in elected representatives without abolishing elections altogether. Shortening terms can, it seems, enable elections to defy the gravity of their supposedly oligarchic tendencies. We see here a clear and striking example of this mechanism in operation in the real world, in a case with immense social and economic consequences. Annual elections therefore seem to reconfigure the relationship between constituent and representative in ways that reduce slack in the system, shorten chains of accountability, and empower society's poor and marginalized members. Shorter terms may thus even be able to restore trust in elected officials, particularly since citizens would not have to trust them for very long. There are of course other concerns about annual elections that would need to be considered if offering them as a concrete proposal; above all, we would need to do a deeper dive on the trade-off between governance and campaigning. Here, however, I have meant merely to suggest that the critique of elections as unavoidably oligarchic, in its strongest forms, is parochial to institutional designs that generate lots of unaccountable power through long terms in office.

Conclusion

This chapter has explored the utility of elections to a democracy for busy people. Elections turn out to have advantages that make them uniquely well suited to such a democracy. They can, first, be made extremely easy, simple, and undemanding for busy citizens to take part in. Elections can also be brought very close to where citizens are through convenient polling sites and mail voting. In conjunction with parties and mandatory voting, they can actually make contact with even the most disconnected citizens who lack the innate motivational resources to attend to politics, thereby reaching citizens where they are. Elections also generate a socially focal event that induces the production and dissemination of information and attracts the attention of citizens.

Because voting can be made undemanding, elections also embody the precept of concentrating power in the least demanding modes and institutions of participation. Compared to alternative ways of organizing mass political power like pluralism, elections make the simplest forms of influence the most authoritative and powerful while at the same time attenuating the influence of more difficult and demanding ones. Campaign finance represents a key concern on this point since those focused on the United States in particular are likely to see elections as uniquely empowering donors rather than voters. But this is a parochial view since the US's system of campaign finance is uniquely unregulated and privatized by the standards of other advanced democracies.

Mandatory voting represents an electoral institution that can, through the medium of law, help to cultivate stand-by citizenship among a vast swath of the public, contributing a key element to a democracy for busy people that reaches people where they are. Empirical evidence suggests that mandatory voting promotes the political awareness of less advantaged citizens in particular, without raising the overall level of politicization in society. As a tutelary institution, mandatory voting can serve dual aims of improving representation and promoting stand-by citizenship, both of which are key for a democracy for busy people.

Finally, there is reason to doubt that elections are inherently oligarchic because a relatively simple manipulation of the length of term in office seems to enable radical and previously unthinkable policy making that serves the interests of the majority. By manipulating time, we can induce responsiveness against the most dire expectations of oligarchic capture, in other words. This suggests that there remain unexplored avenues of electoral reform that might help to address the emerging critiques of elections without excising them from democracy.

CHAPTER SIX

Engines of Inclusion

Political Parties in Competition

There is little love lost between the people and the political parties that represent them in many democracies today. Parties are often rated as the least trusted major democratic institution (Van Reybrouck 2018, 3). Nancy Rosenblum (2008) documents the long history of antipartyism from the ancient world down into our own time and finds that attitudes toward parties have tended to range from skeptical to profoundly hostile. Some of the most influential founders of the American democracy—including George Washington, James Madison, and Alexander Hamilton—saw parties as fatal to the nation's budding republican experiment. With apologies to Rodney Dangerfield, political parties don't get no respect.

Yet since the advent of mass representative democracy in the late nineteenth century, it has been clear that modern democracy is unthinkable save in terms of parties (Schattschneider 2004). It is not my task to rehearse the reasons for this conclusion. What I propose to do is to highlight the underappreciated ways that parties contribute to the health of democracy by cultivating the political interest of the people and enabling their understanding of politics, thus promoting stand-by citizenship. Parties help democracy avoid the dangers of citizens engaging with politics too little, as discussed in chapter 2, and help forestall the paradox of empowerment by making politics cognitively tractable and accessible to the casual citizen.

The ways that parties do this are fourfold: (1) they directly provide information to citizens to help them navigate the political world, (2) they create an informational ecology that informs and thereby empowers ordinary citizens, (3) parties serve to constitute political groups and constituencies, and (4) they serve to organize groups politically, particularly new and politically disconnected citizens. In these ways, parties reach citizens where they are and help bring them up out of impermissible forms of political apathy and passivity and arm them with the knowledge, skills, and motivation necessary to participate in politics.

One purpose of this chapter is to provide an institutional response to worries about the informedness of citizens. Democracy has long faced the objection that it empowers people who do not know how to properly use power. Contemporary versions of this objection abound (Caplan 2007; Somin 2013; Brennan 2016; Freiman 2021). Common to these modern versions is an individualistic paradigm in which citizens individually choose to become politically informed or not based on the costs and benefits of doing so. Though there is some utility in this approach, it places excessive focus on the individual and neglects the institutional environment and informational ecosystem in which they are embedded. It suggests that individuals are on their own in the task of becoming informed, as if the institutional context played no role. This book emphasizes the immensely important role of institutions in helping citizens solve the information problem. By helping constitute a politics that is more or less easy for citizens to understand, institutional design can make a huge difference in whether busy citizens are able to navigate it successfully. Chapter 5 discussed ways elections can do this, such as through simplifying lines of accountability. Here I focus on the ways that parties help simplify politics, make politics more attractive to draw in citizens' interest, and provide citizens with information.

There is, however, nothing inevitable about parties serving these salubrious purposes. The virtues I shall claim for parties are importantly *contingent* on the wider systemic conditions in which they operate. This marks an important contribution to the emerging body of research in political theory about political parties (Rosenblum 2008; Muirhead 2014; White and Ypi 2016; Rosenbluth and Shapiro 2018). Theorists like Nancy Rosenblum, Russell Muirhead, Lea Ypi, or Jonathan White who celebrate parties for their contributions to democracy may overstate their case insofar as the benefits they point to only apply in certain limited circumstances.

I argue that parties only serve the ends of democracy when they are forced to compete with each other, and that to the extent that they do not have to compete, they transform into the oligarchic cartels they are often accused of being. Theorists of parties have not entirely neglected competition, but their discussions do not emphasize how it transforms the behavior of parties. Rosenblum (2008, 228–33) offers the only substantial discussion of competition, and for her, it is mainly part of the discourse of progressive antipartyism and its worry about parties as cartels. She does not argue it constitutes an important condition of parties serving pro-democratic functions. None of the recent theorists of parties therefore center competition as a core element of the political theory of parties and partisanship. My discussion of parties below makes clear how this neglect of competition omits the most important factor in making parties democratic. In emphasizing the contingency of the value of parties, I therefore contribute an important caveat to a growing body of laudatory research on parties.

Yet I also want to suggest that some of the most damning lines of criticism against parties are contingent on attainable systemic conditions as well. In particular, those who view parties as corrupt cartels that monopolize power and resources for themselves miss that these behaviors may themselves be contingent. In certain conditions, these behaviors might be stoppered, and parties might be pressed into doing good democratic service — in particular, by reaching more citizens where they are and drawing them into political awareness.

When Forced to Compete, Parties Are Powerful Engines of Inclusion

I emphasize competition as the specific contingent systemic feature that unlocks parties' democratic potential. My argument is that parties can serve as powerful institutions for engaging more citizens in politics and helping to promote stand-by citizenship and inclusion, but only when they face a robustly competitive electoral environment. When competition is curtailed or incomplete, it creates conditions in which commonly derided pathologies of parties can arise.

What I mean by competition requires some explanation because it is easily misunderstood. I do not mean only that there are real choices available to every voter, though that is one part of it. I emphasize two criteria for a party system to be competitive: first, as just mentioned, that every voter has a real choice, and second, that there must be robust opportunities for new entrants into the party system.

The first criterion of competition is that voters must have a real choice in the sense that they should be able to participate in a race whose outcome is unclear beforehand. This sort of competitiveness addresses one major failure of American democracy; namely, that during any given election, in only a small minority of districts or states is the outcome in any serious doubt. Ninety percent or more of congresspeople are routinely reelected in the House of Representatives, with slightly lower rates in the Senate (OpenSecrets n.d.). Those 10 percent or fewer of races, plus the five or six toss-up states during the quadrennial presidential election, are, effectively, the only sites of competition in the entire national political system. All other votes in all other states and districts—comprising the vast majority of Americans in virtually every election—are effectively taken for granted.

Someone accustomed to living in any of the majority of noncompetitive districts and states who travels to a competitive one during election season steps into a different world, one bombarded with persuasive appeals, political advertising, and targeted mobilization efforts the like of which they may have never seen. My point is not that such efforts are an unalloyed good but rather that the concentration of such efforts on arbitrary segments of the country highlights how competition changes parties' behavior, and this in turn transforms the lived experience of politics for citizens. Politics literally comes to the door of those living in competitive places but leaves those in noncompetitive places completely untouched. This drastic segmentation of competition in American elections consigns most Americans to living without meaningful political competition in the national polity and to having little or no efforts expended by parties to reach them.

This segmentation marks one kind of failure of competition. Yet it is not the only kind. Another kind of failure comes from facing no new competitors. This failure highlights the importance of another criterion of competition, which is that there must be robust opportunities for new entrants into the party system (Bagg and Bhatia 2021). It is all too easy for established parties to relax in easy unresponsiveness when alternative actors who might upset a closed noncompetitive dynamic are barred from competing. For this reason, allowing for new entrants is centrally important for any adequate conception of competition.

This criterion also adds a critical edge to the notion of competition in a proportional representation (PR) context. It might seem that most schemes of PR would easily remedy the problem of insufficient choices that is faced by Americans. Yet not all PR systems make it easy for new parties to enter electoral competition. Many systems make use of electoral thresholds—a certain percentage of the vote a party must earn before gaining any representation—which, if set high enough, can stymie new party formation. It is generally thought that there is a difficult choice involved here between affording new parties a real shot to flourish via low thresholds and avoiding political fragmentation—including the empowerment of fringe parties—via high ones. The trade-off seems to be that we improve representation with low thresholds, but only at the risk of instability and dysfunction, and vice versa. It is not my intention to address this issue here. I merely mean to highlight that not all PR systems are equally accommodative of new party formation, and that it is possible to have PR systems with high thresholds that, for all intents and purposes, bar new parties from competition. If my argument about the importance of competition is right, then it bolsters the case for seeking ways to ensure new entry is guaranteed, even in PR contexts.

So, how does competition affect the behavior of parties? There are likely to be a whole litany of effects, but we are interested only in those that have to do with the way parties interact with citizens, specifically with making them willing and able to participate in politics.

I want to focus on a hard case: urban political machines. Machines refer to the urban political parties, or factions thereof, which dominated politics in many of the largest American cities and came to be seen by many in the late nineteenth and early twentieth century as a hugely deleterious force in public life. They get their "mechanical" name from the unprecedented ways that they organized and regularized the operation of urban politics compared with earlier eras—from the provision of public services, to the distribution of patronage, to political succession, to, crucially, popular political mobilization.

Urban machines are the ur-example of political parties as cartels that seek to capture and monopolize political power and resources for themselves. This remains one of the most widespread objections to political parties in general, and it is against this line of critique that I aim to object. The problem, to elaborate, is that parties seek above all to win office and then use the powers of office to close off competitors' access to power by, among other things, using public resources to reward and cultivate supporters. I argue that even these much-maligned machines are capable of expanding political engagement, particularly among the least engaged, at least when they face a competitive electoral environment.

The main support for this contention comes from Steven P. Erie's landmark study of American political machines, *Rainbow's End*. Erie sets out to check a counterintuitive argument, what he calls "rainbow theory." Rainbow theory argued machines, far from being irredeemably corrupt, actually served to lift impoverished immigrants, particularly the Irish, into the middle class. They allegedly did this by directing public resources like public sector employment to them in exchange for political support. A key part of Erie's reply to rainbow theory is to introduce a "life cycle" theory of urban machines. Erie argues that machines pass through two distinct phases in their development. During the formative or embryonic stage "fledgling machines face strong competitive electoral pressures from the opposition party and from rival factions within their own party" (Erie 1988, 10). The second "consolidation" phase occurs when "machines have triumphed over their opponents and have built minimal winning voter coalitions" that allow them to durably control government.

My main concern is with the unique behavior of political machines during the embryonic stage. Erie argues that during this phase, machines engage in titanic efforts to mobilize and politically socialize new voters, especially immigrants. For example, during the formative period of the most famous political machine, Tammany Hall in New York City, the machine went to astounding lengths to enfranchise newly arrived immigrants. Between 1856 and 1867, when the city electorate initially consisted of only about 60,000 voters, Tammany naturalized 9,207 immigrants *per year* (Erie 1988, 51). This pace would only quicken in the years to come. Tammany would print 105,000 blank naturalization applications and 69,000 certificates of naturalization to fuel its drive, adding in the single year 1868 over 41,000 naturalized voters.

Yet the machine was not only supplying paperwork. It also paid the requisite court fees and even supplied false witnesses to perjure themselves in testifying that the immigrants had been in the country for the five years required for naturalization. These remarkable efforts profoundly reshaped the electorate. In the eight-year reign of Boss Tweed (1865–1872), the New York electorate nearly doubled, increasing 89.7 percent from 71,101 to 134,878 (Erie 1988, 52). By 1886, Tammany had naturalized nearly 80 percent of all of the city's Irish, German, and other Western European migrants (Erie 1988, 53). But naturalization was not the end of the story.

Machines also engaged in a form of political mobilization that socialized these newly enfranchised immigrants into American politics. Machine cities were generally organized into wards, in which representatives of the party, under the ward captain or ward boss, would provide public services to residents and, at election time, ensure that the recipients of their help repaid the favor by voting for the machine (Merton 1968, 128–29). This ward-based form of retail politics brought politics to—and *through*—peoples' front doors. Urban political parties thus reached people where they were in the most literal possible sense, nudging into action those who might otherwise fall into political passivity. Machines also thereby helped forge a connection between individuals' own good, as well as that of their neighborhood, and the otherwise remote politics of the city, state, and nation via party solidarity. By forging local connections between new voters and political parties, machines helped to socialize new citizens into the nation's politics writ large, rendering politics legible to them through their connection to the party.

The proof of parties' inclusionary force was in the pudding, as they say. All these efforts succeeded in building a truly mass democracy. During the middle of the nineteenth century, when most political machines were in their embryonic stage, American democracy posted the highest turnout rates in its history, regularly achieving rates of 70 or 80 percent (Broxmeyer 2020, 10). Such rates compare favorably with other present-day democracies, whereas the present-day US has nearly the lowest rates of voting of all established democracies.

Yet these impressive efforts at inclusionary mobilization would not last. The frenetic activity of making new citizens ceased when the urban machine reached the consolidation phase. Erie (1988, 69) explains that when urban machines faced strong competition in the late nineteenth century, they had been "mobilizers of the immigrant vote." But once they faced only token opposition in the twentieth century, machines shifted to merely selectively bringing out the vote. The mobilization efforts of the formative stage helped build a constituency—or in political science jargon, a minimal winning coalition—that mature machines could rely upon for control of government. With this coalition in hand and the threat of serious competition neutralized, machines turned to husbanding public resources for their key supporters, offering little or only token support to later arrivals such as Black migrants from the US South or immigrants from eastern and southern Europe. Where an embryonic machine would see such new and politically disconnected denizens as potential supporters, a consolidated machine sees them as potential leeches on limited public resources needed to maintain their winning coalition.

My aim here is not to cast a spell of sentimentality over urban political machines, nor to excuse their vast corruption. Indeed, it is the very venality of the machine that I seek to invoke. Even a deeply corrupt institution like a political machine can be made to go to great lengths to reach new and disconnected citizens *where they are*.[1] I emphasize this phrase, "where they are" because it marks a unique power of political parties compared to most other democracy promoting institutions. Whereas innovative democratic institutions like participatory budgeting or deliberative forums require citizens to find their own way to them either by hearing about and attending them or accepting an invitation to one, parties actively and laboriously seek out citizens literally where they already are—in their homes and in public places.

This feature of parties helps to answer one of the biggest issues with existing efforts to innovate democracy—democratic innovations almost uniformly require citizens to *already possess* some degree of civic motivation and political interest. But this leaves behind those who are most in danger of falling into political apathy: those who currently lack any connection to politics, or indeed lack any reason to even want to forge such a connection. Parties' democratic superpower is that their greed for power drives them to reach these citizens where they are and turn them into active supporters, along the way bringing them up out of apathy and transforming them into stand-by citizens. No other democratic institution can make this same claim, with the possible exception of mandatory voting.

The crucial condition forcing this behavior is competition. The embryonic machines sought to make new voters—indeed, whole new constituencies— and succeeded massively. The consolidated machines, having won secure control of the government, ceased such efforts and seriously concerned themselves only with the welfare of their core supporters. We can see similar dynamics today in American politics, where partisan office holders from noncompetitive districts neglect not only their constituents who support the other party, but also political independents and even moderate members of their own party. Thus, competition is revealed to bring about a remarkable change in urban political parties. In its presence, they are motivated to go to exuberant lengths to build a wider citizenry. Without it,

---

1. This is also distinct from the functionalist arguments of "rainbow" theorists like Dahl or Merton, which are the target of Erie's critique, in that their concern is how machines functioned to promote the *welfare* of lower-class groups while mine is specifically with machines' democracy-promoting abilities.

they want to circle the wagons and deny everyone but their core support-ers' political significance.

I contend that this historical example illustrates the fundamental logic of political parties when it comes to unlocking their capacity to reach citizens where they are and draw them into political awareness. It also illustrates that this logic is empirically plausible. Parties that must compete with others organize themselves, shape their activities, and direct their resources in ways that target *potential* supporters—not just current ones. Moreover, this example shows the lengths to which parties will go in this pursuit. The cost and effort expended by Tammany Hall is an expensive way to build a constituency, but they did it because they saw it as the best way to win. Rather than seek to persuade members of what V. O. Key (1961) calls the "attentive public," or the *existing* body of engaged and attentive citizens, they sought to mobilize a *new* group into political consequence. Modern political science might have provided support for this strategy insofar as it suggests that enduring persuasion is vanishingly rare. Politically socialized citizens have generally found their place in the political system and so are rarely in play during a given election. But the same is not true for less politically aware citizens. They are persuadable precisely because they do not have well-established political views or affiliations. In a competitive political environment, these citizens become the most realistic and cost-effective opportunity for parties to gain new supporters. As a result, therefore—and *only* in the presence of real competition—parties have a strong incentive to do the work to mobilize precisely those citizens who are most at risk of impermissible political apathy. A competitive party environment turns parties into engines of inclusion targeting the citizens about whom we should be most concerned. Competition is the all-too-often missing keystone of party democracy, enabling it to achieve its potential for reaching every citizen.

Party-Driven Mechanisms of Inclusion

It is important to be clear about how, exactly, parties make these new citizens, and make politics open to them. This is because, although it is widely understood that parties can serve as powerful political mobilizers, the mechanisms by which they do so are often left unclear or only partially explored. Moreover, some of these mechanisms are intrinsically systemic, indirect, and obscure, and so are easily overlooked. Finally, political theorists have yet to clearly identify the ways that parties mobilize and socialize, even when they laud the mobilizing functions served by parties.

So, how do parties help to make new, stand-by citizens? First and most directly, they do so through organizing groups politically, particularly new and politically disconnected individuals. This is perhaps the most direct means by which parties mobilize, other than actual get-out-the-vote (GOTV) efforts. Political organizing is the process of articulating connections between the party and groups or individuals. This process often occurs through mediating institutions, such as unions or churches (Stout 2010). Some of the most effective types of organizing seem to involve long-term engagement in the community, including providing ordinary forms of social (nonpolitical) support and service (Hersh 2020). Another common vector of organizing is canvassing, where supporters knock on doors or otherwise engage people in public spaces to urge their support (García Bedolla and Michelson 2012). Such canvassing is often part of conventional GOTV efforts, yet these efforts shade into organizing when targeted at habitually disengaged citizens because of how they serve to transform these citizens' view of themselves and their relationship to politics. Lisa García Bedolla and Melissa Michelson explain how this process works using what they call a Sociocultural Cognition model of mobilization that works by tapping into ideas the individual already has to encourage them to adopt "a new cognitive schema as a 'voter'"—or active democratic citizen (García Bedolla and Michelson 2012, 6). Focused canvassing efforts induce these individuals to develop new understandings of themselves and of their relationship to the wider political community, one in which they take an active role. Individual transformation of this kind, I would argue, serves as a seedbed not just of turnout but also of partisan attachment, as citizens newly coming into political awareness reach out for a scaffolding or foundation to support their developing political identity.

This scaffolding effect is distinct from, and foundational for, the more familiar argument that party labels serve as information shortcuts for voters (Bullock 2020). Party identification can help citizens to situate themselves in politics, learning whom to ally themselves with and whom to oppose. It helps them align their affinities and antipathies; it helps socialize them into politics, in other words. This new social identity then serves as the motivational core of their activities as citizens. This process is distinct from party labels as information shortcuts, since shortcuts are not primarily about identity, but rather information, and also because they presuppose political motivation, whereas the scaffolding is constitutive of such motivation.

A second mechanism by which parties help to make attentive citizens is through serving to *constitute* groups and constituencies. This is distinct from organizing groups because organizing presupposes groups as pre-existing entities waiting to be mobilized; it is about forging connections between things that already exist. Here, the idea is that parties help groups to *form*, providing the seed crystal around which groups form. This occurs through a form of representation that Lisa Disch (2011, 107) has called a "mobilization" conception of representation. In this conception, representatives "participate in forming demands and social cleavages, not merely reflect them." Representatives' aim is thus not to follow the preferences or interests of their constituents as if they were set and preformed, as is assumed in rational choice theory and much political science influenced by it. Rather, they seek to "call forth a constituency by depicting it as a collective with a shared aim." Representatives *call into being* constituencies by anticipating and, indeed, formulating the political claims of their supporters, thereby providing the glue that makes them cohere as a group in the first place (Disch 2021, 21). Representation becomes a "reflexive" process wherein representatives stake claims and moot divisions that would-be constituents accept or reject, cleave to or disregard (Disch 2011, 111). This gives rise to a two-way dynamic exchange, the ongoing process of which constitutes representation itself (Urbinati 2006).

Parties, though Disch says little about them, qualify as representatives in her sense — and may even constitute the prime representatives in democratic systems. They often create political groups, commonly by originating the claims around which groups form. Indeed, the articulation and coordinated dissemination of claims is a central function of parties according to several political theories of parties (Rosenblum 2008; Muirhead 2014; White and Ypi 2016). Here I extend that analysis to groups. Parties articulate claims that create groups, not just that appeal to individuals. They help introduce certain ideas into the polity's bloodstream which cause individuals to bunch up and separate socially, not just in partisan terms. This is a large part of the story of polarization in the United States, for instance.

Recall also the function of urban political machines that consists in literally creating new constituencies by enfranchising masses of immigrants. Though this was mostly not achieved through programmatic messaging as when parties articulate claims, it did function to conjure new political groups into existence and invest them with power. This too is therefore another instance of how parties make new constituencies.

The third mechanism by which parties build inclusion and stand-by citizenship is substantially more indirect than the previous two because it occurs at the level of the political information ecosystem that is created by parties competing with each other. This means it is mostly a byproduct of the efforts of parties to win and so is not a direct aim of parties' purposive action as are building new constituencies and organizing groups. The idea here is that stand-by citizenship requires not that citizens be informed but that *the political realm itself* be understandable. If politics were unfathomably complex in every facet, it would be flatly impossible for citizens to intelligibly engage with it. This is an important and profound claim and requires explication.

In the vast literature on citizen informedness, which asks whether citizens know enough to discharge their duties as citizens (see, e.g., Delli Carpini and Keeter [1996]), it is assumed that the main dependent variable—the thing whose variation is to be explained—is individual citizens' knowledge. This implies that it can vary from person to person, or in a single person over time. At the same time, however, the complexity of the information environment is generally assumed to be fixed. But this is a profound mistake. Politics can itself be more or less intelligible, more or less *legible* to the casual observers that are the majority of citizens. The understandability of politics is not mainly a product of the interventions of intentional policy, moreover, but rather of the incidental byproduct of interactions of the major actors on the political stage, especially parties, as well as the complexity of the regime within which they operate. Through their competition, they draw and make publicly known lines of ideological division and policy disagreement. They then relate these divisions and disagreements to upcoming elections, investing them with significance and, above all, with understandable *stakes*. They and their members articulate what the election means for each citizen and for the polity.

When parties interact in a competitive context and so seek to distinguish themselves from others to win votes, parties in competition can thereby *make* a politics that is easy to understand. By contrast, when parties can take their supporters for granted in a noncompetitive environment, or when competition is whittled down to a single cleavage as in two-party systems, parties in flawed competition often make a politics that is personalized, factionalized, or informal, or some combination of all three. Such a politics, like those of a small town, can be highly opaque to ordinary citizens because its machinations are often difficult to report on and only understandable with a long contextual memory stuffed full of the proper names of particular individuals and their personal and political dealings with each other over years or decades. Like a long-running soap opera, such personalized or factional politics is highly difficult for casual observers to understand.

This is where competition makes all the difference. It induces parties to *publicly*—and with the highest clarity and salience—mark out the ground of political contestation. When you stand with us, the party says, it means *this*; when you stand with them, it means *that*. Each party makes contrasting claims of this kind, sending competing messages to citizens about what different electoral choices mean. It is over this ground, prepared and divided by parties in competition, that citizens then sort themselves into groups and coalitions. Parties in competition thus generate an informational ecology that helps citizens to understand the scope and meaning of their choices. That simplifies those choices, in ways that would be all but cognitively impossible without parties.

We can call this the "ecological simplification function" of parties. As explained by Paul Sniderman:

> The ecology of the party system affords partisans an opportunity to make ideologically coherent choices without exceptional effort on their part. The parties do the work for them. They organize the alternatives on offer along ideological lines, and just so far as the choice set [facing citizens] is already ideologically organized, it is easier for voters in general, and a party's supporters in particular, to make consistent choices among them (Sniderman 2017, 43).

By organizing politics ideologically, parties make consistent choices not just possible, but easy for ordinary citizens. This view contrasts with that of Philip Converse, who thinks that citizens "must bring meaning" themselves to ideological terms like "liberal" and "conservative" (Sniderman 2017, 52). Sniderman's point is that the wider environment shaped by the parties *provides* meaning to citizens rather than requiring them to supply it themselves, and thereby economizes on the effort citizens must put forth to make sensible political choices.

To bring out what this effect means, consider a context that lacked parties as we know them: a liquid or delegative democracy. In a full liquid democracy, citizens either vote directly on public policies or delegate their vote on some issue area to a trusted "issue-competent" proxy (Blum and Zuber 2016). This delegation is instantly revocable, however, leaving the delegation perpetually provisional. In this design, parties would likely not exist in any recognizable form since, among other things, there would be no office-seeking competition to stimulate their organization and consolidation.

The most important consequence of this for us is that rather than having a relatively small number of parties determine the policy bundles on offer in elections, all possible combinations of every position on every issue would become open to each citizen to determine for themselves—indeed, making up their minds on this vast array of options would be obligatory to exercise their democratic voice. For voters then, liquid democracy causes what is bloodlessly called the "unbundling" of issues. A more accurate description would be that it triggers an explosion in the complexity of democratic choice so dramatic as to issue forth a politics different in kind, not degree, to that existing before. From the perspective of voters, this constitutes a veritable "big bang" in democratic complexity, as all the considerations bearing on every issue explode into their awareness at once, each calling for their attention and to be integrated into their comprehensive political outlook. This only occurs, moreover, because parties would no longer be doing the enormous service for citizens of taking all of the vast array of individual issues and packaging them together in more or less sensible ways. Instead, citizens would have to undertake this immense labor for themselves.

Whatever other merits liquid democracy might afford democratic regimes, there can be little doubt that the effect on the political inclusion of citizens, particularly busy ones, would be catastrophic. Recall Walter Lippmann's admission of being unable to follow the totality of public affairs in the United States of the 1920s, when societies and states were incomparably less complex than today. Lippmann was an immensely well-educated and well-connected man who, in his words, devoted all of his time and attention to public affairs as a matter of his occupation, yet even he was left utterly behind by the politics of his time. Imagine how much more outclassed would be the more disadvantaged among us today, in an even more complex world. Citizens would flee like rats from a sinking ship such a punishingly demanding politics as that generated by liquid democracy, particularly busy ones because they have a limited budget of time and attention to devote to politics. And they could do so not necessarily because they are incapable of meeting its burdens, as Blum and Zuber (2016) address, but because citizens have a claim of justice against such a demanding politics, as I argued in chapter 3. An infinitely complex politics is one that is not cognitively tractable and, for that reason, not even effectively open to busy or casual citizens. Political parties, then, serve as the great bulwark against weaponizing complexity to effectively exclude busy citizens. Through the ecological simplification effect generated by their competition, parties slay complexity as far as voters are concerned, making democratic politics tractable and thus inclusive.[2]

Parties thus promote stand-by citizenship by enabling citizens to both efficiently and effectively monitor what is happening in politics and to step in when they understand their interests are at stake, or when political need requires it. These are core features of stand-by citizenship. Moreover, making politics understandable makes it easier for citizens who intrinsically care less about politics to be able to profitably pay attention to it and thus, ultimately, to participate in it, making their voices and interests matter. It makes politics accessible to busy, casual citizens. This too is an essential part of stand-by citizenship and the goal embedded in it of effectively including everyone in democratic politics.

The final way that parties promote stand-by citizenship overlaps somewhat with the last one but is more direct. This is the way that parties directly provide information to citizens about what is happening in politics and why it matters. They do this mainly through news coverage of their public statements as well as through political advertisements and other direct media. This information can help citizens navigate the political world. Whereas the ecological simplification function I just described is an indirect, spontaneously generated effect of the competitive interactions of parties, here parties invest directly in getting information to citizens. Parties spend immense sums and expend monumental effort on political advertising and the other tools of political communications—communications staff, press releases, interviews with party members, the distribution of pamphlets, fliers, and books, holding public speeches and rallies, etc. Though these efforts also help generate the ecological effect, that effect is often a function of *contrasts* between these information streams. Here we are concerned with the content of the messages themselves, not the environment that grows up around competing sets of such messages.

---

2. One concern about this line of argument is that simplifying politics will inevitably channel it in some ways rather than others; some issues will be emphasized and others ignored, and this cannot be done in a neutral way. It is surely correct to say that one cannot divide up the space of political contestation in neutral ways—doing so partly constitutes what ordinary politics is all about. Yet I worry about cognitive overload and disengagement more than bias in this channeling. I also hope that a more competitive political environment can reduce our worry about the non-neutrality of this process by giving us more choices and opportunities to contest particular divisions.

These messages help supply a key element of the civic skills that are an essential part of the package of stand-by citizenship. They often include information about who the party supports and why, how to go about registering and voting, the rules for voter identification or requesting absentee ballots, or even running for office. They also tell us the party's stance on direct democracy votes and the daily minutiae of politics. These are crucial inputs for stand-by citizens' critical attention and help make politics more tractable for busy citizens especially.

Two Parties or More?

The importance of competition for turning parties into engines of inclusion raises the question of what kind of party system is most likely to trigger competition with these effects. The key issue here is multipartyism — does competition in a two-party system have the same power to engage and mobilize citizens as a multiparty system? Do both generate similar ecological information effects?[3] I argue that there is substantial reason to think that multipartyism is better when our main concern is building a democracy for busy people and bringing the most disengaged up to the level of stand-by citizenship.

The fundamental theoretical reason for this is that a multiparty system allows for greater dimensionality in political competition, which generates more opportunities for party competition to hook the attention of citizens with issues they care about. One of the great pathologies of two-party competition is the way it reduces all political conflicts to a single dimension. This means that there are never more than two sides to a political issue, however complex, due to the imperatives of this kind of competition. Yet not all issues end up truly dividing the parties at any given time. When there are only two parties in a stable two-party system, an informal agreement about the central issues dividing them generally develops over time. This agreement implicitly keeps every other issue off the political

3. One might ask whether the question here is properly about the number of parties or, rather, about electoral system design. For the reasons explained in this section, I think the number of parties is independently important, but there can be no doubt that the number of parties is closely linked to the design of the electoral system. There is likely much to be said about electoral system design for a democracy for busy people, and I hope to be able to address it in the future. For the time being, I must bracket it because the inevitably complex particulars would take us too far afield from the present discussion.

agenda, effectively rendering those issues politically invisible. Such issues thus fail to attract any public attention, and the parties can together tacitly collude to exclude certain issues from the political agenda. Moreover, there might end up being no very clear distinction between the parties in these other policy areas since they do not form part of the mutually agreed upon ground of political competition.

The key reason that this is problematic is that it leaves citizens who see those excluded issues as vitally important with little reason to concern themselves with politics at all. Since they do not see what really matters to them at stake in politics, they come to lack motivation to pay attention to it in the first place. Two-party competition generates the sense that there is no difference between the parties when the issues one cares about are excluded from the narrow sliver of issues that define it in a particular place and time. I suspect that this deep pathology of the two-party system explains much dissatisfaction with the functioning of American democracy in particular, since the US is the purest two-party system on earth.

The argument I have laid out in this book illustrates why this is so hugely damaging to democracy and does so in ways that have largely evaded emphasis. What I describe is an institutional arrangement that systematically demobilizes citizens by teaching them that the things they care about are of no concern to the only real contenders for political power in their polity, the two main parties. It effectively *induces* political apathy of the impermissible kind discussed in chapter 2. What is happening is not just that citizens are told that the things they care about are only *intermittently* of public moment, but rather that they do not concern the powerful *at all*. It is difficult to imagine a more optimal message for undermining the motivation to pay attention to and participate actively in politics. As I discussed, however, these motivations constitute a necessary institutional minimum inherent to the office of democratic citizen. The two-party system thus constitutes an ongoing attack on the democratic citizenship of a vast share of the people.

Skeptics of multipartyism are likely to retort that citizens in multiparty democracies can also be unhappy with the sparsity and bias of the political agenda, and so that multiparty democracy is no foolproof prophylaxis against it. Yet this neglects that we are engaged in an inquiry of institutional design, in which nothing is foolproof. We are necessarily concerned instead with tendencies and likelihoods.

Multipartyism may not immunize democratic citizens from a politics that minimizes their personal concerns, but it does systematically reduce its likelihood. This is because a multitude of parties multiply the possible dimensions of electoral competition. Consider a simple model consisting of any number of parties arrayed along the left-right spectrum. Each party system generates a certain number of lines of contestation at the point that parties border each other. Along these frontiers of competition are where parties articulate their disagreements and compete for the voters occupying that space on the spectrum. Considered this way, a two-party system has one line of contestation. A three-party system has double that number—two. A four-party system generates three, five parties generate four, and so on.

Moreover, a *stable* two-party system excludes the entry of new parties, whereas multiparty systems, where designed to facilitate new party formation, have additional possible cleavages throughout the spectrum, adding at minimum two more lines of contestation at either end of the party spectrum, for extreme left and right parties. There is also the possibility of new party formation in the center, which would provide an additional pair of competitive fronts. The possibility of emergent competition from new parties therefore adds even more space to the political agenda.

Whereas in a two-party system, each party has only one "flank" from which to expect serious electoral competition, in a multiparty system, each party has at least two. Center-left parties, for instance, must be concerned not only with center-right parties, but also with those of the left. Even parties of the left must be concerned that new or currently marginal parties even further to their left might outflank them on some salient issue and burgle supporters from them. Center-left and center-right parties must likewise fear the formation of a purely centrist party on their other flank.

Any of these fronts might become the defining ground of competition in a given election, potentially adding uncertainty, novelty, and even a salutary sense of drama to politics. As events unfold and issues emerge and are accentuated by events, different points of political contestation will gain salience. So, an election might turn on a set of conflicts between centrist parties at one time and between the left and center-left at another. Moreover, because multiparty systems are created by PR electoral systems, and PR ensures that every vote can always affect who wins, multiple flanks are imbued with political competition simultaneously. What this means is that many more issues can receive substantial attention by the parties in election campaigns, since each of them is potentially concerned with challenges from both the left and right. The more flanks the parties must contest means more dimensions to political competition, and more dimensions means more issues have a shot at making it onto the political agenda. This is why multiparty systems have an inherent tendency that is directly contrary to that of two-party systems with respect to cognitively mobilizing voters. Two-party systems impoverish the political agenda and thereby chase citizens away from politics. Multiparty systems enrich the agenda, thereby attracting them.

According to the picture I just presented, multidimensionality seems to imply no natural limit to the salubrious effect of adding more parties to political competition. This seems to suggest that we should aim to infinitely multiply them. Yet endlessly multiplying parties runs into an obvious problem. It might be said in two-party systems' favor that they *simplify* the decision facing voters vis-à-vis multiparty systems in precisely the kinds of ways likely to aid inclusion. Two-party politics, we might think, is maximally understandable to everyone, reducing the complexity of the cognitive tasks of citizenship as well. To be sure, we do want parties to help make the political arena understandable, and too many parties could conceivably hinder that. A fragmented political scene would certainly be more difficult to keep tabs on. We end up therefore with two conflicting imperatives; to keep the number of parties low to promote cognitively undemanding political simplicity and increasing their number to generate the new dimensions of political contestation that will in turn generate a politics that appeals to a wider swath of the citizenry.

Luckily, these countervailing imperatives suggest a natural solution, and this solution definitively answers the question we set out to answer in this section. The solution is a sort of Aristotelian mean—not too many parties, and not too few. What constitutes too many parties need not concern us here since we are considering only the other end of the spectrum: two parties, or more than two? Two-party systems define one extreme endpoint with respect to the number of parties in competition with each other, since of course a one-party regime would have no competition at all. Framing it this way suggests the conclusion we have already reached; that two-party systems likely do not generate enough competition to trigger the salutary effects that parties can have in cultivating stand-by citizenship. Multipartyism is to be preferred if we are concerned to prevent unacceptable forms of citizen apathy and promote stand-by citizenship.

Don't Two Parties Make Everything Simpler?

Frances Rosenbluth and Ian Shapiro (2018) have recently risen to the defense of two-party systems on the grounds that parties in them have the strength and incentives needed to take long-view time horizons and accomplish the trade-offs necessary for programmatic policy making. The core of their case therefore concerns the systemic functioning of parties. They are little concerned with the interface of parties and citizens, which is my primary concern. Nonetheless, two key implications of their argument present a formidable challenge to the idea I suggested that multipartyism is needed to promote the cognitive engagement of citizens.

Their first argument comes from the way that two-party systems enable single parties to rule. Because of this, two-party systems clarify the lines of accountability in a way that makes it easy for voters to hold parties accountable for their policies (Rosenbluth and Shapiro 2018, 233). Making this point plausible requires clarifying that their ideal is the Westminster model represented by the Parliament of the United Kingdom, not the United States. A Westminster-style parliamentary majority faces no serious constitutional checks on carrying out its programmatic goals, whereas in the US, a tangle of checks and divided powers prevents even robust national majorities from governing. Because parties in a Westminster-style parliamentary two-party system can govern without constraint, it also means that the incumbent government can be blamed without complete injustice for serious problems that arise or go without redress during their tenure. This simplifies electoral accountability along the lines discussed in chapter 5, putting it within easy reach of even the busy, casual citizen.

Rosenbluth and Shapiro's second argument is that two-party systems present voters with comprehensive bundles of issues that have had the trade-offs computed and considered for them. This makes it easier for voters' choices to reflect a rational consideration of the trade-offs inherent in policy making. Moreover, in constructing the policies that make up the bundle, parties have strong incentive to consider their long-run impact, since the party will be held responsible for the results. This likewise helps to discourage shortsighted policy from finding its way to voters. Finally, the comprehensiveness of these bundles helps to clearly distinguish those on offer, making for a distinct choice.

To readers of Rosenblum on parties, these advantages may sound familiar since she argues for parties partly on the basis of them presenting to the electorate "comprehensive public stories" about the direction of policy (Rosenblum 2008, 357). Yet Rosenblum claims that this is a feature of parties as such, not of parties only in two-party systems. According to Rosenbluth and Shapiro, two-party systems are uniquely good at telling such comprehensive stories, and multiparty systems are specifically bad at it. The reasons for this are threefold. First, multiparty systems create space for more specialized parties who care about a relatively small portion of the political agenda instead of a more comprehensive one. Second, smaller parties tend to represent discrete social groups and interests rather than expansive constituencies, encouraging narrow and partial approaches to policy. Finally, multiparty systems tend to empower coalition governments composed of several parties, leading to bargaining between them regarding the direction of policy. The result is that small parties seek to capture benefits for their supporters or policy in line with their narrow concerns at a cost that is externalized to other segments of society. This is because there is no overarching organization who has reason to internalize all the costs, at least not in a multiparty system.

Two-party systems are different, because they empower single parties to rule without being in coalition with others. This gives them the incentive that coalition governments lack to consider the full gamut of policies and the trade-offs between them ahead of time, since their electoral support is on the line in a way that small parties' support is not.

The bottom line here is that two-party competition seems to generate a more understandable political environment in which parties have prepackaged a comprehensive policy program that will be more fully and systematically considered than anything a citizen could do on his or her own. Moreover, citizens in multiparty systems are seemingly faced with the daunting task not just of choosing from among parties who may not offer a complete picture of what they would do in power, but also of calculating the likelihoods of different coalitions emerging after the election and anticipating the often opaque process of coalitional bargaining. Two-party competition, Rosenbluth and Shapiro suggest, offers high-quality, clear alternatives to voters.

Two Parties or More: Three Empirical Checks

It seems then that we have two plausible yet competing stories regarding which type of party system—a multiparty one or a two-party one—generates a more tractable and involving democratic politics for ordinary citizens. So, how are we to determine which of these stories is more nearly correct? One way would be to look at empirical indicators of stand-by citizenship to see which one has the advantage. Stand-by citizenship is precisely the type of undemanding cognitive engagement that these alternate stories would stimulate if they were at all true. Consulting them, we shall see, suggests the superiority of multipartyism.

Recall that there are three reasonably good indicators of stand-by citizenship: turnout, political interest, and political knowledge. The questions we are now considering, then, are: (1) Is there higher turnout in multiparty systems or two-party systems? (2) Are very low levels of political interest avoided more robustly in multiparty or two-party systems? (3) Are very low levels of political knowledge better avoided in multiparty or two-party contexts?

Question 1 is in one sense straightforward to answer—turnout is higher in multiparty systems (Blais 2006, 116; Geys 2006a, 650–51; Karp and Banducci 2008)—yet there has been a wide-ranging debate surrounding this question. The core challenge in determining whether multipartyism[4] encourages greater turnout is that although PR systems with multiple parties have higher turnout rates than two-party systems based on single-member electoral districts, turnout does not increase as the number of parties increases (Blais and Aarts 2006; Grofman and Selb 2010). This puzzle leads some to confidently assert the overwhelming consensus in favor of multipartyism, while others claim the evidence is mixed.

Yet the emphasis I place on the tractability of citizens' political choices suggests a natural solution to this dilemma, and it is one that has found some empirical support. When the number of parties increases without limit, the cognitive complexity of such a fragmented political scene becomes overwhelming for citizens and demobilizes many of them as a result. We thus should not expect turnout to increase linearly with the number of parties due to the accompanying increase in cognitive complexity. Yet the attraction of offering a nonbinary choice set—with more than two parties—remains, driving turnout up as the number of parties passes two. It is because both of these effects are happening at the same time that there is no observed relationship between the effective number of parties and turnout. Instead, turnout is comparatively high in a "sweet spot" between two parties and the point at which there are too many parties for citizens to make sense of. Thus, we should expect to see a *curvilinear* relationship between the effective number of parties and turnout, where turnout increases as the number of parties passes two, but then peaks or plateaus

---

4. There is some debate about how to operationalize what I call here "multipartyism," since, as Blais observes, the number of parties is an output of the institutional context, meaning things like the proportionality of electoral rules and district magnitude (Blais 2006, 112). Subsequent research has used a variety of measures—including the effective number of parties, political fragmentation, and disproportionality in seats—to capture the basic phenomenon I am interested in here.

and then decreases as the number of parties reaches cognitively unmanageable dimensions. Such a curvilinear relationship is precisely what one team of prominent scholars has found (Taagepera, Selb, and Grofman 2014).

Thus, there is a widespread and well-established consensus among scholars that multiparty systems have higher turnout rates than two-party systems. What debate there is can be well explained by the limitations of simple linear relationships for accounting for the effects of the number of political parties. These findings suggest that more voters find something worth voting for in multiparty environments, in line with the argument I laid out above.

The second question about political interest is essentially unanswerable with the current state of knowledge about the interaction of institutions and political interest. Although political interest has long been recognized as an important and powerful determinant of a host of political behaviors, it has largely evaded direct study until quite recently. Moreover, the studies in recent years—above all those of Markus Prior (2018)—have tended to investigate political interest as an individual-level phenomenon, with roots in one's family background, education, financial situation, or personal experiences of politics. What is needed, however, is evidence regarding how different kinds of institutions, such as multiparty and two-party systems, influence political interest. I am not aware of any substantial research into the comparative influence on political interest of different institutional arrangements.[5]

Finally, we come to political knowledge. Recall that we are interested here in political knowledge as an indicator not of what people know, but rather of cognitive engagement with politics. What we want to know is whether political knowledge is higher in two-party systems or multiparty ones, as an indication of which story about the effects of parties on mass engagement is most likely.[6] The evidence again here indicates that citizens in

5. It is entirely possible that there are no such effects, or none worth taking seriously. If political interest is truly an individual-level phenomenon, that would be what we expect. Yet this seems implausible given the powerful yet subtle effects of institutions in shaping citizens.

6. There are important methodological issues with comparing levels of information across countries. The main concern in this area stems from the use of nonidentical questions in some prominent surveys, such as the Comparative Survey of Electoral Systems (CSES). Because political context differs, it has sometimes been left to local investigators to construct questions appropriate to the country, meaning the content of the questions used to gauge informedness vary by country. This means respondents are not asked the same questions across countries, raising worries about comparing the results cross-nationally. For our purposes, however, this

multiparty systems have more political knowledge and so are more engaged (Gordon and Segura 1997; Berggren 2001; Fraile 2013; Grönland, Bächtiger, and Setälä 2014). Indeed, we even see additional confirmation of the curvilinear relationship between the number of parties and the stimulating effect found by Taagepera et al. since the amount of knowledge increases when there are more than two parties but then decreases as the number goes up past about five parties (Gordon and Segura 1997, 140; Fraile 2013, 130–33).

Taken together, these empirical checks point in the same direction. Though the jury is still out on political interest, the empirical evidence regarding turnout and political knowledge seems to suggest that a multiparty environment will do a better job than a two-party one promoting citizens' engagement with democratic politics.

Conclusion

This chapter has argued that political parties serve vital and underappreciated roles in making democracy inclusive of busy citizens. By articulating connections between themselves, their programmatic goals, and social groups, parties organize groups politically. Group members thereby come to understand how politics relates to them and find their place in the otherwise confusing webs of affinity and antagonism that define the politics of any place and time. Parties not only forge connections between themselves and pre-existing groups, but they also can help constitute groups and constituencies in the first place. They can do this both through intensive mobilization efforts, as did Tammany Hall, and through articulating claims and issues. By bringing certain issues forth into the public square, parties can cause groups to form around them.

Parties are also responsible for generating a cognitively tractable information ecosystem for citizens who might otherwise struggle to under-

---

is less of a worry because we are using political knowledge as a proxy for being cognitively engaged with the politics of one's place and time. We can therefore use cross-national comparisons of "information levels" with fewer concerns than those who are actually interested in comparative amounts of information per se because we are only interested in what they reveal about citizens' cognitive engagement with politics. Moreover, most of the cited studies use *identical* questions across regime types (Gordon and Segura 1997; Berggren 2001; Fraile 2013). For instance, both Gordon and Segura and Berggren use data in which citizens everywhere were asked to gauge the left-right placement of the political parties and compared this with the "correct" placement of population averages and the average of country experts.

stand what is happening and what the stakes are of political conflict. Their competition constitutes and divides up the ground of political competition in ways that citizens can understand, and then use to guide their own decision-making. In fact, party competition acts as a bulwark against using complexity as a weapon to deter busy citizens from taking part in politics. In addition to this indirect ecological simplification effect, parties also provide information directly to voters, similarly enriching the information ecosystem.

Yet all these mechanisms are only likely to operate when parties are forced to compete. I insist upon the contingency of parties' usefulness to democracy because it helps to make sense of the powerful critique of parties as self-interested cartels. Every party contains the potential of becoming a cartel, but this potential can be kept at bay indefinitely by the pressure of competition. Parties in competition operate according to fundamentally different incentives, and these incentives cause them to serve democracy well in the ways I describe.

The importance of competition required us to consider whether the number of parties matters for the functions I ascribe to parties. I conclude that it does. Two-party competition is systematically likely to be flawed and partial, generating parties that only imperfectly operate as they should for democracy. Multiparty competition seems more likely to generate the effects I suggest are key for parties to advance a democracy for busy people.

CHAPTER SEVEN

Putting Deliberation and Sortition in Their Place

When deliberative democracy first emerged in the 1980s and 1990s, it was largely the idealistic dream of philosophers and normative democratic theorists. Yet it wasn't long until institutional reformers were self-consciously attempting to put deliberative democracy into practice. After much experimentation, the favored form has largely settled upon what Archon Fung (2003) calls "deliberative mini-publics," or small, ideally randomly selected groups of ordinary citizens convened to deliberate on some problem or issue, usually with input from experts. A 2020 OECD report, suggestively subtitled "Catching the Deliberative Wave," counts 289 such mini-publics between 1986 and 2019 across the world. The original trickle of scholarly work by philosophers and democratic theorists on the idea has become a tidal wave, now including political scientists, political psychologists, and scholars of political communication, among others. It is perhaps not saying too much that deliberative mini-publics, in one form or another, have conquered the imagination of those who today dream of a more perfect democracy.

In this chapter, I am interested in what contributions deliberative mini-publics can make to a democracy for busy people. I argue that they cannot be mass-scale aids to the cultivation of stand-by citizenship without crippling the institutions that make democratic citizenship tractable for most citizens: namely, elections and political parties. There is a drastic trade-off here between deliberation and sortition on one hand, and inclusion on the other. This trade-off should come as something of a surprise to theorists who have come to see mini-publics as a way to increase the inclusivity of government.

The basic argument is as follows. Though mini-publics seem to be able to cultivate stand-by citizenship for those who participate in them, they cannot do so for the mass public through their deployment at the national or state level. To do so at mass scale, they would have to be multiplied enormously for citizens to have a decent chance of being selected. Multiplying the number of mini-publics, though, would require a more thorough renovation of democratic institutions than most imagine; doing so would require going far beyond the most successful examples to date. Most importantly, multiplying mini-publics would almost certainly involve displacing elections and political parties as the cardinal institutions of democracy. Yet this would hobble the institutions that currently do the most to reach citizens where they are and make politics cognitively tractable. These tasks are, as we have seen, the core needs of a democracy for busy people. I conclude then that mini-publics are not likely to be a major element in a democracy that empowers ordinary people equally.

Before beginning the argument, I must clarify a couple of things. First, I treat deliberation and sortition together, and this requires some explanation. Sortition, or lottocracy, refers to the filling of offices by lot or random selection. Its recent recovery in democratic theory has little directly to do with deliberation, but rather stems from imaginative exploration of the democratic past, particularly ancient Athens (Hansen 1999). Advocates point to sortition's fairness and its ability to circumvent elite domination of other avenues to political power, among other things. Yet by far its most prominent institutional deployment today is in the selection of those who would attend deliberative forums. Here sortition promises to select a representative group, one that reflects the diversity of the population. Though we can no doubt imagine other applications of sortition, such as for executive offices, such proposals have been rare, and experiments doing so basically nonexistent. I therefore take sortition for all intents and purposes as an integral part of deliberative institutions.

Recall also that there are three indicators of stand-by citizenship: political interest, political knowledge, and turnout. I shall use these to gauge mini-publics' ability to cultivate stand-by citizenship. Though there are certainly other services institutions can provide to a democracy for busy people, cultivating stand-by citizenship is the first one I consider for mini-publics because of widespread claims that deliberation can durably transform the civic habits and attitudes of participants. These claims suggest that mini-publics might be able to do the hard work of bringing impermissibly apathetic citizens into political awareness, just as political parties in competition have done.

Deliberative Participation and Stand-By Citizenship

We shall see in this section that there is good reason to think that deliberative mini-publics have the ability to induce stand-by citizenship among those who participate in them. Yet we shall also see that this power seems not to extend to inspiring it among nonparticipant citizens. This drastically limits the utility of mini-publics for promoting stand-by citizenship at the level required by putting inclusion first and the other design principles discussed in chapter 5.

In supporting these claims, I draw upon existing empirical evidence and analyses of deliberative institutions and offer secondary analysis of some of it. I also offer an original statistical analysis of data from Canada in attempting to detect the indirect effects of deliberative mini-publics on the wider public. Together, this evidence suggests that deliberative mini-publics can only cultivate stand-by citizenship in ways compatible with putting inclusion first if everyone is afforded the opportunity to participate in one. This sets the stage for the next section, where we explore the implications of redesigning democracy in that direction.

There are some important caveats about this evidence, however. Despite hundreds of deliberative mini-publics and their being the subject of often intense contemporaneous scholarly study, there remain significant limitations regarding what we know about their effects on participants and on the wider public. One recent review found sixty studies presenting empirical research on the spillover effects of deliberation on participants and the wider public and concludes that the evidence "remains tentative because the relevant body of empirical evidence is still small" (Van der Does and Jacquet, forthcoming). This relatively small reservoir of evidence exacerbates three further challenges with the evidence. First, few studies have sought to document the long-term effects of deliberative participation. Rather, they tend to assess effects immediately after participation, or at most a few days afterward. There are very few follow-ups weeks or months later, making it difficult to speak confidently of lasting effects. Second, the evidence only rarely comes from experiments, where control groups allow us to control for extraneous environmental effects and make reliable inferences about the causal effect of deliberation. This is especially important when deliberative mini-publics occur in the context of electoral or referendum campaigns, wherein media coverage, informal discussion, or other ordinary influences may affect participants beyond the deliberation. Finally, relatively few studies are concerned with the variables I center as indicators of stand-by citizenship, particularly those of political interest and turnout. There is nonetheless some evidence that avoids these defects—by including long-term evidence, control or quasi-control groups, and evidence on political knowledge, interest, or turnout—and it is from these studies that I draw in what follows.

The strongest evidence consistent with these requirements for deliberation's promotion of stand-by citizenship comes from civil and criminal juries. Although juries are not always thought of as deliberative mini-publics, they should be. Not only do they involve the sort of face-to-face discussion that deliberative theorists emphasize, but they do so with a proximate authoritative decision in mind. This is significant because some theorists only count discussions oriented toward a decision as deliberation, as opposed to more general political talk (Thompson 2008, 502). Yet jury deliberation qualifies by even this narrow standard.

Juries are an excellent place to look for the effects of deliberation because participation on them is legally mandated and based on the voter roll. This means that jurors constitute a wide and largely representative population compared to the heavily self-selected groups that fill many other kinds of deliberative forums.

In a series of studies, John Gastil and various coauthors have found that jurors who don't usually vote and who engage in jury deliberations are 4 to 7 percent more likely to vote afterward (Gastil, Deess, and Weiser 2002; Gastil et al. 2008, 359). We can see that this is a substantively large effect if we compare it to that of other institutions' effect on turnout. On the lower end of the estimate, the deliberation effect is larger than that of having a unicameral legislature or having nationally competitive electoral districts, both of which increase turnout on the order of 2 or 3 percent (Jackman 1987). The higher end of the estimate of deliberation's effect, 7 percent, compares favorably to that of the single most powerful institution that promotes turnout, mandatory voting, the most conservative estimates of which are on the order of 7 percent as well (Jackman 2001).

Interestingly, the effect seems to apply only to non-habitual voters, as judged by their voting record prior to jury service. This is exactly what we would expect to find if critical attention were indeed the habit of mind described in chapter 4, since people who vote are already oriented toward the political realm, whereas nonvoters are not and need an external impetus to come to an interest in politics. It appears that deliberating on a jury provides that impetus, at least for some participants.[1]

Other evidence for deliberative mini-publics promoting stand-by citizenship among participants comes from James Fishkin and Robert Luskin and draws from their extensive experience with deliberative polling. Deliberative polls invite a representative sample of the population to spend a few days consulting with experts and deliberating with other citizens about a preselected political issue. Most of the evidence gathered in the course of deliberative polling is oriented toward showing that deliberation changes the substantive opinions of participants and that the participants are representative of the population as a whole. But Fishkin and Luskin have also sometimes accumulated information about political knowledge and political interest among both participants *and* nonparticipants, offering quasi-control groups for our variables of concern.

Regarding political interest, the best evidence comes from the National Issues Convention deliberative poll (NIC), held during election season in 1996 in the United States, and the deliberative poll on the Australian Constitutional Referendum of 1999. Participants in the NIC showed substantial and statistically significant increases in their levels of political interest when re-interviewed ten months after the event (Luskin and Fishkin 2002, 13). The increase amounted to 0.2 on a 4-point scale, moving participants about 5 percent of the scale from their pre-participation level. There is also evidence that participants were significantly more likely to participate in politics in a variety of ways after taking part in the deliberation (Luskin and Fishkin 2002, 7). As mentioned above, these data are important because they are among the only rigorous measurements we have of the effect of mini-public participation on political interest in the medium to long term even today.

There are however two important drawbacks to the NIC data. First, it is not clear that deliberation was the cause of the boost in political interest since there was no control group with whom we could compare the

---

1. One might question these findings on the grounds that it might not have been deliberation that caused the change but some other feature of the experience. This is unlikely, however, because the authors differentiate between a number of jury experiences — hung jury, deliberated to a verdict, cancelled trial, etc. — and find that the effects are strongest for those who completed substantial deliberation. The effect of jury service on those who were empaneled but did not deliberate was indistinguishable from zero (Gastil et al. 2008, 359).

participants' increase; it is possible that external factors—such as, in both cases, the elections—may have generated a uniform increase among the entire population. Second, the treatment group of participants was subject to substantial self-selection. For although a representative sample on the order of a thousand was *invited* to participate, a much smaller group of just a few hundred actually showed up. This probably makes participants different from those who didn't show up in important ways, particularly in terms of their busyness and political interest. These limitations are why the data from the Australian deliberative poll is helpful.

For the Australian deliberative poll, those from the original group of invitees who did *not* participate were polled on their political interest, among other things, a few weeks after the referendum took place, along with an independently selected random sample of the Australian public. This creates two "quasi-control groups," allowing us to better assess the effect of participation on political interest. What we observe is an increase in political interest among participants that is almost the same magnitude to that of the NIC participants between the beginning and end of deliberation (0.2 on a 4-point scale) (Luskin and Fishkin 2002, 13). A few weeks later, this increase had worn off slightly but even after this decline, it remained significantly higher than among the sample of Australians who hadn't been invited to participate at all.

There was no statistically significant difference in the level of interest of nonparticipant invitees and participants, however. But the nonparticipants are probably not a good comparison group because they were influenced by the mini-public, through being invited to participate. There are indications that merely inviting nonparticipants boosts their levels of political interest, particularly since they were being invited to deliberate in the atmosphere of the novel electoral mechanism of a national referendum, moreover one on the highly salient issue of Australia's relationship to Great Britain and its monarchy. Nonparticipants who were nonetheless invited might therefore actually constitute a second treatment group rather than a quasi-control group. For this reason, the independent random sample probably constitutes a better comparison group to that of the participants. In sum, the increases in political interest among participants are significant and last at least a few weeks, indicating some lasting growth in their cognitive engagement with politics.

Deliberative polls also provide evidence that participation in this kind of mini-public improves performance on knowledge surveys. Much of this evidence is short term, showing that between first contact and the end of a weekend-long deliberation and consultation with experts the level of specific information about the topic of the poll increased (Luskin and Fishkin 1998, 13–15; Luskin et al. 1999, 10–11; Fishkin and Luskin 1999, 29–31; Luskin, Fishkin, and Plane 1999, 6–7; Luskin, Fishkin, and Jowell 2002, 474–76; Fishkin and Luskin 2005, 291). It would be amazing if this experience failed to increase such specific knowledge. What we want, however, is data that these gains were enduring in the medium to long term, several months at least, and that they induced wider information gains as regarding other political issues since only such gains would signal the general cognitive re-orientation toward politics involved in stand-by citizenship.

There is some evidence of months-long duration in knowledge gains from the Danish deliberative poll on the euro, in which information gains on the topic of the euro were retained for at least three months (Andersen and Hansen 2007). Other deliberative polls have shown gains in general political knowledge—not just the specific topic of the deliberation—but these have been in the very short term, immediately after deliberation. On the whole, then, deliberation in information-rich settings like a deliberative poll does increase knowledge, but it remains unclear to what extent we can take that as an indication of increased critical attention and thus stand-by citizenship. The evidence is nonetheless suggestive and hardly trivial.

There is also evidence that deliberation in mini-publics promotes political interest and political knowledge, and so stand-by citizenship, from the experience of participants in citizen assemblies. These mini-publics feature substantial, prolonged deliberation about a major public issue such as redesigning the constitution or electoral system and include the input of experts as well as nonparticipant members of the public. Citizen assemblies generally meet over the better part of a year, making them probably the most intensive deliberative experience of any mini-public.

Participants in the two Canadian and Dutch citizen assemblies were surveyed at several times throughout their service, including before the deliberations began. Compared to their pre-service levels of political interest and knowledge, participants had large, statistically significant increases in both measures. On a regularized scale, the participants' level of interest increased by about 8 percent, and their scores on information surveys increased by nearly 12 percent (Fournier, Van der Kolk, et al. 2011, 115–17). Because of the lengthy duration of the citizens' assembly deliberations—which ran between eight and eleven months—we can probably treat these as medium-term measures of the effect of participation.

There are at least two issues with this evidence that might limit our confidence in it. As with some of the evidence from deliberative polling, there is no control group to which we can compare these effects; the comparisons above are with the assembly's participants before they began the deliberation and after. Likewise, participation was subject to substantial self-selection since participants were generally chosen by lot from among those who attended initial public meetings about the assembly, after being randomly invited from the voter roll. The lack of random assignment and of control groups must temper our confidence in the results because the effects of deliberation might be different between those with enough initial political interest to accept an invitation to participate. But this tempering need not extinguish the findings' evidentiary value. The superlative duration and quality of citizens' assembly deliberation lends face validity to these results, since it is difficult to imagine that a year-long process of drafting a referendum about amending the constitution or reforming the electoral law — and deliberating with experts and other citizens about it — would have no lasting effects on its participants.

In sum, and despite the methodological quibbles registered above, there is reasonably good evidence from a variety of mini-publics that deliberative participation does indeed increase turnout, political interest, and to some extent political knowledge among participants. This in turn suggests that deliberative mini-publics can indeed encourage those who directly take part in them to meet the minimum standard of stand-by citizenship.

Yet mini-publics are by their nature small institutions with few participants compared to the size of any polity. Most mini-publics accommodate just a few dozen participants, while the largest ones have included a few thousand. When compared to the population of a modern polity, mini-publics thus only ever directly reach an infinitesimally small minority, at least so far. I return to alternatives in the next section.

In light of the limited scale of mini-publics, we want to know whether they can inspire engagement not just from participants, but from members of the wider public (Jacquet and Van der Does 2021; Van der Does and Jacquet, forthcoming). Do mini-publics have spillover effects sparking stand-by citizenship among nonparticipants? In addressing this question, I offer an original analysis rather than recourse to existing analyses, contributing to the kind of study recently called for by Vincent Jacquet and Ramon van der Does (Jacquet and Van der Does 2021; Van der Does and Jacquet, forthcoming).

It may seem odd to some to think that mini-publics could affect nonparticipants at all, but the mechanism for doing so is not especially mysterious. Media coverage and informal discussion of the citizens assemblies can serve to publicize new ways to be democratic and to exercise

TABLE 2 **Effects of citizens' assemblies on indicators of stand-by citizenship in Canada**

	Turnout	Knowledge	Interest
2006*	Null effect	[No data]	Null effect
2008	Null effect	[No data]	Null effect
2011	Null effect	Significant negative effect	Significant positive effect
2015	Null effect	Significant positive effect	Null effect

*2006 analysis includes British Columbia only; Ontario's assembly had not yet occurred.

democratic citizenship. Awareness of citizens assemblies could kindle the political imaginations of those who dislike conventional politics and participation by concretely showing them how democracy can be done differently. In expanding the democratic imaginations of citizens who may not normally engage with politics, mini-publics could convert them to regular political engagement, and so to stand-by citizenship.

In seeking to test this mechanism, I turned to Canada. Two Canadian provinces held high profile citizens assemblies in the first decade of the twenty-first century: British Columbia in 2004 and Ontario in 2006–2007. I analyzed survey data from the Canadian Election Study (CES) — a large, high-quality academic survey of Canadians conducted during election years since 1965 (Blais et al. 2012; Fournier, Cutler, et al. 2011; Fournier et al. 2015) — from the years 2006 to 2015 to seek any indication of differential performance on turnout, political interest, and political knowledge between these two provinces and those that did not hold citizen assemblies.

Table 2 reports the results of ten multivariate ordinary least squares (OLS) regressions using the CES data (see appendix for complete results). After controlling for standard demographic variables (education, income, gender, age), I found mixed to null results. There was never a statistically significant effect on turnout, and only in 2011 was there a significant effect on political interest. All other tested years (seven of eight) showed null results. Political knowledge could not be tested in 2006 or 2008 due to data unavailability, but I found a significantly negative effect on knowledge in 2011 and a significant positive effect in 2015. Overall, these data do not suggest that holding a citizens' assembly like the Canadian ones has spill-over effects to the mass public.

There are serious limitations to this analysis. First, it is possible that there is an effect that is simply too small to be detected using these analytical tools. Experimental designs are better for detecting the small effect sizes we would expect with a mechanism as indirect as the one I tested. Second, there might be heterogeneous effects that this analysis cannot test. For instance, many residents of British Columbia—roughly 40 percent—reported not knowing anything at all about the citizens' assembly (Cutler et al. 2004, 174). These citizens could not have their imaginations sparked by something they had no knowledge of. Thus, it could be that there was an effect, but that it was exclusively found among those who knew something about the assemblies, and not among those who knew nothing about them. Such an effect might be undetectable without differentiating these groups, but unfortunately the CES data does not allow us to test this possibility.

Bearing these limitations in mind, we have seen here no evidence of a spillover effect on the mass public from holding a citizens' assembly. This result is in line with the meta-analyses by Jacquet and Van der Does of existing empirical studies of mini-publics, which do not find robust spillover effects of this kind (Jacquet and Van der Does 2021; Van der Does and Jacquet, forthcoming). It is of course possible that other designs in other countries might have a different outcome; for instance, the success of the Irish citizen assemblies in actually changing major laws in that country may be a promising case (Elkink et al. 2017; Farrell and Suiter 2019). For the time being, however, we cannot assume that deliberative mini-publics—virtually all of which have a much lower public profile than these citizen assemblies—would inspire stand-by citizenship among anyone beyond participants. I conclude that mini-publics can cultivate stand-by citizenship among participants but not among nonparticipant co-citizens. What role, then, can they play in a democracy for busy people?

Open Democracy or Inclusive Democracy?

If deliberative mini-publics can build stand-by citizenship among participants but not nonparticipants, and if cultivating stand-by citizenship is an important part of building a democracy for busy people as I have argued it is, a solution naturally presents itself: multiply mini-publics to the point that everyone has a real chance to be a part of one. Then the power of deliberation might reach everyone. Yet we shall see that this seemingly simple idea threatens to undermine the core institutions making democracy an ordinary part of people's lives, thus dealing a catastrophic blow to democratic inclusion.

For the sake of argument, I largely set aside concerns about whether citizens who are randomly invited to participate would accept such invitations in ways that disadvantage busy citizens. Though I am concerned that busy people would be less available for such service, even if childcare and payment is provided, I shall not press the point here. This is mostly because I think making service on mini-publics mandatory, as with jury service, is a powerful solution to this concern and I do not want to get bogged down on this point. I also recognize the underappreciated power of invitation as a tool for political mobilization. One of the most striking conclusions of Verba, Schlozman, and Brady's (1995) classic analysis of why Americans fail to participate in politics is because nobody asked them. They conclude that reaching out to people where they are and inviting them to participate in political activity can be a powerful stimulant to lasting participation, even among the most politically disengaged citizens. I take Verba et al.'s insights on the power of invitation as an important but often neglected reason to think more people would be willing to accept invitations to participate in deliberative mini-publics than we might otherwise think. There are, finally, ways of designing mini-publics that can in fact reverse the traditional patterns of participatory bias, as Michael Neblo and coauthors have found, such as by mediating the deliberation through online forums, rather than holding them in person (Neblo, Esterling, and Lazer 2018, 63). Such models are very much in keeping with the institutional design principles collected in chapter 5, particularly those of making participation undemanding and reaching citizens where they are.

All that being said, we are still left with the proposal of vastly expanding the number of mini-publics to counter their otherwise limited reach in promoting stand-by citizenship. The practical problem arising from this suggestion that I want to focus on regards what to do with the outputs of these bodies.[2] Assuming that we build out a host of mini-publics, the result will be, at minimum, that these mini-publics issue forth recommendations, plans, opinions, and decisions regarding policy questions. What are we going to do with this veritable tidal wave of outputs?

I am purposefully eliding many questions of institutional design here in order to focus on what I think is the central issue when we center inclusion and democratic equality in our thinking about democratic institutions. This is because we face a stark choice with these outputs; they can either feed *authoritatively* into the rest of the political process—such as by requiring parliamentary action, triggering referenda on their propos-

---

2. There are other important objections, such as those from Lafont and Pevnick and Landa (Lafont 2019; Landa and Pevnick 2021).

als, or directly enacting policy—or they can be merely *advisory*, providing informative input into—but without authoritative standing within—formal political processes. Here advocates of deliberative reform run into a dilemma.

One horn of the dilemma comes from making outputs merely advisory, whereby mini-publics debate public issues but have no authoritative connection to wider political institutions like elections, nor provide influential input to more formal decision-making bodies like legislatures or bureaucracies. The main problem here is not directly that advisory mini-publics are pointless, since examples like the Oregon Citizens Initiative Review panels show that advisory mini-publics can, when integrated with elections, enrich the democratic information environment (Gastil and Knobloch 2020, 125–42). The issue from the perspective of promoting stand-by citizenship is that participation in more purely advisory bodies will seem pointless *to many participants*, creating motivational problems for citizens expected to take part in them and potentially damaging the cultivating effects we aim for. If the deliberation doesn't really matter, and if participation is not mandated, who will choose to participate in them? Voluntary participation in these circumstances will likely replicate the immense self-selection problems documented in chapter 3's discussion of the paradox of empowerment, privileging the wealthier and better educated as in the Canadian and Dutch citizen assemblies (James 2008, 112; Fournier, Van der Kolk, et al. 2011, 55).[3]

Making participation mandatory in a merely advisory mini-public, however, might undermine deliberation's quality, and so its ability to cultivate stand-by citizenship, as unwilling participants view participation as a meaningless chore, and thus fail to evince the requisite collaborative spirit. Deliberation requires a carefully maintained atmosphere of mutual respect, civility, and staying on topic, among other things, and compelled participation could harm this atmosphere by gathering disgruntled spoilers who resent the imposition. A mandatory process that is purely advisory might, in other words, spark psychological reactance, whereby people manifest opposition to and resentment against perceived limitations of their choices (Brehm and Brehm 1981). We might expect this reactance to, in particular, blunt the stand-by-citizenship-cultivating effects of deliberation

---

3. Landemore seeks to defend the democratic credentials of self-selection (Landemore 2020, 93–7), yet I remain unconvinced that her response adequately answers the powerful consensus that it matters immensely who is present in decision-making processes (Sanders 1997; Phillips 1998; Young 2000).

canvassed in the last section, which for us is primary.[4] With the exception of jury service—which is of course not merely advisory—all of that evidence came from mini-publics with voluntary participation. We have *no evidence whatsoever* about the effects of mandatory service on an advisory mini-public. This point bears emphasis: we know *nothing* about the effect of legally requiring people to participate on an advisory, non-authoritative mini-public. Such designs have not been tried, and it is not clear that the infringement of liberty involved could be justified (Landa and Pevnick 2021, 57).

Jury service, which otherwise closely resembles a mini-public with mandatory participation, is fundamentally different from participation on an advisory mini-public, since juries determine *authoritatively* the fate of plaintiffs and defendants. Imagine how different the conduct of juries might often be if all the jurors knew that they had been taken away from their ordinary lives—technically under threat of fine and imprisonment— just to render a verdict that judges could ignore entirely as they please. The seriousness of making an authoritative decision can have a disciplining effect on jurors and their deliberations, as anyone who has taken part in one can attest. Thus, mandatory participation may solve the problem of biased self-selection, but only at the cost of taking us into uncharted waters where we know nothing of its likely effects.

The other horn of the dilemma stems from making the outputs of a huge array of mini-publics an authoritative part of ordinary political processes. When mini-publics' decisions make policy—or when their proposals must be voted on by the electorate in a referendum or debated by the legislature—mini-public participation looks a lot more like service on a jury and would more systematically avoid the concerns just discussed. Yet it would also require a wholesale redesign and rethinking of democratic government itself.

Hélène Landemore (2020) has recently undertaken just such a rethinking of democracy in her theory of "open democracy." Landemore is cen-

---

4. Jon Elster (1986, 120–7) has argued that one cannot justify institutions on the basis of their side effects because doing so is motivationally self-defeating. This is not, however, an issue with deliberative mini-publics convened with a concrete purpose or question in mind, since that purpose provides the motive for the participants. If we take up the perspective of institutional designers, we can then use side effects of that participation to justify the institution, so long as there is another freestanding justification for it that is accessible to participants and not premised on side effects. Deliberative theory surely has surfeit of such justifications (Cohen 1997; Gutmann and Thompson 1996).

trally concerned with what she sees as the oligarchic or aristocratic bias of elections, following Manin. On her account, elections render political power the exclusive property of an elite who have shown themselves in recent years to be systemically unresponsive and irresponsible. Open democracy is intended to formally open up power to ordinary citizens, who come to exercise it through randomly selected deliberative institutions.

Open democracy thus decenters elections in democracy in favor of deliberative mini-publics. Though Landemore is careful not to rule electoral institutions out of her model, it is clear they must surrender their central place in all existing democratic regimes for open democracy to flourish. This includes not only elections themselves, but also closely affiliated institutions—most importantly, political parties. Landemore is strikingly indifferent to the survival of political parties in open democracy (Landemore 2020, 145–49). She seems instead to favor "transitory, fluid, and self-reconfiguring associations of citizens" or "spontaneous ad hoc alliances" rather than stable party institutions (Landemore 2020, 147–48). Yet nowhere does Landemore grapple with the cognitive challenge that parties—and the wider political information ecosystem they help constitute—assist ordinary citizens in meeting.

Politics is complex and ordinary citizens need help to navigate it, particularly those with little time or interest to devote to politics. Making politics cognitively tractable is therefore one of the most important, and least discussed, tasks for making democracy truly inclusive. This is the core function of political parties in competition; their competition for political support results in clarifying political choices and their stakes, as well as simplifying and filtering the options citizens face, as I emphasized in chapter 6. Media coverage of their competition and their own efforts to reach supporters spreads these simplified understandings to citizens, who thereby receive political information that has been contextualized for them. In so doing, choices are given meaning, rather than citizens needing to independently supply it at their own expense. In this way, party competition makes the choices citizens face comprehensible and renders democratic citizenship itself tractable for them.

Landemore does not reckon with this vital function of parties in democratic systems, yet it is of utmost importance to any project of replacing electoral democracy with deliberative mini-publics. If we want democratic politics to be even minimally approachable for ordinary citizens who do not or cannot devote all their time to politics, we must conserve the institutions that stabilize and order political competition and choice. A world of ever-shifting spontaneous associations of citizens pursuing atomized decisions sounds attractive insofar as it promises that issues receive individualized consideration, rather than being wrapped up in comprehensive ideological conflict between parties. Yet to those entering politics for the first time or returning to it after time spent attending to other parts of life, such ever-shifting ground promises befuddlement and confusion, as familiar polestars move or disappear. It drastically raises the cost of being even minimal stand-by citizens, since the difficulty of tracking many, many independent issues is immense when they have not been stably forged together via coalitional politics. Displacing the structural helpmates of democratic choice results in the mystification of politics and promises the demobilization of vast swathes of the population who simply cannot keep up with politics' burdens while also giving other parts of their lives appropriate care and attention.

This brings us back to the dilemma. Here we find at last the point of its other horn: multiplying mini-publics and making them authoritative would almost certainly mean eviscerating the epistemic ecosystem generated by elections and parties, rendering politics a huge buzzing confusion that is cognitively intractable for most citizens, particularly busy ones. Thus, the dilemma is that, if we make mini-publics advisory, they will be sterile, unrepresentative, or spoiled, and if we make them authoritative, we will cripple the epistemic substructure of an intelligible democratic politics, with devastating results for democratic inclusion. I argue that if we put inclusion first, we will probably want to seek other ways to improve democracy. Deliberative mini-publics may have their uses, as I discuss below, but constituting a bulwark of a democracy for busy people is not one of them.

This conclusion might come as something of a surprise since one might think that mini-publics whose few members are selected by sortition would be highly compatible with a democracy for busy people. This is because such institutions seem to economize dramatically on the participatory burdens of citizens. For although those who attend such mini-publics thereby take on a dramatic participatory burden, they are but an infinitesimal share of the population. For all intents and purposes, everyone else is entirely freed from the need to participate.

This reduces the overall social burden of participation, seemingly in line with democracy for busy people, but herein lies the problem. Mini-publics in themselves cut out mass participation and deliberation among the wider public (Chambers 2009). Rather than go through a laborious process of public education and consultation, mini-publics allow for a small group to do all the democratic work for us. This is why Cristina Lafont (2019) criticizes them as objectionable "shortcuts" to truly democratic government, since all of the nonparticipating citizens are expected to blindly defer to their judgment. The way I would put it is that a democracy centered on deliberative mini-publics will involve *less* popular participation than an electoral democracy. Even with many mini-publics, most citizens will not be actively serving on one at any given time. Given the size of modern polities, service might be quite rare, like jury service, occurring at best a few times in a lifetime. Compared to annual elections attended by all citizens via mandatory voting, as I discuss, politics would stand a much worse chance of occupying a regular or enduring place in citizens' lives.

Indeed, another neglected cost of a democracy by mini-public is that it is likely to structurally degrade stand-by citizenship. Randomly selecting citizens to actively participate means that, unless and until their number comes up in the lottery, it is not actually up to citizens whether they step into active citizenship. Government by sortition into mini-publics thereby effectively reduces the number of regular opportunities to participate, and thereby sabotages the fundamental structure of stand-by citizenship. Recall that the core of stand-by citizenship is surveillance of the public realm via critical attention. But this surveillance is oriented toward action. When we are only called upon by our democratic institutions to do anything as citizens when our number comes up in a lottery, we can totally ignore politics at all other times, since we have no ordinary responsibilities—like voting—that require that we keep up to date. What would be the point? It is a perverse possibility that government by mini-public might speed the progress of the privatization of social life, as the public realm becomes one that I do not have *any* regular share in governing, a trend which many democratic theorists understandably lament. Regular voting, in other words, gives us a stake in day-to-day politics in a way that random selection would not.

The Place of Deliberation and Sortition

Even if randomly selected deliberative mini-publics are unlikely to be a mainstay in a democracy that puts inclusion first, this does not mean they are useless. We are, in other words, still left with the question that concluded the first section: What role can deliberative mini-publics play in a democracy for busy people? The last section advanced a negative answer to this question: they are unlikely to serve as the mainstays of any democracy that puts inclusion first, largely because they would undermine the powerfully inclusionary institutions of electoral-representative democracy. This section advances a more positive answer that focuses on one key way that they can aid or improve electoral processes rather than supplant them. The key idea here is that deliberation and sortition's role should be *supplementary* to existing electoral-representative institutions rather than duplicative of them to avoid disabling the inclusion-enhancing functions of parties and elections. This role is best fulfilled, I argue, through integration with the electoral system, particularly direct democracy.

What does it mean for a deliberative mini-public to be integrated with the electoral system? There have been numerous salient examples that can illustrate different ways of doing so. Integration can mean that some portion of the membership of the body is composed of elected officials, as with the Irish Convention on the Constitution (ICC), wherein about a third of the membership were members of the Oireachtas (Irish parliament). Integration could also mean that mini-publics determine the content of referenda, such as by drafting the text that is then voted on by the whole electorate, as happened with the Irish and Canadian citizens assemblies. Another example of electoral integration is where mini-publics review ballot initiatives, or other electoral choices (Gastil 2000, 8), and write recommendations for them that are sent to every voter via the voter pamphlet, as in the Oregon Citizens Initiative Review panels (OCIRs). A final example that has not been tried but arises as a natural combination of the latter two would be a mini-public that drafts or edits the text of ballot initiatives whose topic is chosen by citizens via an adjusted version of the initiative process (Gastil and Richards 2013).[5] Holding a deliberation at the same time as an election, as Fishkin piloted in 1996 (McCombs and Reynolds 1999) and Ackerman and Fishkin (2004) suggest, does not inte-

5. The idea of giving an initiative's proponents the power to amend its text in light of public (or deliberative) input was strongly supported by one California deliberative poll (Fishkin et al. 2015, 1036). According to Fishkin et al., participants were responding to concerns about drafting errors or unintended consequences, though another common worry is that the immense expense of the initiative process has led to it becoming a potent tool for wealthy organized interests (cf. Matsusaka 2004). Although participants in the deliberative poll opposed giving this power to the legislature, the concern that initiatives might be badly written or corruptly motivated could be answered by running the text through a deliberative oversight body.

grate them together in the relevant sense because the deliberation lacks a formal procedural link to the election, and thus can be overlooked or ignored by citizens, activists, and politicians. It may seem that CIRs lack such a procedural connection as well, yet advocates for initiatives often feel strategically pressured to engage them because CIRs' recommendations can affect electoral outcomes due to their penetration into the electorate via the voter pamphlet (Gastil and Knobloch 2020, 111–13). This brings us to a main advantage of electoral integration.

Integration with elections is crucial to deliberative mini-publics achieving mass reach because elections elicit, when properly designed, input from all, and so impose an expectation of participation on all citizens. By "mass reach," I mean that ordinary citizens are at minimum aware of mini-publics. When mini-publics are integrated with elections in any of the ways just discussed, they become relevant not just to those who participate in them, but to voters as well. When mini-publics decide what is being voted on, offer easily accessed advice about what is being voted on, or include elected officials, they become directly useful to the task facing voters. Reflecting over the conclusions reached by mini-publics about electoral choices can help voters to make their own voting decisions. This applies even to elected representatives, both when they serve on mini-publics, as in the Irish case, and at other times, since representatives are often key to enacting mini-publics' decisions (Gastil 2000). Making mini-publics directly relevant to voters' task in mass elections is what *most* extends their reach. We can see this logic in action in some of the most successful mini-publics.

Three of the mini-publics with the greatest success in reaching mass awareness, and in many other regards, are the ICC, the British Columbia Citizens' Assembly (BCCA), and the OCIRs. All of these were electorally integrated in one or more of ways discussed above. The Irish Convention was composed of a mix of politicians and randomly invited citizens who deliberated on several provisions of the Irish Constitution, eventually recommending the legalization of same-sex marriage via referendum, among other things. Awareness of the ICC was high among the Irish, as judged by a knowledge survey composed of four true or false questions. About half (46 percent) were able to answer three or more of the questions correctly, and two of the questions—regarding whether the convention recommended a referendum on marriage equality and whether politicians served on it—were answered correctly by 77 and 67 percent of respondents, respectively (Elkink et al. 2017, 371). BCCA convened 160 citizens to redesign the province's electoral system and had their recommendation voted on in a referendum.[6] In polls leading up to the vote, almost 60 percent of respondents claimed to know something about the citizens' assembly (Cutler et al. 2004, 174). The Oregon CIRs achieved similar results. OCIRs consisted initially of twenty-four-person (now twenty-person) panels that review state ballot initiatives and produce a brief, one page report and recommendation on each, which is then included in the voter pamphlet. Polls show that 40 percent of voters were aware of the panels by the time they submitted their ballots in 2010, the OCIRs' inaugural year, but that number rose to "between 52 and 54 percent in 2012 and 2016" (Gastil and Knobloch 2020, 135).

Though awareness of the OCIRs seems to have plateaued at that level—at a little more than half the electorate—this is nonetheless an impressive number in both an absolute and relative sense, as are those of the ICC and BCCA. In an absolute sense, it means that millions of citizens know about these new innovative institutions. If there is anything at all to the inspiration effect discussed in the first section, reaching such a wide public is a major plus. Relatively speaking, moreover, we usually know nothing about the reach of mini-publics into the awareness of ordinary citizens. There is generally no data on the penetration into popular awareness of mini-publics since there is little reason to think they had any reach beyond their immediate membership.[7] A notable exception to this lack of data illustrates just how much electoral integration seems to boost awareness. Fishkin's NIC, briefly discussed earlier in this chapter, was a very successful non-electorally-integrated mini-public, both in deliberative terms and in terms of its reach. Yet it seems to have reached only a small fraction of the share of the electorate compared to the BCCA or OCIRs. The NIC was built from the ground up as a media event, airing a few segments on national television early in the election season of 1996. It is estimated that some 9.8 million Americans watched some portion of the more than

6. Technically, the BCCA recommendation was voted on in two referenda. The first only narrowly failed to secure the double supermajority requirement imposed by the legislature (60 percent overall, plus a majority in at least 60 percent of province's 79 districts). It was thought this failure was due to there being virtually no effort at public education about the citizens' assembly and its recommendation, so a public outreach campaign was conducted and the proposal put to another vote in 2009, where it was soundly defeated (Fournier, Van der Kolk, et al. 2011).

7. Some might contest the relevance of mass awareness for the assessment of mini-publics since their legitimacy is not linked to mass participation but rather the quality of deliberation and sortition. This may help explain why so few studies seek out this kind of data.

four hours of programming it generated (Rasinski, Bradburn, and Lauen 1999, 161). Yet even this large number was but a tiny sliver of the possible electorate that year—about 5 percent, less than a tenth the reach of the ICC, BCCA or OCIRs.

Because of their electoral connections, the ICC, BCCA and OCIRs were relevant to voters in a way the NIC was not. They determined the questions or advised voters on the questions they were to answer, and so voters had reason to pay attention to them. This is what boosted the reach of these mini-publics so dramatically. When we put inclusion first in the design of democratic institutions, this element of reach is, in a way, a minimum criterion of success. Indeed, it might even be required by a more basic criterion of publicity, insofar as most mini-publics are effectively both opaque and invisible to the wider public. Increasing the reach of these institutions opens the door to their being accepted by the mass public as a valuable piece of the overall democratic tapestry (Parkinson and Mansbridge 2012).

Such popular acceptance of randomly selected mini-publics cannot be taken for granted. Empirical studies of citizen's hypothetical support for different deliberative and sortition-based institutions shows decidedly mixed results (Vandamme et al. 2018; Rojon, Rijken, and Klandermans 2019; Bedock and Pilet 2020, 492; Christensen 2020; Garry et al. 2021). Though this evidence suggests an openness to these institutions, it does not indicate a populace bursting with enthusiasm at the prospect of deliberative or sortition-based reform. Some evidence, moreover, indicates that support goes up as the authority to make binding decisions goes down, suggesting less powerful or merely advisory mini-publics would be seen as more legitimate (Jacquet, Niessen, and Reuchamps 2020; Bedock and Pilet, forthcoming). This, of course, triggers the concerns discussed in the last section about degrading the quality of mini-publics' deliberation and thus their power to cultivate stand-by citizenship.

One possible reason for trepidation about deliberation and sortition among the mass public shows up repeatedly in theorizing about them: the lack of accountability. Randomly selected citizens—in all actual institutions so far attempted as well as in most plans for democratic innovations—are subject to no accountability mechanisms whatsoever for their performance in office. This raises valid concerns that they may engage in self-interested activity, particularly once interested parties—like wealthy and corporate interests—seriously mobilize to influence their (hypothetically) increasingly important deliberative processes (Landa and Pevnick 2021). All this suggests there are likely to be legitimacy gaps in deliberative innovations, at least in the medium term.

Electoral integration may be able to shore up these gaps by unlocking a potent source of legitimacy for deliberative processes. Like it or not, elections convey legitimacy. This is why even authoritarian states hold sham ones. Under the status quo, representative institutions monopolize electoral legitimacy when mini-publics are convened by them with no provisions for referenda on the mini-publics' work. Integrating mini-publics with elections in general—and direct democracy in particular—thereby provides an alternate source of legitimacy for mini-publics, one that may redeem one of the key historical justifications for direct democratic institutions.

In the early twentieth century United States, reformers proposed giving citizens a right to make law directly, via the initiative, as a way to circumvent legislatures that were captured by business interests and to enable popular measures blocked by those interests to become the law of the land (Goebel 2002). Yet it has long been worried that legislation made in this way would be poorly designed and ill-considered, reflecting in particular what we might today call a lack of deliberation. This is because direct democratic elections often lack the rich ecosystem of information shortcuts generated by political parties competing with each other (cf. [Lupia 1994]). Adding deliberative elements to the process can at least partially address these concerns, as there is good evidence that they can help better inform electorates on ballot initiatives (Suiter et al. 2020; Gastil and Knobloch 2020). The specific design matters a great deal here, especially regarding the stage of the process when the mini-public steps in. Should they identify the problems, write initiatives' text, edit the text, or review it for voters (Gastil and Richards 2013, 266–69)? Yet so long as we safeguard ordinary citizens' ability to initiate the process, the check on captured elected officials can function.

Moreover, by combining deliberation and direct democracy, we can thereby strengthen the legitimacy of deliberative mini-publics while at the same time answering a major objection to direct democracy. In this way, we retain and improve the escape valve function of citizen-initiated legislation, which in turn bolsters electoral-representative democracy against precisely the concerns of unaccountability and unresponsiveness that have moved recent advocates of deliberative reform. Direct democracy shorn of concerns about being the tool of the wealthy works much better as a tool for securing responsiveness. In addition, integration with the electoral system answers concerns about the accountability of deliberative mini-publics while retaining deliberation and sortition.

Even in California, where direct democracy finds its most widespread use, it remains a *supplementary* institution to those of electoral-representative democracy. So long as that remains the case when integrating them into a more deliberative direct democracy, the information ecosystem-shredding effects of empowering mini-publics should be largely avoided. I conclude, then, that this is the best place for deliberation and sortition in a democracy for busy people: helping to improve an element of the democratic system that creates a plausible check on electoral-representative institutions without displacing them from their central place. Deliberation and sortition would not thereby reinvent democracy, as their most ardent defenders allege, but rather, in the words of John Gastil and Katherine Knobloch (2020, 141), "fulfill a narrow purpose."

Conclusion

This chapter sought out a place for deliberative mini-publics in a democracy for busy people. I started out by looking for evidence that they could promote stand-by citizenship, in line with long-standing claims that deliberation can cultivate better citizens. The results there were mixed: mini-publics do seem to promote it among participants, but not among the wider public. This pattern might not worry devotees of deliberation, but for those who put inclusion first, it triggers serious concerns.

These concerns were brought to fruition in the dilemma of what do with the outputs of mini-publics that are numerous enough to cultivate stand-by citizenship among a large share of the public. On the one hand, if the outputs of mini-publics are kept advisory, it might undermine the quality of deliberation and so degrade or eliminate the cultivation effect. On the other hand, if the outputs are made binding, the result will be to shred the informational ecosystem generated by parties and elections that helps to make politics cognitively tractable and accessible for ordinary citizens, especially those who are busy. The blow to inclusion of such a course would be severe. There does not therefore seem to be a clear way to take advantage of mini-publics' power to cultivate stand-by citizenship, at least not without doing massive damage to inclusion.

If, however, we view mini-publics as making elections better by integrating them, there might be a role for mini-publics in improving the functioning of direct democracy. There they can help ballot initiatives to either be better written or improve the information of the electorate about them. This can help to maintain a useful check on legislatures that might otherwise be captured and bottle up popular legislation. Pairing direct democracy with mini-publics can, moreover, help to bridge legitimacy gaps that beset freestanding mini-publics. As aids to electoral-representative democracy, then, deliberative mini-publics can be a part of a democracy for busy people.

Too Much Democracy?

*D*emocracy for Busy People* has tried to develop the values, principles, and institutions that would help prevent those with little time for and interest in politics from becoming effectively dominated by more active and engaged citizens. It highlights the problem of unequal busyness, which arises from the fact that in every imaginable future, people's real opportunity to participate in politics is going to vary widely due to variations in interest and life circumstances. The problem is that, without redress, this results in an unacceptable violation of democratic equality through the development of something like an aristocracy of activists. Rather than naturalizing this development as an inevitable result of differing tastes for politics, I have argued that we must take seriously the challenge it presents to core democratic values by developing new ideas and using them to take a fresh look at democratic institutions.

I first searched for the ideas we need to address the problem of unequal busyness by exploring the limits of democratic citizenship—its minimum and its maximum. Throughout, I conceived of citizenship as an office, providing a link between individuals' ethical demands, institutions, and system-level theories of democracy. In investigating the minimum of democratic citizenship, I considered whether apathy in the sense of completely ignoring politics is ever defensible. I argued that it was not, and that democracy demands at least some of citizens' attention at least some of the time. With regard to citizenship's maximum, I argued that democracy does us an injustice when it fails to take our nonpolitical commitments into account in constructing its expectations for citizens. I laid out two moral limits to those expectations, one based on a right to control one's time and the other on the paradox of empowerment, the latter of which turns demanding avenues of participation into ways for advantaged people to gain further political power. Together, the maximum and minimum of what democracy can ask from citizens provided vital guidance for outlining a conception of democratic citizenship optimized to empower busy people.

This conception, stand-by citizenship, defines a maximally inclusive idea of democratic citizenship that puts all citizens into a position to step into active participation when they judge it worthwhile. Inclusion, I argued, should be the first value in a democracy for busy people within a wider ideal of democratic equality. Stand-by citizenship defines what is needed to be included in politics. It consists, in the first instance, in devoting some of one's attention to politics, and subjecting what one sees to reflection. This critical attention is the first component of stand-by citizenship. Its second element is the civic skills necessary for participation, such as embodied information about how to participate. The final element is upward flexibility, which means citizens can do more than simply watch and judge should they so choose. Together, these elements define a conception of citizenship that is as undemanding as possible given democracy's needs and puts all citizens in a position to make real choices regarding their participation in democracy.

These discussions of citizenship's minimum and maximum and of stand-by citizenship yielded a series of principles for the design of democratic institutions. The second part of the book considered three categories of institutions in light of these principles: elections, political parties, and randomly selected deliberative assemblies. Elections were found to have considerable promise for a democracy for busy people due to the (potentially) low costs of participation and immense reach through the social environment. A series of reforms—including simplifying the delegation of authority, reducing the administrative burdens of voting, mandatory voting, and annual elections—could help answer contemporary criticisms of elections as elitist while enhancing their inclusive power. Political parties, I argued, have an enormous capacity to build inclusion and cultivate stand-by citizenship so long as they are forced to compete with each other, particularly in multiparty environments. Many of the most serious pathologies of parties today are, I suggest, a product of segmented or lacking competition, which if remedied could transform the representativeness of elections while also augmenting parties' inclusionary force. A key feature of both elections and parties is that, when well designed, they make democracy cognitively accessible to ordinary citizens by simplifying participation and enriching the information environment.

With respect to deliberative assemblies, the picture was not so bright. Though they can powerfully cultivate stand-by citizenship among participants, there is little evidence they can do so for wider audiences. Their best function is likely to be as helpmates to the institutions of electoral democracy, most promisingly to improve the workings of direct democracy. With this sketch of the whole argument fresh in mind, there are two objections to it that I want to consider before closing with a discussion of the challenges facing democracy from the emerging political economy of attention.

The Rhetoric of Reaction in Democracy for Busy People

Much of this book could be thought to partake of two of the species of reactionary political argument adumbrated by Albert O. Hirschman (1991) in his book, *The Rhetoric of Reaction*. In it, Hirschman spells out three types of arguments that have dominated conservative and reactionary political rhetoric since the French Revolution: the perversity thesis, the futility thesis, and the jeopardy thesis. Two core arguments of this book might be thought to be instances of the perversity and jeopardy theses. The argument that many democratic reforms popular today, particularly those based on deliberation and sortition, are likely to backfire via the paradox of empowerment could fairly be seen as a version of the perversity thesis. That thesis posits that attempts to push society in a certain direction will result in change, but in the opposite direction to that intended by advocates of reform (Hirschman 1991, 11). Since I understand myself as interested in progressive reform to build a more inclusive and egalitarian democracy, this possibility concerns me.

Moreover, my argument that democratic citizenship must be limited lest it encroach on the nonpolitical parts of life from which most of us derive the lion's share of our satisfaction seems to smack of Hirschman's jeopardy thesis. The jeopardy thesis posits that hard-won accomplishments of the past cannot be taken for granted and might be jeopardized by some proposed innovation (Hirschman 1991, 84). One of the key instances of this thesis Hirschman discusses is the old worry that democracy will undermine liberty through some version of the tyranny of the majority. My argument can be seen as exploring this old tension insofar as the nonpolitical parts of life correspond to "liberty," and the demands of citizenship correspond to "democracy." Within this tension, my argument takes the side of liberty. This concerns me since I generally dismiss the worry about majority tyranny as a mere theoretical possibility that is almost never borne out. Modern tyranny is much more often a matter of minorities imposing their will on majorities, as in authoritarianism, colonialism, and imperialism. Even cases like Jim Crow apartheid in the US South are much more complicated institutionally than just "democracy did this," since ambiguously democratic institutions like federalism and the minority-empowering filibuster often play central roles.

Am I thus arguing that progress will backfire, and so should not be attempted? That democracy must be limited for the sake of liberty? These are not at all my views. As I mentioned in chapter 1, I feel the thrill of invention in studying democratic innovations. Their novelty has fired my imagination and driven me to explore the democratized futures they promise. That thrill is why this book exists.

It is nonetheless the case that misguided reforms can, in fact, discredit not just specific reforms that fail, but the project of reform in general. The resources for reform—above all political organization for it and popular interest in it—are finite and easily dissipated, so misguided projects must be identified before too many resources are wasted. I want democratic regimes to avoid reforms that would serve to lock in the power of activist elites at the expense of busy citizens. That is my agenda. What makes the rhetoric of reaction explored by Hirschman so powerful is precisely that the lines of critique they spell out can be used not just by democracy's enemies out to destroy it, but by its friends to improve it. All I can do is identify myself as one of democracy's friends and hope that the occasional formal similarities of my arguments to those of democracy's critics does not cause the arguments to be ignored.

Dethroning the Active Citizen?

This book champions the busy against the politically active. But does this stance constitute a form of inverted snobbery, or the contempt of those at the bottom of social hierarchies for those at the top (Shklar 1984, 121)? After all, active citizens conform more closely to democracy's ideals, conventionally understood, and this proximity grants them an elevated status among those concerned with politics, as we see in countless homilies to their civic virtue. When we champion the busy, however, we may seem to turn up our noses at these active citizens as busybodies. Championing those who are traditionally seen as falling short of democratic ideals runs counter to established sentiments and calls the value of active citizens' virtue into question. Indeed, it might even be seen as an attempt to transform their virtue into vice, pushing them off their thrones of virtue to be replaced by busy people. Elevating busy people may thus constitute a Nietzschean inversion of democracy's value system, putting the busy and passive at the top of concern rather than the active and engaged (Nietzsche 1967, 36). Yet wouldn't such an inversion leave behind much of what we value about democracy? Haven't the politically involved earned the honor usually afforded them for their dedication?

At least since the emergence of the New Left and its participatory reimagining of democracy in the 1960s and 1970s, those who involve themselves deeply in politics command a kind of civic status above those who do not. Their easy familiarity with the ways of power, questions of the day, and key players set them apart as a distinct kind of elite—a paradoxically democratic one. Their civic virtue in living up to the democratic ideal of the engaged, active citizen is what elevates them. Yet the elevation of any group of citizens above others without institutional checks or authorization is inherently suspect in democracy, rendering the existence of this elite paradoxical. Though of course in principle their civic type of virtue is open to all in ways that the classical and aristocratic virtues were not, we know that it is not in fact open to all on anything like equal terms. This is just to restate the problem of unequal busyness. The civic virtue of good democratic citizens—which makes them better than citizens who lack it— can thus be seen as a currency of inequality concentrated within a social clique defined by a shared interest in politics. In championing the busy, then, I am challenging this implicit democratic hierarchy. This challenge is likely to spark at least discomfort among members of the active civic elite, and perhaps stronger reactions. It is nonetheless the stand I take, as should those likewise concerned with democratic equality and collective self-rule. The thought of my mother, and of the millions like her, allows me to take no other.

Moreover, the concerns highlighted in this book in no way prevent the celebration of active citizenship. Recall that the upward flexibility of stand-by citizenship allows for a clearer account of "political saints" who undertake difficult and arduous service in the political sphere. By articulating a coherent set of minimum expectations for citizens, stand-by citizenship helps us sort out saints from those doing the minimum, as well as both from the people not even doing the minimum. So, although I elevate the busy, this does not mean those who do more cannot be appreciated for doing so. What is needed nonetheless are institutions that allow them to enact their virtue while fencing in their ability to use it to the detriment of the busy. We want institutions that allow civic virtue to be its own reward rather than a means to power, and that is what part II of this book has tried to provide.

The Political Economy of Attention

We are living in an age where information is plentiful and attention is, by comparison, scarce (Simon 1971, 40ff; Williams 2018, 13–14). This reverses an age-old situation of attention being plentiful compared to the information that is available to engage it. The new relative scarcity of attention raises many fundamental questions about the organization of our lives and of our social institutions, including democracy. In closing, I want to highlight a few of these challenges for democratic theory and point out how democracy for busy people has sought to address some of them. Many questions nonetheless remain to be answered and it is an area of investigation that requires (with apologies for the pun) a great deal of additional attention.

Attention being a scarce resource can be framed in at least two distinct ways, each of which raises distinct sets of questions for democratic theory. The first framing emphasizes the *scarceness* of attention. It encourages us to see attention as something that must be rationed, inviting tropes of shortage and consequent questions of proper distribution. To what should we pay our limited stock of attention? What kinds of concerns are important enough to demand it? The second framing focuses on the resource part of attention as a scarce resource, and concerns who *controls* it. This framing follows from resources being classic sources of conflict over who controls them. It encourages us to see attention as something that is under someone's thumb, perhaps ours or perhaps not, raising questions regarding where attention should flow, who should be in control of where it flows, and what kinds of influences may be diverting it from where it properly belongs.

In democratic theory, these two framings invite different kinds of questions. The scarcity framing invites us to ask what kinds of things citizens ought to be paying attention to. We can think about this first within our quotidian politics—should we be paying more attention to climate change or the immediate well-being of the poor? To health care or tax policy?

Should we wage a culture war against celebrity culture for soaking up so much precious attention? We can also inquire about attention's distribution "externally," regarding whether politics itself should receive more attention compared to other concerns in life. We may become concerned, for example, about how the private realm and its concerns can crowd out political and civic concern. We can worry, along with Benjamin Constant (1819 [1988]), about private life dominating people's attention to such an extent that they neglect democratic citizenship. All this can be intensified by the phenomenon of scarcity (and busyness!) that I already mentioned. Poverty can take over so much of one's attention, it may damage their prospects for citizenship (Mullainathan and Shafir 2013).

Democracy for Busy People has focused a great deal on the latter question, suggesting that politics deserves at least a portion of our attention, though we must be careful not to let its just share grow unduly. Robert Talisse (2019) has also warned against a strong, all-pervading politics. He argues that we might "overdo" democracy by allowing it to saturate our social environment such that we can never divert our attention away from politics, cutting us off from nonpolitical ways of relating to each other and so sabotaging social life. Where Talisse has suggested purely social responses to this challenge, I have suggested institutional ones. One way to see my suggested suite of electoral reforms—that simplify the voting task for citizens—is, precisely, as a means to economize on citizens' attention. Mandatory voting too operates in this regard since it eliminates the burden of deciding *whether* to turn out to vote, freeing up attention to focus on *how* one will vote, even if it is a protest vote. Moreover, the entire framework of cognitive scaffolding provided by parties competing in elections can be seen as serving an attention-saving function. Finally, the overall skepticism regarding demanding forms of participation recommended by democracy for busy people helps us to notice and raise doubts about all strategic efforts to mystify and complexify democratic politics. This skepticism can help combat efforts to weaponize the scarcity of attention to insulate the powerful from scrutiny and accountability.

The former question regarding what issues within politics we should be paying attention to also merits consideration. I have argued elsewhere that it can be good for democracy if citizens specialize the issues that they pay attention to, because it can help to constitute discrete specialist publics dedicated to surveilling every issue (Elliott 2020a). Yet this line of argument raises questions of importance—surely there some issues that are so important that everyone should pay attention to them. What might

make an issue important in the first place? Is there an ethics of importance we should consult in choosing how to distribute our attention? Are
there limits to our ability to control our attention that might attenuate
such an ethics? All these questions and more remain open and all but un-
addressed regarding the distribution of attention within democracy.

The framing of attention as an issue about control rather than scarcity
raises a distinct set of questions and challenges for democratic theory. An
obvious question arises almost immediately within this framing: If we are
not in control of our attention, who is? It may sound odd or even implausible that anyone but ourselves would be in control of it. Yet key features and institutions of our present political economy of attention have
diverted control of attention to "attention merchants" (Wu 2016; Williams
2018). Think here of app designers, social media companies, and other
tech giants whose advertising-based business models are premised on
capturing attention at industrial scale. James Williams asks specifically
whether our new internet-connected devices, and the online services they
connect us to, are diverting too much attention from the things we care
about most. He worries that our devices and the apps that populate them
interfere with our fundamental human agency by obstructing our abilities
(1) to do what we want to do, (2) to identify who we want to be, and (3) to
want what we want to want. Our apps and devices rewire the reward centers of our brains—they remake our minds—in ways that make these core
features of agency more difficult.

This redirection of our attention presents existential issues for democracy. Fundamental democratic ideas are premised on assumptions about
attention that the industrial-scale capture of attention calls into doubt.
Democratic accountability, for instance, assumes that citizens pay enough
attention to the doings of representatives and other power holders to hold
them accountable. Consent—problematic as a basis of legitimacy though it
is—also assumes that citizens attend to politics sufficiently to form an intention to consent or not. Both these issues have often been discussed in terms
of informedness—are citizens informed enough to hold officeholders responsible, and what information would be needed to meaningfully consent
to a social contract, or to a policy made via direct democracy? If attention is
being systematically diverted—"harvested" is the word Williams (2018, 87)
uses—then how are democratic citizens going to do any of the things they
must for democracy to subsist?

All three of the concerns Williams highlights regarding individual
agency have democratic equivalents that might also be sabotaged. If citi-

zens' attention is being systematically siphoned by attention merchants, how are citizens going to decide what they want their government to do? Second, how can citizens identify the kind of polity they want if their attention is diverted elsewhere? Third, how can they reflect on whether the policies they want are in fact the ones they ought to want if they are entranced by meticulously engineered distractions? The systematic hijacking of citizens' attention starves democracy of the attention it needs for these essential activities.

Democracy for busy people provides some conceptual resources for approaching these issues of who controls attention. First, it suggests that attention is a specifically *democratic* resource because of the case it makes that democracy demands attention from all citizens. This provides democracy a claim to control that resource, particularly against other sources of demands with no such well-grounded claim. This could help justify democratic efforts to regulate or reform the current political economy governing the flow of attention in society to ensure it receives its share. The institutional reforms I suggested for a democracy for busy people can be seen as doing exactly that, particularly those that seek to cultivate stand-by citizenship. These reforms could be seen as efforts to ensure that at least some attention flows to politics from everyone. Further work might be done in this area regarding media regulation and perhaps public education.

The idea of our lives consisting of a moral economy can help us to think about the deep implications of how our attention is divvied up by connecting our ultimate concerns and conceptions of the good life to much more prosaic concerns of apps, social media, and a more highly mediated social life. Moral economy can, in other words, help stitch together conceptually the different dimensions of agency Williams sees being frayed by the attention capture industry. Moreover, the right to control our time might easily be recast as a right to control our attention. It might thereby supply a normative foundation to push back against all efforts to impress our attention into the service of anyone else. Though I argued that democracy has a strong enough claim on our attention to overcome this entitlement of control, it would be difficult for anything so trivial as advertising to make a similar claim. Nonetheless, as in the case of the scarcity framing, there remain many other questions to be answered and conceptual innovations to be made to fully address who controls the people's attention.

All three sections of this conclusion have addressed in different ways the worry that there is too much democracy: so much that it endangers reform, so much that it displaces the virtuous civic elite, and so much that it dominates our attention. In closing, I want to clearly state my position on whether there can be too much democracy. There is a cottage industry of works in recent years alleging in one way or another that there is too much democracy. I have talked about some of these works in this book. At the same time, there are many who blithely assume maximizing democracy along one dimension or another, in one form or another, is the remedy for all our ills. Interestingly, both those who worry about too much democracy and those who want to maximize it look to replace existing democratic structures with some alternative, thinking either that having too much democracy means we should have less or that we can never have too much. Neither of these is my view. I worry that democracy might be overdone out of a desire to see it survive and flourish. That is my goal, as it is for all true democrats. But like many goals, running blindly toward it may trip us up or land us in a ditch. We must survey the landscape we traverse, taking note of its chasms and swamps. It turns out, we must be wary both of too much democracy and of not having enough of it. Thus, to ask simply whether there is too much democracy is to pose a badly formed question. It is at least as important—and probably more so—to consider whether there is too little. I look, then, to find the right amount of democracy, of the right kind, as should we all.

Acknowledgments

They say success has many parents, but failure is an orphan. Insofar as this book succeeds in any of its aims, it is because of the support and help of many people. I hope that it has the good fortune of some of them laying claim to their influence on it, but its flaws remain my own.

Foremost on the list of creditors is Melissa Schwartzberg, whose tireless support has helped guide my formation as a scholar and teacher, and even as a parent. When I came to her in my first year in graduate school and told her I was going to have a baby, she didn't bat an eye but instead laid out what parenthood at that point in my career meant, and immediately set to work outfitting us with the necessaries of parenthood in a New York City apartment. She has been there for me at every major step of my career, and I doubt I would have been able to manage even one of them without her.

David Johnston played an enormous role in helping shepherd me through graduate school and into my calling as a scholar. His lessons have been foundational to my approach to scholarship. Robert Y. Shapiro has likewise offered his mentorship and help on this and other projects, and in my transition from student to scholar. Andy Sabl has been a mentor of mine since my undergraduate days at UCLA, where he supervised my honors thesis. He has since supported my scholarly ambitions all through my time at Columbia, served as a reader on my dissertation, and helped on the academic job market. Just as he has been a formative presence in my development as a scholar, so too his work and approach to political theory has likewise been formative for this book. I also owe thanks to Rahul Sagar for support in the early stages of this project when it was easy to lose confidence that I could do it. I would also like to thank Simone Chambers, Lisa Disch, and Michael Neblo for their support throughout the period when I was thinking about and writing the book. Support from scholars like them whose work has so influenced me—and whose influence is so apparent in my scholarship—has helped keep me in the game.

I owe an immense debt to Jeffrey Friedman as an interlocutor, editor, and scholar. His tireless work in political epistemology has helped spur the distinctive approach I take throughout this book in focusing again and again on the epistemic dimensions of democratic citizenship and institutions. His support of my career has likewise helped to keep me from losing confidence at crucial moments and enabled me to complete this and other works.

The book has benefited from numerous helpful and challenging comments during the years of its gestation at many conferences. An early draft of chapter 3 received helpful feedback from Michael Neblo and Julie Rose at the Association for Political Theory meeting at the University of Michigan. John McGuire invited me to a conference called "Doing Democracy Differently" where I encountered some very helpful feedback from, among others, John, Jennie Ikuta, Ainsley LeSure, Kevin Duong, and James Muldoon. Thanks are also due to Phil Parvin for convening a conference on the Ethics of Participation at Loughborough University, where I benefited from conversations with all the attendees, particularly Phil, Sarah Birch, and Ben Saunders. I have also benefited from conversations and exchanges at various times with Ashraf Ahmed, Eric Beerbohm, Étienne Brown, Chiara Destri, Sean Ingham, Jeffrey Lenowitz, Julia Maskivker, Tim McCarty, Benjamin McKean, Ben Mueser, Eric Oliver, Zeynep Pamuk, Luise Papcke, Daniel Weinstock, and Fabio Wolkenstein. I'd also like to thank my colleagues at Murray State for their feedback at the department's Research Colloquium, where I presented portions of chapter 3.

Hélène Landemore has been a helpful interlocutor from the incipient stages of this project, and I benefited immensely from conversations with her and from her work. Though we have sometimes reached different conclusions, this book would not be the same without her influence. Conversations with Turku Isiksel during my time at Columbia led to my developing the argument on stability in chapter 2. Jeff Broxmeyer supplied useful pointers to work in the historiography of the Gilded Age political machines that helped me think through their role in expanding democracy, even if I reach somewhat different conclusions from him in this regard. Conversations with Sean W. D. Gray, and engagement with his work on political silence, helped stimulate my thinking about the meaning of political apathy for democracy. Emilee Chapman has been an invaluable interlocutor on mandatory voting and democratic theory more widely. I have benefited so much from conversations with her and from engaging with her work.

James Han Mattson provided vital support during the most active period of the writing process. Trading commiseration and advice with a writer of his caliber helped me keep the faith that something meaningful could be shaped from the pile of words I was accumulating. Ben Schupmann, Brett Meyer, Andreas Avgousti, and Luke MacInnis have been great friends and offered comradely support through grad school and into the process of writing this book. Andy Guess has offered vital help in the last moments of two major projects, including this one.

I also owe thanks to Elizabeth F. Cohen for her help in illuminating for me the obscure business of academic book publishing during the last stages of bringing the book to light, as well as her pathbreaking work on the political value of time. It was she who introduced me to my editor at the University of Chicago Press, Sara Doskow, whose professionalism and efficiency made the review and publication process a breeze. Jacob Levy has been a mentor whose scholarship has influenced how I think about the tasks of political theory, as well as about liberalism and its relationship to democracy. His support has also lent me a lifeline in a difficult period of my career. His influence on my work runs deep, including in the present book.

Thanks also to my wife, Katie Axt, whose support made this book in every way possible. My daughters, Iris and Quincy, have no doubt delayed its publication, but I would not have had it any other way.

Last but by no means least, I want to thank and acknowledge my mother, Deborah Coatsworth, to whom this book is dedicated. In searching my heart for what impelled me to write and persist on this project, I eventually discovered it was her. I could not get over my sense that democratic theory had nothing useful to say about the kind of citizen she was for most of her life — namely, a busy and inattentive one. It seemed wrong to me that a body of thought devoted in part to inclusion and equality was silent about those, like her, who through fate and circumstance had shaped their lives around demands that could not be deferred. For her, being a single parent to me was just such a demand. It turns out that I cannot accept that a just democracy would punish with neglect and marginalization a mother's love.

Appendix

This appendix reports and explains the detailed results of analyses summarized in Table 2. As described in chapter 7, the data are drawn from the Canadian Election Study (CES) series, using the years 2006, 2008, 2011, and 2015 (Blais et al. 2012; Fournier, Cutler, et al. 2011; Fournier et al. 2015). These were the four surveys completed after the initiation of citizens assemblies (CAs) in British Columbia in 2004 and Ontario in 2006–2007. The chief variable of interest was whether a respondent lived in one of these provinces. For the 2006 analysis, only residents of British Columbia were so coded since the Ontario CA had not yet met. Residents of Ontario and British Columbia were coded as "CA Canada" for all other years.

The tables below show the association between the main independent variable of living in a province that held a CA and the dependent variables of turnout, political knowledge, and political interest. Each regression deploys a standard set of demographic control variables: age, education, income, and gender.

For years 2011 and 2015, the control variables were coded as follows. Age was coded into six ascending categories: birth years 1900–1940 = 6, 1941–1950 = 5, 1951–1960 = 4, 1961–1970 = 3, 1971–1980 = 2, 1981–1990 = 1, 1991–1997 = 0. Education was coded into four groups: high school or less = 0, some college = 1, college graduate = 2, and postgraduate degree = 3. Income was coded into five groups: those making $29,999 per year or less = 0, $30,000–$59,999 = 1, $60,000–$89,000 = 2, $90,000–$109,000 = 3, and more than $110,000 = 4. Gender was coded as 0 = female, 1 = male.

For years 2006 and 2008, the control variables were coded as follows. Age was coded by numerical age, ascending from 18 to 97. Income was coded into three terciles: 0, 1, and 2. Education was coded into ten

TABLE 3　**Relationship between living in a citizens'
assembly (CA) province and turnout, by demographic
variable, 2006**

	Coefficient	SE
CA provinces	0.0124	0.0274
Education	0.0099*	0.005
Income	0.0177	0.0125
Gender	0.0378*	0.0189
Age	0.0031***	0.0006
Constant	0.6789***	0.0486
R^2	0.0467	
N	682	

* $p < .05$
** $p < .01$
*** $p < .001$

TABLE 4　**Association between living in a citizens'
assembly (CA) province and turnout, by demographic
variable, 2008**

	Coefficient	SE
CA provinces	−0.0068	0.0139
Education	0.0216***	0.0037
Income	0.0227*	0.0092
Gender	−0.0388**	0.014
Age	0.0041***	0.0004
Constant	0.5538***	0.0344
R^2	0.0586	
N	2,047	

* $p < .05$
** $p < .01$
*** $p < .001$

TABLE 5　**Association between living in a citizens'
assembly (CA) province and turnout, by demographic
variable, 2011**

	Coefficient	SE
CA provinces	0.0005	0.013
Education	0.0284***	0.0067
Income	0.0003**	0.0001
Gender	−0.0093	0.0128
Age	0.0298***	0.0043
Constant	0.7466***	0.0207
R^2	0.0319	
N	2,191	

* $p < .05$
** $p < .01$
*** $p < .001$

TABLE 6 **Relationship between living in a citizens' assembly (CA) province and turnout, by demographic variable, 2015**

	Coefficient	SE
CA provinces	−0.0123	0.0076
Education	0.0224***	0.0042
Income	0.0174***	0.003
Gender	−0.0062	0.0077
Age	0.0227***	0.0024
Constant	0.7788***	0.0139
R^2	0.0336	
N	4,552	

* $p < .05$
** $p < .01$
*** $p < .001$

categories ascending from 0 = did not complete elementary school to 9 = doctoral degree. Gender was coded as 0 = female, 1 = male.

The tables below report the results of ten OLS regressions performed in Stata17. The coefficients reported here are unstandardized. SE in each table stands for standard error.

These first four tables report the relationship between living in a CA province and turnout, as measured by self-report on the CES.

This second set of tables reports the relationship between living in a CA province and political knowledge. Political knowledge in 2015 was measured using four knowledge questions that are all about naming relevant political figures: the federal finance minister, the provincial premier, the governor general, and the Russian president. I constructed a simple additive index for these items ranging from 0 to 4. Each correct answer bumped respondents up one unit in this index. Knowledge was measured in 2011 with the same index, except for the Russian president question, which was not asked, yielding an index between 0 and 3. These knowledge indexes are the dependent variables in tables 7 and 8. Because the knowledge questions were only included in the 2011 and 2015 CES, there are only two tables for this variable.

Notice that the coefficient for CA province is significant in both 2011 and 2015, but in opposite directions. The effect in 2011 is negative, while it is positive in 2015. The similar absolute sizes of these effects in both years made me think the opposite sign might be due to a coding error but numerous checks revealed no evidence that was the case. Moreover,

TABLE 7 **Relationship between living in a citizens' assembly (CA) province and political knowledge, by demographic variable, 2011**

	Coefficient	SE
CA provinces	−0.2221***	0.0378
Education	0.267***	0.0196
Income	0.0011***	0.0003
Gender	0.2142***	0.0371
Age	0.1037***	0.0123
Constant	0.9504***	0.0596
R^2	0.1081	
N	2,713	

* $p < .05$
** $p < .01$
*** $p < .001$

TABLE 8 **Relationship between living in a citizens' assembly (CA) province and political knowledge, by demographic variable, 2015**

	Coefficient	SE
CA provinces	0.2241***	0.0399
Education	0.4165***	0.0217
Income	0.1536***	0.0152
Gender	0.6471***	0.0398
Age	0.1550***	0.0116
Constant	1.0849***	0.0637
R^2	0.1061	
N	9,796	

* $p < .05$
** $p < .01$
*** $p < .001$

TABLE 9 **Relationship between living in a citizens' assembly (CA) province and political interest, by demographic variable, 2006**

	Coefficient	SE
CA provinces	0.1138	0.2538
Education	0.2869***	0.047
Income	0.1706	0.116
Gender	0.9362***	0.178
Age	0.0362***	0.0056
Constant	1.8512***	0.4392
R^2	0.1117	
N	811	

* $p < .05$
** $p < .01$
*** $p < .001$

TABLE 10 **Relationship between living in a citizens' assembly (CA) province and political interest, by demographic variable, 2008**

	Coefficient	SE
CA provinces	0.0761	0.101
Education	0.3580***	0.0264
Income	0.1106	0.0664
Gender	0.5267***	0.1008
Age	0.0341***	0.0031
Constant	1.7555***	0.2431
R^2	0.1066	
N	2,652	

* $p < .05$
** $p < .01$
*** $p < .001$

TABLE 11 **Relationship between living in a citizens' assembly (CA) province and political interest, by demographic variable, 2011**

	Coefficient	SE
CA provinces	0.2187*	0.0974
Education	0.3573***	0.0503
Income	0.0025**	0.0008
Gender	0.4590***	0.0956
Age	0.2971***	0.032
Constant	4.5862***	0.155
R^2	0.0782	
N	2,188	

* $p < .05$
** $p < .01$
*** $p < .001$

TABLE 12 **Relationship between living in a citizens' assembly (CA) province and political interest, by demographic variable, 2015**

	Coefficient	SE
CA provinces	0.0499	0.058
Education	0.4030***	0.0319
Income	0.1602***	0.0225
Gender	0.6173***	0.0581
Age	0.2745***	0.018
Constant	4.1596***	0.1008
R^2	0.0907	
N	6,445	

* $p < .05$
** $p < .01$
*** $p < .001$

coding problems in 2011 would have led to puzzling results for the other 2011 regressions on turnout and political interest, yet those findings have no similar anomalies compared to the other years.

The final set of tables, tables 9–12, reports the relationship between living in a CA province and political interest. Political interest was measured with a single question asking respondents their level of interest in politics on a ten-point scale.

References

Abizadeh, Arash. 2021. "A Recursive Measure of Voting Power with Partial Decisiveness or Efficacy." *Journal of Politics* 39 (4): 31–55.

Achen, Christopher H., and Larry M. Bartels. 2016. *Democracy For Realists: Why Elections Do Not Produce Responsive Government*. Princeton: Princeton University Press.

Ackerman, Bruce, and James S. Fishkin. 2004. *Deliberation Day*. New Haven: Yale University Press.

Agrawal, Arun, and Krishna Gupta. 2005. "Decentralization and Participation: The Governance of Common Pool Resources in Nepal's Terai." *World Development* 33 (7): 1101–14.

Agrawal, Bina. 2001. "Participatory Exclusions, Community Forestry, and Gender: An Analysis for South Asia and a Conceptual Framework." *World Development* 29 (10): 1623–48.

Allen, Ann, and David N. Plank. 2005. "School Board Election Structure and Democratic Representation." *Educational Policy* 19 (3): 510–27.

American National Election Studies. 2021. ANES Time Series Cumulative Data File (data set and documentation). https://electionstudies.org/data-center/anes-time-series-cumulative-data-file/.

Amnå, Erik, and Joakim Ekman. 2014. "Standby Citizens: Diverse Faces of Political Passivity." *European Political Science Review* 6 (2): 261–81.

Andersen, Vibeke Normann, and Kasper M. Hansen. 2007. "How Deliberation Makes Better Citizens: The Danish Deliberative Poll on the Euro." *European Journal of Political Research* 46 (4): 531–56.

Anderson, Elizabeth. 1999. "What is the Point of Equality?" *Ethics* 109 (2): 287–337.

Anderson, Elizabeth. 2017. *Private Government: How Employers Rule Our Lives (and Why We Don't Talk about It)*. Princeton: Princeton University Press.

Anzia, Sarah F. 2014. *Timing and Turnout: How Off-Cycle Elections Favor Organized Groups*. Chicago: Chicago University Press.

Appiah, Kwame Anthony. 2006. *Cosmopolitanism: Ethics in a World of Strangers*. New York: W. W. Norton.

Arendt, Hannah. 1968. *The Origins of Totalitarianism.* New ed. New York: Harcourt.

Bachrach, Peter, and Morton S. Baratz. 1962. "Two Faces of Power." *American Political Science Review* 56 (4): 947–52.

Bagg, Samuel, and Udit Bhatia. 2021. "Intra-party Democracy: A Functionalist Account." *Journal of Political Philosophy* 30 (3): 347–69.

Bajpai, Rochana. 2011. *Debating Difference: Group Rights and Liberal Democracy in India.* New York: Oxford University Press.

Bastani, Aaron. 2019. *Fully Automated Luxury Communism: A Manifesto.* New York: Verso.

Bechtel, Michael M., Dominik Hangartner, and Lukas Schmid. 2015. "Does Compulsory Voting Increase Support for Leftist Policy?" *American Journal of Political Science* 60 (3):752–67.

Bedock, Camille, and Jean-Benoit Pilet. 2020b. "Who Supports Citizens Selected by Lot to be the Main Policymakers? A Study of French Citizens." *Government and Opposition* 56 (3): 485–504.

Bedock, Camille, and Jean-Benoit Pilet. Forthcoming. "Enraged, Engaged, or Both? A Study of the Determinants of Support for Consultative vs. Binding Minipublics." *Representation*, forthcoming. DOI: 10.1080/00344893.2020.1778511.

Beerbohm, Eric. 2012. *In Our Name: The Ethics of Democracy.* Princeton: Princeton University Press.

Berelson, Bernard R., Paul F. Lazarsfeld, and William N. McPhee. 1954. *Voting: A Study of Opinion Formation in a Presidential Campaign.* Chicago: Chicago University Press.

Berger, Ben. 2011. *Attention Deficit Democracy: The Paradox of Civic Engagement.* Princeton: Princeton University Press.

Berggren, Heidi M. 2001. "Institutional Context and Reduction of the Resource Bias in Political Sophistication." *Political Research Quarterly* 54 (3): 531–52.

Berman, Ari. 2015. "How the 2000 Election in Florida Led to a New Wave of Voter Disenfranchisement." *The Nation*, July 28. https://www.thenation.com /article/archive/how-the-2000-election-in-florida-led-to-a-new-wave-of-voter -disenfranchisement/.

Berman, Sheri. 1997. "Civil Society and the Collapse of the Weimar Republic." *World Politics* 49 (3): 401–29.

Bessette, Joseph M. 1994. *The Mild Voice of Reason: Deliberative Democracy and American National Government.* Chicago: University of Chicago Press.

Birch, Sarah. 2009. *Full Participation: A Comparative Study of Compulsory Voting.* New York: United Nations University Press.

Blais, André. 2006. "What Affects Voter Turnout?" *Annual Review of Political Science* 9:111–25.

Blais, André, and Kees Aarts. 2006. "Electoral Systems and Turnout." *Acta Politica* 41:180–96.

Blais, André, Joanna Everitt, Patrick Fournier, Elisabeth Gidengil, and Neil Nevitte. 2012. Canadian Election Study, 2004–2008 (data set). https://ces-eec.arts.ubc.ca /english-section/surveys/.

Blum, Christian, and Christina Isabel Zuber. 2016. "Liquid Democracy: Potentials, Problems, and Perspectives." *Journal of Political Philosophy* 24 (2): 162–82.

Bond, Robert M., Christopher J. Fariss, Jason J. Jones, Adam D. I. Kramer, Cameron Marlow, Jaime E. Settle, and James H. Fowler. 2012. "A 61-Million-Person Experiment in Social Influence and Political Mobilization." *Nature* 489 (7415): 295–98.

Bonica, Adam, Jacob M. Grumbach, Charlotte Hill, and Hakeem Jefferson. 2021. "All-Mail Voting in Colorado Increases Turnout and Reduces Turnout Inequality." *Electoral Studies* 72:102363. DOI: 10.1016/j.electstud.2021.102363.

Botchway, Karl. 2001. "Paradox of Empowerment: Reflections on a Case Study from Northern Ghana." *World Development* 29 (1): 135–53.

Boyd, Richard W. 1986. "Election Calendars and Voter Turnout." *American Politics Quarterly* 14 (1–2): 89–104.

Brehm, Sharon S., and Jack W. Brehm. 1981. *Psychological Reactance: A Theory of Freedom and Control.* New York: Academic Press.

Brennan Center for Justice. 2021. Voting Laws Roundup: March 2021. New York: Brennan Center for Justice.

Brennan, Jason. 2011. *The Ethics of Voting.* Princeton: Princeton University Press.

Brennan, Jason. 2016. *Against Democracy.* Princeton: Princeton University Press.

Brennan, Jason, and Lisa Hill. 2014. *Compulsory Voting: For and Against.* New York: Cambridge University Press.

Broxmeyer, Jeffrey D. 2020. *Electoral Capitalism: The Party System in New York's Gilded Age.* Philadelphia: University of Pennsylvania Press.

Bullock, John G. 2020. "Party Cues." In *The Oxford Handbook of Electoral Persuasion,* edited by Elizabeth Suhay, Bernard Grofman and Alexander H. Trechsel, 129–50. New York: Oxford University Press.

Cain, Bruce E. 2015. *Democracy More or Less: America's Political Reform Quandary.* New York: Cambridge University Press.

Caplan, Bryan. 2007. *The Myth of the Rational Voter: Why Democracies Choose Bad Policies.* Princeton: Princeton University Press.

Carreras, Miguel. 2016. "Compulsory Voting and Political Engagement (Beyond the Ballot Box): A Multilevel Analysis." *Electoral Studies* 43:158–68.

Chambers, Simone. 2009. "Rhetoric and the Public Sphere: Has Deliberative Democracy Abandoned Mass Democracy?" *Political Theory* 37 (3): 323–50.

Chapman, Emilee Booth. 2019. "The Distinctive Value of Elections and the Case for Compulsory Voting." *American Journal of Political Science* 63 (1): 101–12.

Chapman, Emilee Booth. 2022. *Election Day: How We Vote and What It Means for Democracy.* Princeton: Princeton University Press.

Christakis, Nicholas A., and James H. Fowler. 2013. "Social Contagion Theory: Examining Dynamic Social Networks and Human Behavior." *Statistics in Medicine* 32 (4): 556–77.

Christensen, Henrik Serup. 2020. "How Citizens Evaluate Participatory Processes: A Conjoint Analysis." *European Political Science Review* 12 (2): 239–53.

Coates, Ta-Nehisi. 2014. "The Case for Reparations." *The Atlantic*, June. https://www
.theatlantic.com/magazine/archive/2014/06/the-case-for-reparations/361631/.

Cohen, Elizabeth F. 2018. *The Political Value of Time: Citizenship, Duration, and Democratic Justice*. New York: Cambridge University Press.

Cohen, Joshua. 1997. "Deliberation and Democratic Legitimacy." In *Deliberative Democracy: Essays on Reason and Politics*, edited by James Bohman and William Rehg, 67–92. Cambridge, MA: MIT Press.

Cohen, Joshua, and Joel Rogers. 1995. "Secondary Associations and Democratic Governance." In *Associations and Democracy: The Real Utopias Project*, vol. 1, edited by Erik Olin Wright, 7–98. New York: Verso.

Constant, Benjamin. 1819 (1988). "The Liberty of the Ancients Compared with That of the Moderns." In *Political Writings*, edited by Biancamaria Fontana, 307–28. New York: Cambridge University Press.

Cutler, Fred, Richard Johnston, R. Kenneth Carty, Andre Blais, and Patrick Fournier. 2004. "Deliberation, Information, and Trust: the British Columbia Citizens' Assembly as Agenda Setter." In *Designing Deliberative Democracy: The British Columbia Citizens' Assembly*, edited by Mark E. Warren and Hilary Pearse, 166–91. New York: Cambridge University Press.

Dahl, Robert A. 1956 (2006). *A Preface to Democratic Theory*. Expanded ed. Chicago: University of Chicago Press.

Dahl, Robert A. 1961. *Who Governs? Democracy and Power in an American City*. New Haven: Yale University Press.

Delli Carpini, Michael X., and Scott Keeter. 1996. *What Americans Know about Politics and Why It Matters*. New Haven: Yale University Press.

Disch, Lisa. 2011. "Toward a Mobilization Conception of Democratic Representation." *American Political Science Review* 105 (1): 100–114.

Disch, Lisa Jane. 2021. *Making Constituencies: Representation as Mobilization in Mass Democracy*. Chicago: University of Chicago Press.

Doppelt, Jack C., and Ellen Shearer. 1999. *Nonvoters: America's No-Shows*. Thousand Oaks, CA: Sage.

Easton, David. 1965. *A Systems Analysis of Political Life*. New York: Wiley.

Eliasoph, Nina. 1998. *Avoiding Politics: How Americans Produce Apathy in Everyday Life*. New York: Cambridge University Press.

Elkink, Johan A., David M. Farrell, Theresa Reidy, and Jane Suiter. 2017. "Understanding the 2015 Marriage Referendum in Ireland: Context, Campaign, and Conservative Ireland." *Irish Political Studies* 32 (3): 361–81.

Elliott, Kevin J. 2015. "Designing Attentive Democracy: Political Interest and Electoral Institutions." PhD diss., Columbia University.

Elliott, Kevin J. 2017. "Aid for Our Purposes: Mandatory Voting as Precommitment and Nudge." *Journal of Politics* 79 (2): 656–69.

Elliott, Kevin J. 2018a. "Against Democracy." *Contemporary Political Theory* 17 (suppl. 2): 94–97.

Elliott, Kevin J. 2018b. "Making Attentive Citizens: The Ethics of Democratic Engagement, Political Equality, and Social Justice." *Res Publica* 24 (1): 73–91.

Elliott, Kevin J. 2019. "Democracy and the Epistemic Limits of Markets." *Critical Review* 31 (1): 1–25.

Elliott, Kevin J. 2020a. "Democracy's Pin Factory: Issue Specialization, the Division of Cognitive Labor, and Epistemic Performance." *American Journal of Political Science* 64 (2): 385–97.

Elliott, Kevin J. 2020b. "A Family Affair: Populism, Technocracy, and Political Epistemology." *Critical Review* 32 (1–3): 85–102.

Elster, Jon. 1986. "The Market and the Forum: Three Varieties of Political Theory." In *Foundations of Social Choice Theory*, edited by Jon Elster and Aanund Hylland, 103–32. New York: Cambridge University Press.

Engelen, Bart. 2007. "Why Compulsory Voting Can Enhance Democracy." *Acta Politica* 42 (1): 23–39.

Erie, Steven P. 1988. *Rainbow's End: Irish-Americans and the Dilemmas of Urban Machine Politics, 1840–1985*. Berkeley: University of California Press.

Farrell, David M., and Jane Suiter. 2019. *Reimagining Democracy: Lessons in Deliberative Democracy from the Irish Front Line*. Ithaca: Cornell University Press.

Fishkin, James, Thad Kousser, Robert C. Luskin, and Alice Siu. 2015. "Deliberative Agenda Setting: Piloting Reform of Direct Democracy in California." *Perspectives on Politics* 13 (4): 1030–42.

Fishkin, James S. 2009. *When the People Speak: Deliberative Democracy and Public Consultation*. New York: Oxford University Press.

Fishkin, James S., and Robert C. Luskin. 1999. "Bringing Deliberation to the Democratic Dialogue." In *The Poll with a Human Face: The National Issues Convention Experiment in Political Communication*, edited by Maxwell McCombs and Amy Reynolds, 3–38. Mahwah, NJ: Erlbaum.

Fishkin, James S., and Robert C. Luskin. 2005. "Experimenting with a Democratic Ideal: Deliberative Polling and Public Opinion." *Acta Politica* 40 (3): 284–98.

Foner, Eric. 2002. *Reconstruction: America's Unfinished Revolution, 1863–1877*. New York: Harper Perennial.

Fortunato, David, Randolph T. Stevenson, and Greg Vonnahme. 2016. "Context and Political Knowledge: Explaining Cross-National Variation in Partisan Left-Right Knowledge." *Journal of Politics* 78 (4): 1211–28.

Fournier, Patrick, Fred Cutler, Stuart Soroka, and Dietlind Stolle. 2011. The 2011 Canadian Election Study (data set). https://ces-eec.arts.ubc.ca/english-section/surveys/.

Fournier, Patrick, Fred Cutler, Stuart Soroka, and Dietlind Stolle. 2015. The 2015 Canadian Election Study (data set). https://ces-eec.arts.ubc.ca/english-section /surveys/.

Fournier, Patrick, Henk van der Kolk, R. Kenneth Carty, Andre Blais, and Jonathan Rose. 2011. *When Citizens Decide: Lessons from Citizen Assemblies on Electoral Reform*. New York: Oxford University Press.

Fowler, Anthony. 2013. "Electoral and Policy Consequences of Voter Turnout: Evidence from Compulsory Voting in Australia." *Quarterly Journal of Political Science* 8 (2): 159–82.

Fowler, Stephen. 2021. "What Does Georgia's New Voting Law SB 202 Do?" Georgia Public Broadcasting, March 27. https://www.gpb.org/news/2021/03/27/what-does-georgias-new-voting-law-sb-202-do.

Fraile, Marta. 2013. "Do Information-Rich Contexts Reduce Knowledge Inequalities? The Contextual Determinants of Political Knowledge in Europe." *Acta Politica* 48 (2):119–43.

Freiman, Christopher. 2021. *Why It's OK to Ignore Politics.* New York: Routledge.

Fricker, Miranda. 2007. *Epistemic Injustice: Power and the Ethics of Knowing.* New York: Oxford University Press.

Fung, Archon. 2003. "Survey Article: Recipes for Public Spheres: Eight Institutional Design Choices and Their Consequences." *Journal of Political Philosophy* 11 (3): 338–67.

García Bedolla, Lisa, and Melissa R. Michelson. 2012. *Mobilizing Inclusion: Transforming the Electorate through Get-Out-the-Vote Campaigns.* New Haven: Yale University Press.

Garmann, Sebastian. 2017. "Election Frequency, Choice Fatigue, and Voter Turnout." *European Journal of Political Economy* 47 (March):19–35.

Garry, John, James Pow, John Coakley, David Farrell, Brendan O'Leary, and James Tilley. 2021. "The Perception of the Legitimacy of Citizens' Assemblies in Deeply Divided Places? Evidence of Public and Elite Opinion from Consociational Northern Ireland." *Government and Opposition* 57 (3): 532–51.

Gastil, John. 2000. *By Popular Demand: Revitalizing Representative Democracy through Deliberative Elections.* Berkeley: University of California Press.

Gastil, John, E. Pierre Deess, and Phil Weiser. 2002. "Civic Awakening in the Jury Room: A Test of the Connection between Jury Deliberation and Political Participation." *Journal of Politics* 64 (2): 585–95.

Gastil, John, E. Pierre Deess, Phil Weiser, and Jordan Meade. 2008. "Jury Service and Electoral Participation: A Test of the Participation Hypothesis." *Journal of Politics* 70 (2): 351–67.

Gastil, John, and Katherine R. Knobloch. 2020. *Hope for Democracy: How Citizens Can Bring Reason Back into Politics.* New York: Oxford University Press.

Gastil, John, and Robert Richards. 2013. "Making Direct Democracy Deliberative through Random Assemblies." *Politics & Society* 41 (2): 253–81.

Geys, Benny. 2006a. "Explaining Voter Turnout: A Review of Aggregate-Level Research." *Electoral Studies* 25:637–63.

Geys, Benny. 2006b. "'Rational' Theories of Voter Turnout: A Review." *Political Studies Review* 4:16–35.

Goebel, Thomas. 2002. *A Government by the People: Direct Democracy in America, 1890–1940.* Chapel Hill: University of North Carolina Press.

Goodin, Robert E. 2009. "Demandingness as a Virtue." *Journal of Ethics* 13 (1): 1–13.

Goodin, Robert E., and John S. Dryzek. 2006. "Deliberative Impacts: The Macropolitical Uptake of Mini-publics." *Politics & Society* 34 (2): 219–44.

Gordon, Stacy B., and Gary M. Segura. 1997. "Cross-National Variation in the Political Sophistication of Individuals: Capability or Choice?" *Journal of Politics* 59 (1): 126–47.

Gourevitch, Alex. 2015. *From Slavery to the Cooperative Commonwealth: Labor and Republican Liberty in the Nineteenth Century.* New York: Cambridge University Press.

Gray, Sean W. D. 2021. "Silence and Democratic Institutional Design." *Critical Review of International Social and Political Philosophy* 24 (3): 330–45.

Gray, Sean W. D. Forthcoming. "Towards a Democratic Theory of Silence." *Political Studies*, forthcoming. DOI: 10.1177/00323217211043433.

Green, Donald P., and Alan S. Gerber. 2019. *Get Out the Vote: How to Increase Voter Turnout.* 4th ed. Washington, DC: Brookings Institution Press.

Green, Donald P., and Ian Shapiro. 1994. *Pathologies of Rational Choice Theory: A Critique of Applications in Political Science.* New Haven: Yale University Press.

Green, Jeffrey Edward. 2010. *The Eyes of the People: Democracy in an Age of Spectatorship.* New York: Oxford University Press.

Green, Jeffrey Edward. 2016. *The Shadow of Unfairness: A Plebeian Theory of Liberal Democracy.* New York: Oxford University Press.

Grofman, Bernard, and Peter Selb. 2010. "Turnout and the (Effective) Number of Parties at the National and District Levels: A Puzzle-Solving Approach." *Party Politics* 17 (1): 93–117.

Grönland, Kimmo, André Bächtiger, and Maija Setälä, eds. 2014. *Deliberative Mini-publics: Involving Citizens in the Democratic Process.* Colchester, UK: ECPR.

Gruber, Judith, and Edison Trickett. 1987. "Can We Empower Others? The Paradox of Empowerment in the Governing of an Alternative Public School." *American Journal of Community Psychology* 15 (3): 353–71.

Guerrero, Alexander A. 2014. "Against Elections: The Lottocratic Alternative." *Philosophy & Public Affairs* 42 (2): 135–78.

Gutmann, Amy, and Dennis Thompson. 1996. *Democracy and Disagreement.* Cambridge, MA: Belknap.

Hansen, Mogens Herman. 1999. *The Athenian Democracy in the Age of Demosthenes: Structure, Principles, and Ideology.* Translated by J. A. Crook. Norman: University of Oklahoma Press.

Herd, Pamela, and Donald P. Moynihan. 2018. *Administrative Burden: Policymaking by Other Means.* New York: Russell Sage Foundation.

Hersh, Eitan. 2020. *Politics Is for Power: How to Move Beyond Political Hobbyism, Take Action, and Make Real Change.* New York: Scribner.

Herzog, Lisa. 2018. *Reclaiming the System: Moral Responsibility, Divided Labour, and the Role of Organizations in Society*. Oxford: Oxford University Press.

Hibbing, John R., and Elizabeth Theiss-Morse. 2002. *Stealth Democracy: Americans' Beliefs about How Government Should Work*. New York: Cambridge University Press.

Hill, Lisa. 2004. "Compulsory Voting in Australia: A Basis for A 'Best Practice' Regime." *Federal Law Review* 32 (3): 479–97.

Hill, Lisa. 2014. "Compulsory Voting Defended." In *Compulsory Voting: For and Against*, edited by Jason Brennan and Lisa Hill, 109–203. New York: Cambridge University Press.

Hirczy, Wolfgang. 1994. "The Impact of Mandatory Voting Laws on Turnout: A Quasi-Experimental Approach." *Electoral Studies* 13 (1): 64–76.

Hirschhorn, Bernard. 1986. "A Progressive Reformer and Two of His Reforms." *OAH Magazine of History* 1 (3/4): 22–25.

Hirschman, Albert O. 1991. *The Rhetoric of Reaction: Perversity, Futility, Jeopardy*. Cambridge, MA: Belknap.

Huntington, Samuel P. 1975. "The Democratic Distemper." *Public Interest* 41:9–38.

Innerarity, Daniel. 2019. "Democratic Equality: An Egalitarian Defense of Political Mediation." *Constellations* 26 (4): 513–24.

Jackman, Robert W. 1987. "Political Institutions and Voter Turnout in the Industrial Democracies." *American Political Science Review* 81 (2): 405–24.

Jackman, Simon. 2001. Compulsory Voting. In *International Encyclopedia of the Social and Behavioral Sciences*, edited by Neil J. Smelser and Paul B. Baltes. Oxford: Pergamon.

Jacquet, Vincent, Christoph Niessen, and Min Reuchamps. 2020. "Sortition, Its Advocates and Its Critics: An Empirical Analysis of Citizens' and MPs' Support for Random Selection as a Democratic Reform Proposal." *International Political Science Review* 43 (2): 295–316.

Jacquet, Vincent, and Ramon van der Does. 2021. "The Consequences of Deliberative Minipublics: Systematic Overview, Conceptual Gaps, and New Directions." *Representation* 57 (1): 131–41.

James, Michael Rabinder. 2008. "Descriptive Representation in the British Columbia Citizens' Assembly." In *Designing Deliberative Democracy: The British Columbia Citizens' Assembly*, edited by Mark E. Warren and Hilary Pearse, 106–26. New York: Cambridge University Press.

Karp, Jeffrey A., and Susan A. Banducci. 2008. "Political Efficacy and Participation in Twenty-Seven Democracies: How Electoral Systems Shape Political Behaviour." *British Journal of Political Science* 38 (2): 311–34.

Key, V. O., Jr. 1961. *Public Opinion and American Democracy*. New York: Knopf.

Keyssar, Alexander. 2000. *The Right to Vote: The Contested History of Democracy in the United States*. New York: Basic Books.

Klarman, Michael J. 2016. *The Framers' Coup: The Making of the United States Constitution*. New York: Oxford University Press.

Lafont, Cristina. 2019. *Democracy without Shortcuts: A Participatory Conception of Deliberative Democracy*. New York: Oxford University Press.

Landa, Dimitri, and Ryan Pevnick. 2021. "Is Random Selection a Cure for the Ills of Electoral Representation?" *Journal of Political Philosophy* 29 (1): 46–72.

Landemore, Hélène. 2013. *Democratic Reason: Politics, Collective Intelligence, and the Rule of the Many*. Princeton: Princeton University Press.

Landemore, Hélène. 2020. *Open Democracy: Reinventing Popular Rule for the 21st Century*. Princeton: Princeton University Press.

Lessig, Lawrence. 2011. *Republic, Lost: How Money Corrupts Congress—and a Plan to Stop It*. New York: Twelve.

Lever, Annabelle. 2010. "Compulsory Voting: A Critical Perspective." *British Journal of Political Science* 40 (4): 897–915.

Levitsky, Steven, and Daniel Ziblatt. 2018. *How Democracies Die*. New York: Broadway Books.

Lijphart, Arend. 1997. "Unequal Participation: Democracy's Unresolved Dilemma." *American Political Science Review* 91 (1): 1–14.

Lippmann, Walter. 1993. *The Phantom Public*. New Brunswick: Transaction Publishers. Original edition, 1927.

Lockhart, P. R. 2019. "How Shelby County v. Holder Upended Voting Rights in America." *Vox*, June 25. https://www.vox.com/policy-and-politics/2019/6/25/18701277/shelby-county-v-holder-anniversary-voting-rights-suppression-congress.

Loewen, Peter John, Henry Milner, and Bruce M. Hicks. 2008. "Does Compulsory Voting Lead to More Informed and Engaged Citizens? An Experimental Test." *Canadian Journal of Political Science* 41 (3): 655–72.

Lupia, Arthur. 1994. "Shortcuts versus Encyclopedias: Information and Voting Behavior in California Insurance Reform Elections." *American Political Science Review* 88 (1): 63–76.

Lupia, Arthur. 2006. "How Elitism Undermines the Study of Voter Competence." *Critical Review* 18 (1–3): 217–32.

Luskin, Robert C., and James S. Fishkin. 1998. "Deliberative Polling, Public Opinion, and Democracy: The Case of the National Issues Convention." Annual Meeting of the American Political Science Association, Boston, MA, September 2–6.

Luskin, Robert C., and James S. Fishkin. 2002. "Deliberation and 'Better Citizens.'" Annual Joint Sessions of Workshops of the European Consortium for Political Research, Turin, Italy.

Luskin, Robert C., James S. Fishkin, and Roger Jowell. 2002. "Considered Opinions: Deliberative Polling in Britain." *British Journal of Political Science* 32 (3): 455–87.

Luskin, Robert C., James S. Fishkin, Roger Jowell, and Alison Park. 1999. "Learning and Voting in Britain: Insights from the Deliberative Poll." Annual Meeting of the American Political Science Association, Atlanta, GA, September.

Luskin, Robert C., James S. Fishkin, and Dennis L. Plane. 1999. "Deliberative Polling and Policy Outcomes: Electric Utility Issues in Texas." Annual Meeting of the Association for Public Policy Administration and Management, Washington, DC, November 4–7.

Lutz, Donald S. 1979. "The Theory of Consent in the Early State Constitutions." *Publius* 9 (2): 11–42.

Manin, Bernard. 1997. *The Principles of Representative Government*. New York: Cambridge University Press.

Mansbridge, Jane. 2003. "Rethinking Representation." *American Political Science Review* 97 (4): 515–28.

Maskivker, Julia. 2019. *The Duty to Vote*. New York: Oxford University Press.

Matsusaka, John G. 2004. *For the Many or the Few: The Initiative, Public Policy, and American Democracy*. Chicago: University of Chicago Press.

Mazzei, Patricia, and Nick Corasaniti. 2021. "Florida Republicans Pass Voting Limits in Broad Elections Bill." *New York Times*, April 29, 2021. https://www.nytimes.com/2021/04/29/us/politics/florida-voting-rights-bill.html.

McCombs, Maxwell, and Amy Reynolds, eds. 1999. *The Poll with a Human Face: The National Issues Convention Experiment in Political Communication*. Mahwah, NJ: Erlbaum.

McMillen, Neil R. 1994. *The Citizens' Council: Organized Resistance to the Second Reconstruction 1954–64*. Urbana: University of Illinois Press.

Medearis, John. 2015. *Why Democracy Is Oppositional*. Cambridge, MA: Harvard University Press.

Merton, Robert K. 1968. *Social Theory and Social Structure*. Enlarged ed. New York: Free Press.

Mill, John Stuart. 1991. *Considerations on Representative Government*. Amherst, NY: Prometheus Books.

Mueller, Dennis C., and Thomas Stratmann. 2003. "The Economic Effects of Democratic Participation." *Journal of Public Economics* 87 (9–10): 2129–55.

Muirhead, Russell. 2014. *The Promise of Party in a Polarized Age*. Cambridge, MA: Harvard University Press.

Mullainathan, Sendhil, and Eldar Shafir. 2013. *Scarcity: The New Science of Having Less and How It Defines Our Lives*. New York: Picador.

Murphy, Liam B. 2000. *Moral Demands in Nonideal Theory*. New York: Oxford University Press.

Mutz, Diana C. 2006. *Hearing the Other Side: Deliberative versus Participatory Democracy*. New York: Cambridge University Press.

Nagel, Thomas. 1986. *The View from Nowhere*. New York: Oxford University Press.

Neblo, Michael A., Kevin M. Esterling, and David M. J. Lazer. 2018. *Politics with the People: Building a Directly Representative Democracy*. New York: Cambridge University Press.

Neuman, W. Russell. 1986. *The Paradox of Mass Politics: Knowledge and Opinion in the American Electorate*. Cambridge, MA: Harvard University Press.

Nietzsche, Friedrich. 1967. *On the Genealogy of Morals.* Translated by Walter Kaufmann and R. J. Hollingdale. New York: Vintage.

Organization for Economic Cooperation and Development (OECD). 2020. *Innovative Citizen Participation and New Democratic Institutions: Catching the Deliberative Wave.* Paris: OECD.

Okrent, Daniel. 2010. *Last Call: The Rise and Fall of Prohibition.* New York: Scribner.

OpenSecrets. n.d. "Reelection Rates over the Years." Accessed August 2021. https://www.opensecrets.org/elections-overview/reelection-rates.

Page, Scott E. 2007. *The Difference: How the Power of Diversity Create Better Groups, Firms, Schools, and Societies.* Princeton: Princeton University Press.

Parkinson, John, and Jane Mansbridge, eds. 2012. *Deliberative Systems: Deliberative Democracy at the Large Scale.* New York: Cambridge University Press.

Parvin, Phil. 2018. "Democracy without Participation: A New Politics for a Disengaged Era." *Res Publica* 24 (1): 31–52.

Pateman, Carole. 1970. *Participation and Democratic Theory.* New York: Cambridge University Press.

Pettit, Philip. 1997. *Republicanism: A Theory of Freedom and Government.* New York: Oxford University Press.

Phillips, Anne. 1991. *Engendering Democracy.* University Park, PA: Pennsylvania State University Press.

Phillips, Anne. 1998. *The Politics of Presence.* New York: Oxford University Press.

Piven, Frances Fox, and Richard A. Cloward. 1988. *Why Americans Don't Vote.* New York: Pantheon Books.

Poama, Andrei, and Tom Theuns. 2019. "Making Offenders Vote: Democratic Expressivism and Compulsory Criminal Voting." *American Political Science Review* 113 (3): 796–809.

Prior, Markus. 2018. *Hooked: How Politics Captures People's Interest.* New York: Cambridge University Press.

Rallings, C., M. Thrasher, and G. Borisyuk. 2003. "Seasonal Factors, Voter Fatigue and the Costs of Voting." *Electoral Studies* 22 (1): 65–79.

Rasinski, Kenneth A., Norman M. Bradburn, and Douglas Lauen. 1999. "Effects of NIC Media Coverage Among the Public." In *The Poll with a Human Face: The National Issues Convention Experiment in Political Communication,* edited by Maxwell McCombs and Amy Reynolds, 145–65. Mahwah, NJ: Erlbaum.

Research Group Elections eV (Forschungsgruppe Wahlen e.V.). 2017. "Federal Election 2017." Accessed June 2017. https://www.forschungsgruppe.de/Wahlen/Grafiken_zu_aktuellen_Wahlen/Wahlen_2017/Bundestagswahl_2017/.

Rojon, Sebastien, Arieke J. Rijken, and Bert Klandermans. 2019. "A Survey Experiment on Citizens' Preferences for 'Vote-Centric' vs. 'Talk-Centric' Democratic Innovations with Advisory vs. Binding Outcomes." *Politics and Governance* 7 (2): 213–26.

Rosanvallon, Pierre. 2008. *Counter-democracy: Politics in an Age of Distrust*. Translated by Arthur Goldhammer. New York: Cambridge University Press.

Rose, Julie L. 2016. *Free Time*. Princeton: Princeton University Press.

Rosenblum, Nancy L. 2008. *On the Side of the Angels: An Appreciation of Parties and Partisanship*. Princeton: Princeton University Press.

Rosenbluth, Frances McCall, and Ian Shapiro. 2018. *Responsible Parties: Saving Democracy from Itself*. New Haven: Yale University Press.

Sabl, Andrew. 2002. *Ruling Passions: Political Offices and Democratic Ethics*. Princeton: Princeton University Press.

Sabl, Andrew. 2015. "The Two Cultures of Democratic Theory: Responsiveness, Democratic Quality, and the Empirical-Normative Divide." *Perspectives on Politics* 13 (2): 345–65.

Sanders, Lynn M. 1997. "Against Deliberation." *Political Theory* 25 (3): 347–76.

Saunders, Ben. 2010. "Tasting Democracy." *Public Policy Research* 17 (3): 147–51.

Schattschneider, E. E. 1960. *The Semisovereign People: A Realist's View of Democracy in America*. New York: Holt, Rinehart and Winston.

Schattschneider, E. E. 2004. *Party Government: American Government in Action*. New Brunswick, NJ: Transaction.

Scheffler, Samuel. 1992. *Human Morality*. New York: Oxford University Press.

Schlozman, Kay Lehman, Henry E. Brady, and Sidney Verba. 2018. *Unequal and Unrepresented: Political Inequality and the People's Voice in the New Gilded Age*. Princeton: Princeton University Press.

Schumpeter, Joseph A. 1942 (1976). *Capitalism, Socialism and Democracy*. New York: Harper Perennial.

Schwartzberg, Melissa. 2014. *Counting the Many: The Origins and Limits of Supermajority Rule*. New York: Cambridge University Press.

Schwartzberg, Melissa. 2016. "Aristotle and the Judgment of the Many: Equality, Not Collective Quality." *Journal of Politics* 78 (3): 733–45.

Schwartzberg, Melissa. 2018. "Justifying the Jury: Reconciling Justice, Equality, and Democracy." *American Political Science Review* 112 (3): 446–58.

Scudder, Mary F. 2020. "The Ideal of Uptake in Democratic Deliberation." *Political Studies* 68 (2): 504–22.

Selb, Peter, and Romain Lachat. 2009. "The More, the Better? Counterfactual Evidence on the Effect of Compulsory Voting on the Consistency of Party Choice." *European Journal of Political Research* 48:573–97.

Shani, Danielle. 2012. "Measuring Political Interest." In *Improving Public Opinion Surveys: Interdisciplinary Innovation and the American National Election Studies*, edited by John H. Aldrich and Kathleen M. McGraw, 137–57. Princeton: Princeton University Press.

Shelby, Tommie. 2016. *Dark Ghettos: Injustice, Dissent, and Reform*. Cambridge, MA: Belknap.

Sheppard, Jill. 2015. "Compulsory Voting and Political Knowledge: Testing a 'Compelled Engagement' Hypothesis." *Electoral Studies* 40:300–307.

Shineman, Victoria Anne. 2018. "If You Mobilize Them, They Will Become Informed: Experimental Evidence that Information Acquisition is Endogenous to Costs and Incentives to Participate." *British Journal of Political Science* 48 (1): 189–211.

Shklar, Judith N. 1984. *Ordinary Vices*. Cambridge, MA: Belknap.

Shklar, Judith N. 1991. *American Citizenship: The Quest for Inclusion, Tanner Lectures on Human Values*. Cambridge, MA: Harvard University Press.

Simon, Herbert A. 1971. "Designing Organizations for an Information-Rich World." In *Computers, Communications, and the Public Interest*, edited by M. Greenberger. Baltimore: John Hopkins University Press.

Singer, Peter. 2010. *The Life You Can Save: How to Do Your Part to End World Poverty*. New York: Random House.

Singh, Shane P. 2021. *Beyond Turnout: How Compulsory Voting Shapes Citizens and Political Parties*. New York: Oxford University Press.

Singh, Shane P., and Jason Roy. 2018. "Compulsory Voting and Voter Information Seeking." *Research & Politics* 5 (1): 1–8.

Smith, Graham. 2009. *Democratic Innovations: Designing Institutions for Citizen Participation*. New York: Cambridge University Press.

Sniderman, Paul M. 2017. *The Democratic Faith: Essays on Democratic Citizenship*. New Haven: Yale University Press.

Somin, Ilya. 2013. *Democracy and Political Ignorance: Why Smaller Government Is Smarter*. Stanford: Stanford University Press.

Stepan, Alfred. 2001. *Arguing Comparative Politics*. New York: Oxford University Press.

Stout, Jeffrey. 2010. *Blessed Are the Organized: Grassroots Democracy in America*. Princeton: Princeton University Press.

Suiter, Jane, Lala Muradova, John Gastil, and David M. Farrell. 2020. "Scaling Up Deliberation: Testing the Potential of Mini-publics to Enhance the Deliberative Capacity of Citizens." *Swiss Political Science Review* 26 (3): 253–72.

Taagepera, Rein, Peter Selb, and Bernard Grofman. 2014. "How Turnout Depends on the Number of Parties: A Logical Model." *Journal of Elections, Public Opinion and Parties* 24 (4): 393–413.

Talisse, Robert B. 2019. *Overdoing Democracy: Why We Must Put Politics in Its Place*. New York: Oxford University Press.

Taylor, Steven L., Matthew S. Shugart, Arend Lijphart, and Bernard Grofman. 2015. *A Different Democracy: American Government in a Thirty-One-Country Perspective*. New Haven: Yale University Press.

Thaler, Richard H., and Cass R. Sunstein. 2008. *Nudge: Improving Decisions about Health, Wealth, and Happiness*. New Haven: Yale University Press.

Thompson, Dennis F. 2008. "Deliberative Democratic Theory and Empirical Political Science." *Annual Review of Political Science* 11 (1): 497–520.

Tocqueville, Alexis de. 2010. *Democracy in America*, vol. 1. Translated by James T. Schleifer. Indianapolis: Liberty Fund.

Umbers, Lachlan M. 2020. "Compulsory Voting: A Defense." *British Journal of Political Science* 50 (4): 1307–24.

Urbinati, Nadia. 2006. *Representative Democracy: Principles & Genealogy*. Chicago: University of Chicago Press.

Urbinati, Nadia. 2014. *Democracy Disfigured: Opinion, Truth, and the People*. Cambridge, MA: Harvard University Press.

Vandamme, Pierre-Étienne, Vincent Jacquet, Christoph Niessen, John Pitseys, and Min Reuchamps. 2018. "Intercameral Relations in a Bicameral Elected and Sortition Legislature." *Politics & Society* 46 (3):381–400.

van den Berghe, Pierre L. 1967. *Race and Racism: A Comparative Perspective*. New York: Wiley.

van der Does, Ramon, and Vincent Jacquet. Forthcoming. "Small-Scale Deliberation and Mass Democracy: A Systematic Review of the Spillover Effects of Deliberative Minipublics." *Political Studies*, forthcoming. DOI: 10.1177/2F0032321721 1007278.

Van Reybrouck, David. 2018. *Against Elections: The Case for Democracy*. Translated by Liz Waters. New York: Seven Stories Press.

Verba, Sidney, Kay Lehman Schlozman, and Henry E. Brady. 1995. *Voice and Equality: Civic Voluntarism in American Politics*. Cambridge, MA: Harvard University Press.

Waldron, Jeremy. 1999. *Law and Disagreement*. New York: Clarendon Press of Oxford University Press.

Waldron, Jeremy. 2016. *Political Political Theory: Essays on Institutions*. Cambridge, MA: Harvard University Press.

Walzer, Michael. 1970. *Obligations: Essays on Disobedience, War, and Citizenship*. Cambridge, MA: Harvard University Press.

Wampler, Brian. 2007. "A Guide to Participatory Budgeting." In *Participatory Budgeting*, edited by Anwar Shah, 21–54. Washington, DC: World Bank/International Bank for Reconstruction and Development.

Warren, Mark E. 2002. "What Can Democratic Participation Mean Today?" *Political Theory* 30 (5): 677–701.

Warren, Mark E., and Hilary Pearse, eds. 2008. *Designing Deliberative Democracy: The British Columbia Citizens' Assembly*. New York: Cambridge University Press.

White, Jonathan, and Lea Ypi. 2016. *The Meaning of Partisanship*. New York: Oxford University Press.

Williams, James. 2018. *Stand Out of Our Light: Freedom and Resistance in the Attention Economy*. New York: Cambridge University Press.

Wilson, James Lindley. 2019. *Democratic Equality*. Princeton: Princeton University Press.

Wolf, Susan. 1982. "Moral Saints." *Journal of Philosophy* 79 (8): 419–39.

Wu, Tim. 2016. *The Attention Merchants: The Epic Scramble to Get Inside Our Heads*. New York: Knopf.

Young, Iris Marion. 2000. *Inclusion and Democracy*. New York: Oxford University Press.

Zacka, Bernardo. 2017. *When the State Meets the Street: Public Service and Moral Agency*. Cambridge, MA: Belknap.

Zaller, John R. 1992. *The Nature and Origins of Mass Opinion*. New York: Cambridge University Press.

Zepeda-Millán, Chris. 2017. *Latino Mass Mobilization: Immigration, Racialization, and Activism*. New York: Cambridge University Press.

Index